PUSH BACK, MOVE FORWARD

Laura R. Woliver

PUSH BACK, MOVE FORWARD

THE NATIONAL COUNCIL OF WOMEN'S
ORGANIZATIONS AND COALITION ADVOCACY

TEMPLE UNIVERSITY PRESS
Philadelphia • Rome • Tokyo

TEMPLE UNIVERSITY PRESS
Philadelphia, Pennsylvania 19122
www.temple.edu/tempress

Library of Congress Cataloging-in-Publication Data

Names: Woliver, Laura R., 1954- author.
Title: Push back, move forward : the National Council of Women's
   Organizations and coalition advocacy / Laura R. Woliver.
Description: Philadelphia : Temple University Press, 2018. | Includes
   bibliographical references and index. |
Identifiers: LCCN 2018006353 (print) | LCCN 2018026357 (ebook) |
   ISBN 9781439916841 (E-book) | ISBN 9781439916827 (cloth) | ISBN
   9781439916834 (pbk.)
Subjects: LCSH: National Council of Women's Organizations. | Women—United
   States—Societies and clubs. | Women—Political activity—United States. | Women's
   rights—United States.
Classification: LCC HQ1904 (ebook) | LCC HQ1904 .W76 2018 (print) | DDC
   320.082/0973—dc23
LC record available at https://lccn.loc.gov/2018006353

To all the brave people who push back against injustice and work to move forward compassionate principles and fair policies.

Contents

Preface

T he biggest worldwide march for women's rights occurred the day after
Donald Trump was inaugurated as the 45th president of the United
States. The size of The Women's March dwarfed the small Trump in-
augural crowd. The nation was subjected to a "whose was bigger" debate
regarding the crowds. Thankfully, DC Metro officials settled this important
issue for us: President Obama's crowd was the biggest, the Women's March
was very big, coming in second to Obama's, and President Trump's was the
smallest of the three (Kutner 2017).

On Saturday January 21, 2017, women marched in protest of the election
results and in support of a wide variety of women's issues in all major American cities and towns and in a wide variety of settings. There was one march
by a handful of cancer survivors up and down the hallway of a cancer ward.
Their IVs rolled beside them ("Feet on the Ground. Not Backing Down!"
2017. *Ms.* [Spring]: 6–27).

Many marchers donned hand-knitted hot pink "pussy hats" as cultural reversals for Trump's bragging about grabbing women by their "pussies" and getting
away with it because he is famous. Women's word of mouth and social media
spread the news about the hats, the march, and the need to resist and fight back.

The women were galvanized to protect hard-won policies, current social
norms, and rights achieved by previous activists and organizers such as the
coalition of women's rights organizations known as the National Council
of Women's Organizations (NCWO). The NCWO's history and advocacy
activities are the subject of this book. The coalition known as the NCWO no
longer exists. However, the women's marches and other forms of activism

by dozens of groups formerly part of the NCWO show their commitment to "never go back" but to push back and move forward the policies of the women's rights movement, including reproductive rights, civil rights, LGBTQ rights, increased protections for workers and the environment, and immigrant rights (Shaw 2017).

Future efforts to protect, enhance, and further women's social and political progress will draw on the lessons learned from women's activism and coalitions discussed in *Push Back, Move Forward*. Many of the achievements partially attributable to women's movement activists, including those in the NCWO, are now in the crosshairs of the Trump administration, the Republican-controlled Congress, and a majority of Republican-controlled state legislatures. These include:

- Women's access to previously male-only organizations (see Chapter 4 for more)
- Measures, such as early voting, that have increased voter participation (Chapter 5)
- Social Security and other social safety net benefit programs (Chapter 6)
- The Affordable Care Act and programs to improve access to health care, including birth control (Chapter 7)
- U.S. government policies that support global human and women's rights (Chapter 8)

The activities of the NCWO and the recent Women's March are part of an ethos of linked fate, a vision wherein society shares assets and risks in order to have a basic safety net for everyone. These efforts are not one-offs but systematic and structural. Part of the coda for progressive social movements like the women's movement is that humans are basically all in the same boat. Contrasted to these community efforts are neoliberal, free market–based theories wherein individuals seeking through market forces to find optimum solutions for themselves will create efficient and just societies. The tension between these two standpoints (one: linked fate; two: neoliberal individualism) is discussed throughout the book.

The intersectionality of women's and gender studies scholarship also weaves throughout the book. The section in Chapter 5 on the Church Ladies Project and working the gender gap displays this further. As spiritual and religious women might explain their sense of linked fate, intersectionality, and civic duty, "There but for the grace of God, go I." Practicing solidarity for social justice and community flourishing is highlighted throughout *Push Back, Move Forward*, weaving each chapter together just as it ties the Women's March to the NCWO and to the entire history of the American women's movement.

Acknowledgments

My thanks to all the women's rights activists especially those studied for this book. I am grateful to the members of the NCWO who have allowed me to join their meetings and observe them while they worked. Activists affiliated with the NCWO graciously gave of their time and expertise to enhance this study. In particular, thanks to NCWO chair Susan Scanlan, the NCWO staff, and Jan Ericson of NOW for their years of support for this research.

As Anna Quindlen put it, concerning the changes to her life achieved through the efforts of the modern women's movement, "The greatest social tsunami of my lifetime, the women's movement, was part fearsome political force, part personal support group. It was hated and feared, and it changed the world completely, so that sometimes I want to send its leaders a note that says, 'Thank you for my life.'" (Quindlen 2012: 126). I second that emotion.

I would like to thank the College of Liberal Arts (now the College of Arts and Sciences) at the University of South Carolina, Columbia (USC), for awarding me a CLASS grant (College of Liberal Arts Scholarship Support award) in 2000–2001, which enabled me to conduct the initial fieldwork for this study. Dean Mary Ann Fitzpatrick provided timely financial support for summer research on this project. In addition, two Carol Jones Carlisle Awards from the Women's and Gender Studies program at USC, for 2014 and 2017, were timely and essential to my fieldwork. Support from the Department of Political Science and the Women's and Gender Studies program at USC has enabled me to conduct fieldwork and expand the interviews from

2007 through 2011. A 2009 talk at the Department of Political Science at the University of Kansas, Lawrence, provided useful feedback on earlier stages of my research.

To support research expenses in Washington, DC, the American Political Science Association's (APSA) Centennial Center for Scholars provided office space and computer support for three summers: 2010, 2011, and 2014. In addition, two APSA Marguerite Ross Barnett Research Fund grants for July 2011 and August through September 2014 allowed me concentrated time in DC for the final stages of the fieldwork.

The Clearinghouse on Women's Issues honored me with an invitation to reflect on my fieldwork in June 2014 at their 40th anniversary meeting in Washington, DC. In "the District" Anne Martin and Sue Klein graciously hosted my stay and supported my work intellectually. The Folger Shakespeare Library also provided timely and needed respite for my trips to DC.

Earlier versions of these chapters were presented at several academic conferences of the American Political Science Association, the Southeast Women's Studies Association, and the Southern Political Science Association. Comments from panel chairs, discussants, and audience members at these events provided me with ideas and critiques that helped move the project along to completion.

Research assistants from the Department of Political Science and the Women's and Gender Studies program at USC—Annie Boiter-Jolley, Scott Chalupa, Jennifer Karash-Eastman, Rachel Krauss, Christian McMaster, Seo Yong Park; Christine Sixta Rinehart, Stephen Ruxton, Kaitlyn Timmerman-Estes, Travis Wagoner, and a very talented undergraduate, Ms. Vivien Tourney—helped me with multidisciplinary literature and understanding the intersectionality of women's political history and activism. Encouragement and feedback from graduate students Annie Boiter-Jolley, Helen Adair King, and Elena Grynberg kept my writing momentum moving forward. Catherine Logan Maples underscored for me the importance of listening to women's lives and valuing their graceful strengths and resilience. My undergraduate students at USC have inspired and strengthened my work. For my entire professional life I have benefited from the wisdom and mentoring of Anne N. and Douglas Costain, Kristin Bumiller, and colleagues in the Women's Caucus for Political Science. It has been an honor to learn alongside all of these scholars.

My Women's and Gender Studies colleagues, especially Drucilla Barker, Lala Carr Steelman, Norman Edward Madden Jr., DeAnne H. Messias, Mary Baskin Waters, and Lynn Weber, were always sources of insight, wisdom, and comic relief during this long-haul project. They read earlier versions of chapters and supported me emotionally, politically, and intellectually.

What a treasure the Women's and Gender Studies program has been to me and many others at USC.

Many members of the Woliver and Binkley extended families visited me during my fieldwork at various "base camps" in DC. Their company and interest in my work made it all even more enjoyable.

Any errors in the book are my own. Mistakes might have persisted even in the face of the high-quality editing and mentorship I received from Temple University Press. Editor-in-Chief Aaron Javsicas recognized potential in the earliest manifestations of this research. His years-long encouragement of my work and wise counsel on writing and editing were foundational, invaluable, and spectacular.

Most of all, my deepest appreciation goes to the loves of my life, Mark W. Binkley and our children Paul and Sarah.

Acronyms and Abbreviations

AARP	American Association of Retired Persons
AAUW	American Association of University Women
ACA	Patient Protection and Affordable Care Act; nickname: Obamacare
ACORN	Association of Community Organizations for Reform Now
AEI	American Enterprise Institute
AFL-CIO	American Federation of Labor and Congress of Industrial Organizations
CARASA	Committee for Abortion Rights and Against Sterilization Abuse
CLUW	Coalition of Labor Union Women
COP	Council of Presidents
CWU	Church Women United
EW	Engaging Women
FMF	Feminist Majority Foundation
IWPR	Institute for Women's Policy Research
IWY	International Women's Year
NACW	National Association of Colored Women
NASA	National Aeronautics and Space Administration
NCADV	National Coalition against Domestic Violence
NCNW	National Council of Negro Women
NCPE	National Committee on Pay Equity
NCPSSM	National Committee to Preserve Social Security and Medicare

NCSSS	National Committee to Save Social Security
NCW	National Council of Women
NCWO	National Council of Women's Organizations
NEA	National Education Association
NGO	Nongovernmental Organization
NOW	National Organization for Women
NWA	National Women's Agenda
NWPC	National Women's Political Caucus
NWRO	National Welfare Rights Organization
OWL	Older Women's League
PPFA	Planned Parenthood Federation of America
SSA	Social Security Administration
SSI	Supplemental Security Income
WAA	Women's Action Alliance
WESCAD	Women's Equality Summit, Congressional Action Day (of the NCWO)
WISER	Women's Institute for a Secure Retirement
WJCC	Women's Joint Congressional Committee
WOW	Wider Opportunities for Women
WREI	Women's Research and Educational Institute

PUSH BACK, MOVE FORWARD

1

Introduction

Easier in Groups: The American Women's Movement and the National Council of Women's Organizations

> It was easy to miss, maybe because it didn't look like male bomb throwing.
> —CARMON AND KNIZHNIK, *Notorious RBG: The Life and Times of Ruth Bader Ginsburg*

> Well-behaved women seldom make history.
> —ULRICH, *Well-Behaved Women Seldom Make History*

Fieldwork is full of surprises and insights. Connections between people pop up in unexpected and humane encounters. Traveling from South Carolina to Washington, DC, to attend National Council of Women's Organizations (NCWO) meetings, conduct interviews, and observe events often reminded me of the movie *Trains, Planes and Automobiles*. Some trips were smooth, some not so much.

In January 2011, I arrived in DC for a council meeting. As I approached the meeting room at the National Education Association (NEA) building on 16th Street, N.W., I saw a yellow sticky note on the door. "NCWO meeting canceled because of snowstorm," the note announced. I looked outside and did not see any snow. I called NCWO chair Susan Scanlan who explained that the NCWO follows the DC public school system on early dismissals or weather cancellations. DC Public Schools' classes were let out early that day because of a possible snowstorm. Susan Scanlan stated, "We are a women's organization and members have children being released from school early and they have to deal with them." She added, "We have a few elderly members of the council. I couldn't live with myself if one of them got hurt on the ice on a sidewalk." Probably only scholars doing fieldwork on compassionate, feminist, and community- and/or family-oriented movements have to deal with research disruptions like a public school system letting out early. It was a frustration for me that day. But for my project as a whole, it was very telling about the worldview of many of these activists.

Americans are diverse, contentious, and individualistic. Some might claim that goes double for American women. Coordinating the messages and energies of citizens engaged in feminist politics, as many participants explained to me, is like herding cats. Amazingly, one coalition in Washington, DC, worked to speak for twelve million women. The NCWO channeled information, strategies, and responses for the now institutionalized women's movement in the United States. *Push Back, Move Forward* is based on my interviews with NCWO activists and my observations at council meetings and events sponsored or cosponsored by the coalition.

Make a Difference

As the motto of the NCWO put it, "One woman can make a difference, but it is easier if we do it in groups." Holding together a large and diffuse coalition is a challenge for any movement. Political organizing in the United States has become more specific and less broad. Coalitions, however, work against this grain. Coalitions bring diverse groups together who live and breathe separate, yet often overlapping and sometimes redundant, existences.

Push Back, Move Forward is a study of a shifting coalition of mouthy women who stood up, showed up, and acted out. My study of the NCWO echoes and builds on social movement scholarship, gender and politics, and public policy analysis. A national coalition like the NCWO was part and parcel of long civil rights, labor, and women's movements. It was intersectional and aware of the dominant power dynamics of well-resourced individuals, groups, and interests who might have disproportionate influence within a coalition. The efforts of groups and coalitions like the NCWO were foundational yet often uncelebrated, as they seemed unspectacular.

Push Back, Move Forward is based on fieldwork conducted in 1999–2001 and again from 2008 through 2014. Gaps in the fieldwork demarcate funding availability (often difficult in the field of women and politics); commitments to teaching, research, and service at the University of South Carolina; and family and cultural responsibilities.

From 1999 to 2014, I attended twenty-five NCWO meetings, which were held every other month in Washington, DC. I also conducted sixty-nine interviews with individuals involved with the NCWO. While doing fieldwork in DC, I was invited along when NCWO members attended events and meetings. My participant observations at more than forty-seven demonstrations, press conferences, congressional committee hearings, NCWO-sponsored trainings, and NCWO task force meetings also inform the research. In the spring of 2017 I verified the direct quotes from interviews, meetings, and events attended.

However, I was not able to reach a small number of people directly quoted. Please see Appendixes A, B, C, and D for lists of fieldwork, interviews, and events.

In addition to fieldwork, I followed the political activities of the NCWO through their email announcements, policy statements, and position papers. In the summer of 2011, I was given access to the files in the NCWO offices in DC and authorized to copy relevant documents, communications, and reports. One step feminist researchers try to take in their work is to give back to the group or people being studied. My small gesture of giving back for the kindnesses of the busy people in the NCWO coalition was to make a catalog or a list of the contents of their files, organize and box them up when appropriate, and leave the NCWO office with better organized archives than they had when I started.

Feminist scholars, as is well known, "frequently engage in participant observation. They are generally suspicious of Cartesian ways of knowing, or the High Science model, which depicts human subjects as solitary and self-subsistent and where knowledge is obtained through measurement rather than sympathy" (Tickner 2014: 103). Feminist methods also situate the researcher in the research process. Researchers periodically need to critically reflect on the power and powerlessness of the researcher in the project (Jaggar 2016b; Ackerly and True 2013: 135–159). As Gloria Steinem explained about the wisdom of many women, "Never having learned to separate mind and body, thoughts and emotion, or intellect from the senses, they trusted their own experience" (1992: 117).

The NCWO sought to empower girls and women as effective advocates for their visions and dreams. For many years the NCWO held an annual conference called "WESCAD" (Women's Equality Summit and Congressional Action Day). Each year attendees were provided with advice from experienced speakers on how to effectively and succinctly advocate for issues on the Hill. In each training session I observed, demystifying politics was a powerful part of the lesson. In 2008, Lisa Maatz, a widely respected policy advocate and strategist at the American Association of University Women (AAUW), told the gathering at WESCAD how to frame an issue, pose an "ask," provide data and research, and then close the deal with a story about a real person. "Your voice can make a difference," Maatz admonished. "The best tool in your arsenal is a personal story. Not the statistics. Tell your story. Let them put a face to the issue. Real people. How it works in the district" (author's observation and notes from WESCAD, March 27, 2008).

A second example was when Eleanor Smeal, president of the Feminist Majority Foundation (FMF), told young people preparing for their summer internships on Capitol Hill that they were all smart and she could demystify the federal budget for them (FMF Intern Briefing, July 21, 2011). Planning sessions I observed regarding proposed reforms to Social Security or health care reform went through similar steps. The last step, to cinch the point, was to find a "real person" to provide a narrative story about the impact events were having on them.

In *Push Back, Move Forward*, I utilized stories about real people. It is part of the ethos in women's politics to break silences and honor women's experiences. When telling stories, I heeded the advice of battle-hardened advocates like Lisa Maatz and Eleanor Smeal. When the meaning of a story is grasped, so are its moral implications (Polletta 2006: 88). The final step should be to link individual narratives to public policies so everyone with similar stories can access resources to relieve their hardships.

Not Dead Yet: Plan of the Book

Chapter 1, this chapter, explains the political and cultural context of the NCWO. The powerful mantra of disability rights activists "Not Dead Yet" reflects a brave, steady stance for citizenship claims that many feminists can relate to. Many feminist activists and scholars have noted the frequent obituaries for the American women's movement offered by various media and pundit sources. As Mark Twain quipped, "Reports of my death have been greatly exaggerated" (1897). The trope here is that, when a movement is declared "dead," the intent is to shut up adherents and reinforce silence (Reger 2012: 3–4).

Silencing women is evoked frequently to maintain dominant discourses and patriarchal powers. U.S. Senate majority leader Mitch McConnell (R-KY) on February 8, 2017, silenced Senator Elizabeth Warren (D-MA) during consideration of President Donald Trump's nomination of Senator Jefferson Beauregard Sessions III (R-AL) for U.S. attorney general. Senator Warren had been reading aloud from a letter Mrs. Coretta Scott King submitted to the Senate years earlier opposing, on the basis of race prejudice, Jeff Sessions's appointment to a federal judgeship. McConnell, to explain his order, said, "She [Warren] was warned. She was given an explanation. Nevertheless, she persisted" (Wang 2017).

T-shirts, bumper stickers, and other celebratory memorabilia for this strong, mouthy woman quickly appeared and sold well. "Nevertheless, she persisted" was emblazoned on the merchandise. Persisting in a difficult environment, speaking up for people who are not equally represented in the halls of power, and maintaining an ethic of linked fate is foundational. Many people do this, often in groups and coalitions like the NCWO, many times without much credit or celebration, since their efforts are unspectacular, without razzle-dazzle, and not media worthy.

Chapter 2 discusses several precursor groups and coalitions whose work enlarged concepts of citizenship and public policy. The context for the NCWO is what came before: previous women's coalitions, often divided by race, which set the stage for actions of new coalitions such as the Leadership Conference on Civil Rights and the NCWO. Their efforts meant subsequent groups like the NCWO did not start from scratch.

Chapter 2 includes a brief overview of conservative mobilizations and the impact of neoliberal market ideologies on communal proposals and policies. As explained throughout the study, free market neoliberalism concomitant with American individualism counters programs and reforms based on a sense of linked fate. Neoliberalism, also discussed, can even make President Donald Trump seem feminist (M. Ferguson 2017).

Chapter 3 explains the origins and operations of the NCWO. After the defeat of the Equal Rights Amendment (ERA) and other setbacks, the women's movement (not dead yet) did not shut up. Leaders of feminist interest groups in DC regrouped and persisted. They started to more formally work together. The first iteration of their cooperation was the Council of Presidents (COP). The NCWO evolved from the COP as smaller feminist groups and individual activists joined the growing coalition.

Chapter 4 theorizes the powers and cultural narratives evident in the NCWO's 2003 query to the Augusta National Golf Club in Georgia about their all-male membership policy. The Masters Golf Tournament dustup led me to examine the cultural givens, contrasting what is neutral and "unmarked" as natural to what is harmful and subjugating. The chapter discusses the money and power aspects of the issues raised. My intersectional analysis of the Masters Golf Tournament includes the examination of unmarked, transparent categories of dominance "where power and privilege constellate on their own terms" and in relation to recognized and forbidden inequalities (May 2015: 23). I also examine in Chapter 4 a tendency in the media to handle complex gender justice issues in a "he said/she said" manner. The events highlighted the cultural and political aspects of the women's movement as adherents continued to push for women to be taken seriously in all aspects of life.

Chapter 5 explores with Annie Boiter-Jolley, the chapter coauthor, the ways the NCWO worked the gender gap in elections. It is axiomatic that group prospects trace with election results. Working the powerful specter of the gender gap was one way the NCWO signaled political potential. Educating and mobilizing core constituencies of the coalition, such as the highly successful Church Ladies Project in 2008, is highlighted in Chapter 5. The long-term efforts to get out "her vote" illustrate the depth, breadth, and heart of the women's movement and the NCWO's part in the historic election turnouts of 2008 and 2012.

Chapter 6 discusses the NCWO's involvement in the politics of Social Security. The NCWO responded to free market, neoliberal reform proposals for Social Security with a barrage of data and stories on the centrality of Social Security to peoples' economic prospects, especially women's. The NCWO highlighted the female face of Social Security. Rather than reform through dismemberment into private accounts, the NCWO helped up the ante for Social Security by advocating that the years of care work that people (usually women) provide outside formal markets be credited to their work life when calculating their Social Security benefits. This and other ways to better reflect women's lives in Social Security were also proposed by the NCWO.

Chapter 7 explores the involvement of NCWO in the Affordable Care Act (ACA), particularly the reproductive health aspects of the act. Health care reform has been an issue in American politics for decades. The huge coalitions involved in the passage of the ACA, including the NCWO, geared up in the early years of the Barack Obama administration and during the policy window of Democratic Party leadership in the U.S. Congress, especially with the House Speakership of Nancy Pelosi (D-CA). The centrality of elections discussed in Chapter 5 echoes here in the policy window for health care reform after the 2008 elections. The ACA included many advancements for women. At the same time, the women's groups in the NCWO and allied partners were asked to "stand down" on a central principle of their movement: coverage of complete reproductive health care, to include legal abortion.

Chapter 8 examines global feminist issues in the NCWO's agenda. The American-based NCWO had a borderless concern about women around the world. My examination of global feminism includes whether nonprofit organizations (NGOs) alleviate or eradicate social problems. The chapter discusses the pros and cons of Western feminist groups, including their concerns and actions and global gender issues.

The Conclusion links the NCWO to other research and issues of the women's movement and the formalization of a diffuse social movement. I review the benefits and perils when a coalition claims to speak for more than twelve million women. A sense of linked fate regarding exclusionary membership policies, political representation, Social Security, health care, and global women weaves through these chapters. A coalition like the NCWO engaged in a lot of unheralded work that secured basic, foundational aspects of women's well-being. Their work was not perfect. Their strength waxed and waned. In fact, as the Conclusion explains, the NCWO experienced hard times, lingered as an abeyance structure, and as of this writing is inactive.

Contrary to dozens of media reports over the past four to five decades that the modern women's movement is "dead," *Push Back, Move Forward* documents the entrenched and "given" nature of modern feminism in our culture and politics. "Women's lib" coexists with counterinterests deriding, denouncing, and denying the accomplishments of the women's movement in many aspects of American and world politics. Stopping the privatization of

Social Security, as Chapter 6 details, is unsexy, marginally newsworthy, and centered in devoted efforts. The Social Security actions were hard won, uncredited successes for groups like the NCWO. As NCWO chair Susan Scanlan explained, "I can't get arrested in this town with a *good* story" (interview, emphasis in original). For the millions of people (mostly women) who consistently receive Social Security despite market volatilities, economic crises, or election outcomes, the good story of continuing the program is bedrock for their well-being. Tillers of change are required for political reform (Steelman, Woliver, and Steelman 2009). Change agents' hard work can also create "life at its most artful" (Jasper 1997: 218). Social movements like feminism are cultural as well as political tillers of change.

Necessary Movement Cultures

Doing the spade work, civil rights activist and social justice leader Ella Baker consistently advised, was required if injustices were to be systematically halted and all people brought into full, deep citizenship (Ransby 2003). Often it's women who work those spades. Working for a cause for the duration, playing the long game for justice, can be a deep pleasure, providing meaning in many people's lives. Those in the women's movement, for instance, have often been described as a community of readers (Sicherman 2010; Rochon 1998; U. Taylor 2010: 71). Women's book clubs, literary societies, and study groups created safe spaces without adult men: "a school not governed by state authorities, the earliest versions of the club form represented a small step toward political action" (Clemens 1997: 196). Women's self-education often included sororal learning and support (Lagemann 1979).

The arts and humanities often reflected the rebellion and resilience of people without official power (Preston 1995). Poets like Emily Dickinson moved the discourse as they also advised, "Tell all the truth, but tell it slant." Audre Lorde explained, "For women, poetry is not a luxury. It is a vital necessity of our existence. It forms the quality of the light within which we predicate our hopes and dreams toward survival and change, first made into language then into idea, and then into more tangible action. Poetry is the way we give name to the nameless so it can be thought" (Lorde quoted in Reed 2005: 89; see also Byrd, Cole, and Guy-Sheftall 2009). The affirmation possible in "'women-identified' culture included musicians, artists, feminist book stores, memorials, and women-only safe spaces" (Whittier 1995: 66). Cognitive frames blending cultural and political activities were hallmarks of many enduring social movements.

When examined closely, movement cultures reveal courage and determination: "what counts as dramatic has often been defined in limiting ways based on male-centered views of heroic performance. If the goal is to change the world, there is reason to believe that publicly performed or privately read poems have been a force as powerful as any other" (Reed 2005: 88). The uncounted girls and women who have taped and pinned copies of Maya Angelou's poem "Still I Rise" to their mirrors and bulletin boards know this rings true. A poem can be a stimulus that empowers readers.[1] The cultural aspects of social movements inspired the mental constructs that energized individuals to work for social change and were as important as physical resources and networks (Jasper 1997: 75). These cognitive frames helped set the "cultural interpretation needed in order to establish the pre-existing meanings organizers can appeal to" for supporter mobilization (Jasper 1997: 78). One activist and NCWO stalwart explained to me, "It [the NCWO] requires a great deal of unseen support and work. I would never miss a meeting for the interaction that we have as women with a common cause. . . . This is the finest contribution of the NCWO, because we do see that we are not standing alone—whether it is unmet needs, what the state of the art is, and moving along from there" (Ruth Nadel, interview, November 29, 2000). Feminist organizations also "develop theory not only *of* the women's movement but *for* the movement" (Ferree and Martin 1995a: 13, italics in original). These processes were often strongly emotional and pleasurable as when bearing witness against evil and doing the right thing lent "dignity to one's life even when stated goals are elusive" (Jasper 1997: 82). In addition, "like artists, activists create new moral possibilities" (Jasper 1997: 97).

The NCWO participated in many culture moves. One explicitly involved "making pests of ourselves," as Martha Burk framed it, until the suffragists' statue and also the statue of Sojourner Truth were elevated from the U.S. Capitol crypt to Statuary Hall. Many voices joined in these efforts. Moving the statues meant a lot to many of the activists I interacted with during the fifteen years of this study. The statue stories were frequently offered up as proud examples of sassy group accomplishments. Measuring the success or failure of social movements is tricky when the cultural and personal aspects of individual involvement is valued. Change agents and protesters "are more like poets than engineers" (Jasper 1997: 379; see also Finney 2011; Madden 2013, 2010; Preston 1995; Rankine 2014). In this instance, to move the two statues took pests, poets, spade work, tillers of change, *and* engineers.

Defend Communal Efforts

Large social movements are shifting and complex. The women's movement is "a messy multiplicity of feminist activism across U.S. history and beyond its borders" (Hewitt 2010a: 7). Standard chronologies are often insufficient; a diverse array of activists are involved; coalitions are built and contested;

dynamic agendas include politics, culture, and economics; and admonitions for multicultural, multiracial, multisexual, and multieconomic positionality while matrixes included in all of the above are part of the mix (Hewitt 2010a: 7; see also Cole 2008). At the core of a coalition is "how people draw attention to and speak about their awareness of difference and multiple lived experiences through gender, race, class, ethnicity, religions, and other differences" (S. Gilmore 2008a: 5). Effectively representing the positions of more than twelve million women in more than 180 separate member organizations added to the complexity, the power but also the weakness, of the NCWO.

Many observers have noted the evaporation of politics, or common good concerns, from many of our social interactions and expectations. People who volunteer to make a difference one person at a time, as concerned individuals, are valued and praised. People who request social policies to address systematically many of the hardships a person could experience in life are "out of bounds," ideological, political, or partisan. Even individuals who volunteer to do good deeds often eschew politics. One scholar crystallized what she observed in community efforts, "At every meeting the vice-mayor passed the hat for a homeless women's shelter. No one mentioned housing policy" (Eliasoph 1998: 53).

Deep political solidarity directed toward systematic social change requires more than personal tolerance of diversity, charitable donations, or acts of public service (Hancock 2011: 63). Political solidarity means willingness to work and perhaps sacrifice for changes that will abide so that injustices and hardships are less likely to happen.

Ameliorative efforts are less controversial than working for social change. Fair housing activism is more likely to create a backlash than is volunteering at a homeless shelter. Backlash includes previously privileged groups who enter a kind of "oppression Olympics" by redefining victimhood to encompass any perceived collateral damage brought about by expanding social justice. One example is when people claim that heterosexual marriages are endangered by gay marriages (Hancock 2011: 14). The mindset here suggests that heterosexual marriage is a neutral given and gay marriage would be a social construction that subtracts from heterosexual institutional power; and the circle is unbroken with the claim that heterosexual marriage is not socially constructed. The zero-sum paradigm means that all you can achieve with addition (of gay marriage) is actually a subtraction (from heterosexual marriages). Seeing through these logical fallacies requires the critical consciousness that theorist bell hooks asserted needs to be central to education. hooks explained that visionary, intersectional feminist politics is about "having a person of any gender who understands deeply and fully the need for there to be respect for the embodied presence of males and females, without subordination" (Alptraum 2017: 59).

People can make peace with a silence about silence, or a metasilence. People can walk over homeless people on sidewalks and then never talk about it and also never talk about never talking about it. "In other words, the very act of avoiding the elephant [in the room] is itself an elephant [in the room]! Not only do we avoid it, we do so without acknowledging that we are actually doing so, thereby denying our denial" (Zerubavel 2006: 53). Class, gender, race, and heteronormative privileges, for instance, can be systematically ignored and masked by willful blindness, ignorance, asset hoarding, and denial (Kruks 2012: 94; D. Thompson, forthcoming; Hancock 2011: 11). The behavior of some privileged people even extends to what is considered knowledge and truth, categorized as epistemic privilege (Kruks 2012: 98; Hancock 2011).

The social norm that talking about politics at the dinner table is impolite spills over into irritation at people who speak up about social policies and politics. If the person discussing politics is a woman, in many communities, the discomfort heightens. The resistant person threatens patriarchal givens. Hence, we hear and understand the trope "strident feminist." "Indeed," Gilligan and Richards argued, "the stability of patriarchy requires the suppression of any voice in women or men that might, on reasonable grounds, contest its terms, a suppression which itself relies on the power of gender by deeming the resisting voice in men unmanly or effeminate and in women unwomanly" (2009: 30).

So, when "mouthy" women speak their truth about incest, rape, domestic violence, discriminatory policies, pay inequity, sexual harassment, sex trafficking, to name a few, their "breaking the silence" is usually not greeted well. Often the speakers are pelted with ad hominem attacks. Women's voices are often ignored and belittled (Karpowitz and Mendelberg 2014; Mendelberg, Karpowitz, and Oliphant 2014) or violently suppressed as threats to patriarchal natural order. One of the transformative roles that many women play in politics, then, is to tell women's stories and set the context of what it is like to be a girl or woman in particular situations. Being secure in the political nature of feminism is important, especially after the 2016 elections. The intersectional theorist bell hooks reminded us, "The challenge to patriarchy is political, and not a lifestyle or identity" (Alptraum 2017: 59).

Nevertheless, in the face of blowback, many people resist, push back, speak out, dissent, advocate, and persist. Oftentimes it is women, including those organized into the NCWO, who defend communal efforts, acknowledge linked fates, and work to help people besides themselves have safety, security, and agency. Fighting movement backlash is hard, however, when zero-sum analysis perpetuates and interlaces with "compassion deficit disorder" and victim blaming (Hancock 2011: 14–17). Many times their efforts are unspectacular and unheralded even while they establish, defend, or expand bedrock social policies and political rights.

Push Back, Move Forward is about formal movement organizations combining their efforts via the NCWO. It is important to remember that these formal organizations are not the entire women's movement. National organizations are more visible and easier for researchers to study. The women's movement is mostly "a broad perspective on the world and women's place in it. Individuals internalize this perspective, and individuals, communities, and social movement organizations put it into action" (Whittier 1995: 23). Keep in mind that the core of the women's movement is not the assortment of formal organizations, which ebb and flow. The women's movement is cognitive, cultural, and politically persistent.

Chapter 2 foreshadows the NCWO with an overview of the context and history of earlier coalitions of women's activists. Chapter 3 focuses on the formation of the COP and its growth into the NCWO and explains the structure and workings of the NCWO. Collectively these feminists worked to put their dreams and aspirations into action.

2

Precursors

Genders, Matrixes, and Coalitions

> I like to say that the women's groups are like a thousand points of light. That is lovely. But, sometimes a flashlight beam is needed to concentrate all our energy and light on one needed area.
> —Susan Bianchi-Sand, interview

> When their voices and authority are challenged within their churches, [black women] sometimes respond, "If it wasn't for the women, you wouldn't have a church."
> —Gilkes, *If It Wasn't for the Women . . . : Black Women's Experience and Womanist Culture in Church and Community*

"Make a Way Out of No Way," my students proclaimed, and as I learned from black feminist scholarship and activist memoirs. The adage helps us envision the development of many organizations for social justice, including the NCWO. As will be discussed, the NCWO operated within a milieu of political negativity, sexism, and a strong neoliberal insurgency that praised market solutions and condemned social programs.

An intersectional feminist standpoint, such as the ethic of care approach, "rests on a thick rather than thin understanding of democracy" (Gilligan 2011: 22). A thick democracy includes the lives of women and people without economic security. It is a democracy with substance, where Anatole France's famous quip, "The law, in its majestic equality, forbids the rich as well as the poor to sleep under bridges, to beg in the streets, and to steal bread," would lose some of its bite (France quoted in Schlozman, Verba, and Brady 2012: 537). Formal equality, while valuable, needs to include agency, economic security, and well-being. Thick democracy asserts that all people are capable of making their own decisions especially concerning their bodies. Deep, intersectional political commitments are recursive intellectually and biased toward achieving collective justice (May 2015: 251).

It is important to teach and remember stories of activists who challenged injustice and worked to prevent it. It fills in some of the willful ignorance about the history of all the people in a society. Evidence of past and current resistance also suggests that people have broken from dominance and envisioned and worked for change (May 2015: 59–60). "Intersectionality is fundamentally committed to the potential that change is possible, meaning that it is conceivable and feasible, though not guaranteed" (May 2015: 59–60).

There were many foremothers and precursors for the NCWO. Space does not permit me to pay full respect to the women and men in the abolition movement and temperance campaigns, efforts to end child labor and to prosecute lynching, and the more than seventy-year campaign to achieve women's suffrage, to name just a few. This chapter covers some of the major women's coalitions operating earlier than the NCWO.

The presidential election of Ronald Reagan in 1980, the Republican takeover of the U.S. Senate, and the consistent opposition of Republican leaders to issues central to the modern women's movement (legal abortion, affirmative action, enforcement of existing gender equity laws, progress on comparable worth, the ERA, to name a few) troubled many progressive groups. The defeat of the ERA in 1982 was an additional impetus for a dozen major women's rights organizations in DC to create an informal coalition, the COP. Eventually, the COP evolved into the much larger NCWO.

Stitching Coalitions Together: Women of Color Bridge Builders

Foregrounding American women of color as bridge builders, as faithful and fearless feminists, is foundational for understanding a coalition like the NCWO. Black women in America have staunchly supported gender equality as well as voted consistently and faithfully for candidates and parties with the highest probability of working for social justice, including gender justice. Dependable, steady, and engaged often beyond their formal educations, social class status, employment patterns, and many socioeconomic status statistics that would predict political apathy or anomie, black women showed up and pushed back. Their long-haul efforts were foundational to gender, racial, and social class progress. In a fair social science discipline, black women would be role models for citizenship, no matter what the socioeconomic circumstances.

Instead, much of the scholarship on American politics is hegemonic because of the focus on white people and formal legal rights. Many accounts of the American women's movement echoed these dominant narratives (B. Thompson 2010: 39–60; see also Giddings 1984; Hull, Scott, and Smith 1982; White 1999; Springer 2005: 65–68; Roth 1999: 70–90). The media, also, has rendered invisible the women of color who pioneered the women's movement and worked steadily for women's rights. "In the way that image can overwhelm reality," Gloria Steinem asserts, "nothing but struggle for decades would keep this from becoming a self-fulfilling prophecy" (2015: 69).

Women often worked in several movements or causes at the same time. Hewitt explains, "Those participants in woman's rights and suffrage movements who envisioned themselves as part of broad campaigns for racial, economic, and gender justice provide a critical bridge between feminism and other initiatives for progressive social change. The largest contingent of nineteenth-century 'bridge women' were radical Quakers and African Americans with deep roots in abolitionism and passionate commitments to racial equality, utopian communalism, Indian rights, health reform, land reform and religious freedom" (2010b: 33; see also Flexner 1974). Early female reformers created the foundation on which later generations of women built antiracist, global, and multicultural coalitions. Whether or not they used the term "feminist" these women included: African Americans, Latinas, Mexican Americans, Jewish women, labor unionists, radical immigrant women, and more (Hewitt 2010b: 33; Bejarano 2013; Klapper 2013).

Many scholars have neglected and overlooked the work of black women. In American history, for instance, "even white historians who have recognized and implicitly castigated the racism of white progressives seem unaware that black women across the country were creating their own brand of 'progressivism'" (Scott 1992: 148). The blank spots in our education are meaningful. The epistemologies of ignorance, or the politics of unknowing, are tied to structural inequality and the willingness of many people not to know (May 2015: 190).

The National Association of Colored Women (NACW), for instance, became the primary means for black women to build race leadership. "Its members saw a set of interlocking problems involving race, gender, and poverty, no one of which could be dealt with independently. They believed that if they worked for the poor, they worked for black women and if they worked for black women, they worked for the race" (White 1999: 24). The NACW asserted that "a race could rise no higher than its women" because the problems of the black race revolved around the problems of black women (White 1999: 24). During the nadir period after Reconstruction, the black church turned inward and the guiding principle behind clubs was racial uplift through self-help (White 1999: 26–27; Springer 1999; Franklin and Moss 1994). The southern black Baptist missionary societies and movements along with the National Association of Colored Women Clubs, which began in 1896, were part of the regrouping during those hard times (Ransby 2003: 18).

The NACW did not hesitate to represent poor black women as reflected in their motto: "Lifting as We Climb" (White 1999: 54–55, 69–70; Ransby 2003: 19). Women in the NACW were more than altruistic. Their motto presumed race and sex sameness but social and cultural distance (White 1999: 78). The results were not either/or but both/and: some elitism but also egalitarianism. Ransby explains, "Elitism coexisted with a commitment to equality, so black women's organizations could support cross-class relationships as well as reinforce class distinctions" (2003: 19). Leaders stressed that the work was a vocation rather than an avocation. Black Baptist women activists "embraced the masses of less fortunate black people and made sacrifices, both material and personal, in order to provide assistance. Missionary women who were advocates of temperance, modesty, and propriety also embraced the principle of providing aid to the downtrodden, irrespective of their status, their sins, or their inadequacies" (Ransby 2003: 19).

Black women of different socioeconomic classes organized (Barnett 1995: 204; see also Giddings 2002, 1984). Several decades earlier than white women's organizing of the 1960s and 1970s, black women's political activism emphasized "participatory democracy, community, collectivism, caring, mutual respect, and self-transformation" (Barnett 1995: 202–203; see also Clark and Brown 1986). Black women lived as well as theorized intersectionality with a liberatory, egalitarian, and radical political vision (May 2015). Black women knew that gender was raced and social classed. Black women understood that intersectionality meant, for instance, that the politics of reproduction could not be disentangled from these power matrixes (Klutchen 2009).

The politics of action, not just words, involve the marriage of theory and practice into the concept of praxis. These communities of feminist and communal praxis emphasized the need for concrete service to others (Ransby 2003: 18, 271, 298). Leaders such as Ella Baker modeled a deliberative lifetime of political praxis and leadership (Ransby 2003: 371). Baker was a master teacher and resident griot (Ransby 2003: 357). "It was her contention that the political was inherently personal long before it was a slogan for Second Wave feminism" (Ransby 2003: 369).

The deliberative, purposeful lives of people like Ella Baker were "of a piece" within a long tradition of African American resistance. Ransby explains, "Each intergenerational organization she joined, each story she told, each lesson she passed on was a part of the connective tissue that formed the body politic of the Black Freedom Movement in the United States from the 1930s into the 1980s" (2003: 6).

Another notable bridge builder, Pauli Murray, worked in tandem in several movements. Murray's activism was always intersectional and liberatory (Murray 1987). She was often ahead of her time and behind the scenes. She advanced both the civil rights and the women's movement by working with labor unions, religious groups, and community organizers (Schulz 2017: 67). Murray deserves much more acclaim than she has received, as do many other African American women who are stellar citizens.

Black women were formidable in the civil rights movement, which encompasses the "long civil rights movement" (Hall 2005) all the way to today's Black Lives Matter movement. "Although the civil rights movement nurtured feminists across the color line, its organic relationship to black feminism was unique" (U. Taylor 2010: 65–66; see also Sullivan 2009). For instance, in 1935 the National Council of Negro Women (NCNW) was launched as an organization of organizations. The NCNW was a clearinghouse for information on women's activities and a supporter of interracial development and progressive labor movements (White 1999: 149). Scholars of black history and politics in America synthesized black feminist consciousness into three central ingredients: "an understanding of intersectionality, a focus on community-centered politics, and an emphasis on the particular experiences of black women" (Simien 2006: 5, 45–46, 54–62; see also Crenshaw, 1989 and 1991; Dawson 2001, 1994; Cole and Guy-Sheftall 2003).

Black women were predisposed to a double consciousness embedded in their interlocking experiences of racism and sexism in the matrixes of oppression. "This notion of double consciousness connotes an acute sense of awareness" of the intersectional nature of power and powerlessness (Simien 2006: 8). An outsider-within standpoint often made for perceptive, all-encompassing analysis of dominant powers and unequal citizenship (Collins 2000). One result was that "black feminists have maintained that feminism benefits the black community by challenging patriarchy as an institutionalized oppressive structure and advocating the building of coalitions" (Simien 2006: 11, 132–133). Collective action through a sense of linked fate was therefore needed and strongly supported by both black women and black men (Simien 2006: 11, 16, 34–39; see also Brown-Guinyard 2013).

Women's Joint Congressional Committee

In 1920, the year women secured the right to vote with the Nineteenth Amendment, the Women's Joint Congressional Committee (WJCC) emerged as a large umbrella organization.[1] The WJCC coordinated and unified the legislative agendas of the most prominent white women's organizations. Within five years the WJCC was a powerful lobbying clearinghouse for the agendas of twelve million women from twenty-one national organizations (Jan Wilson 2007: 1; Muncy 1991: 103–107).

Organized women such as those represented by the WJCC in the 1920s drew on a notion of women as disinterested moral caretakers of the public welfare. The politics of motherhood in this era offered a protective cover: "This politics of oblique infiltration, as opposed to direct challenge, eventually produced changes in both the roster of acknowledged political players and the scope of state intervention, while at the same time inscribing women's traditional family role in new social policies and state agencies" (Clemens 1997: 45; see also T. Brown 1998; Gifford 1995: 7; Knight 2005). Progressive reformers' cumulative efforts, to include white women and women of color, transformed the organization of American politics by expanding the roster of regular political participants from mainly those with partisan loyalties and power to interested citizens often organized into groups (Clemens 1997: 45; see also Scott 1991).

The prospects for their social reform programs benefited from framing their efforts as maternal politics or municipal housekeeping. However, passage of the WJCC marquee bill, the Sheppard Towner Maternity and Infancy Act in 1921, and their subsequent push for child labor laws, frightened some interests. Manufacturers foresaw a forceful women's reform block that could begin to regulate labor and working conditions (Jan Wilson 2007; see also Clemens 1997: 306–308).

Attacks against the WJCC increased. Female reform activists did not counteract conservative, self-styled patriotic groups concerned about the spread of socialism or the oversight and regulation of business (Jan Wilson 2007: 6, 27). One way of disparaging the WJCC and other women's groups included publishing and disseminating the (in)famous "spider chart" that displayed their supposed connection to socialism and radicalism (Jan Wilson 2007: 154; Cott 1987: 242).

Women's groups such as the WJCC became more politically forceful as they moved beyond ameliorative or philanthropic service and worked for federal programs to help solve problems like poverty, disease, labor conditions, and war (Jan Wilson 2007: 163). Toward the end of the 1920s, the WJCC began to lose some influence as it started pushing for more class-based reforms that were less easily attributed to their maternal interests. To make a long story short, by 1930 the WJCC had lost most of its congressional and public support. The coalition began a gradual descent until its demise in 1970 (Jan Wilson 2007: 1).

Women's Work and Empowerment

Female political education and experiences in political effectiveness as well as histories with many powerful future allies made the WJCC vital to women's political culture, liberal feminism of the later twentieth century, and the debates about the role of the state in social reform (Jan Wilson 2007: 173). The WJCC and the women's groups within its coalition "were able to muster public and congressional support by working through strictly nonpartisan, separate female organizations and by forming coalitions with potentially powerful and influential groups, including labor unions, reform organizations, newspaper editors, legal scholars, religious associations, and, most important, progressive-minded politicians in both major political parties"

(Jan Wilson 2007: 3–4). The WJCC was a conduit to progressive reforms from the 1920s to the FDR period (1932–1944). In addition, even though the WJCC waned in political power, like many efforts, it left layered and cumulative residues of reform (Tarrow 1998: 175).

As one WJCC member reflected in 1964, "the committee's failures in the 1920s did not always 'spell ultimate defeat'" (Jan Wilson 2007: 173). Residues of reform and development of women's political stance vis-à-vis the state were engendered also by the NACW, Ella Baker, and thousands of women of color who worked for justice and helped gather in the people of the modern women's movement (Chavez 2010; Simien 2006; Hine and Thompson 1998; U. Taylor 2010; B. Thompson 2010).

Diminutive characterizations of women's political work as "municipal housekeeping" sometimes elided the essential, yet uncelebrated, efforts of women reformers of various classes and races. "'Municipal housekeeping,'" Anne Firor Scott taught, "made communities all over the country healthier and more livable. Perhaps a partial reason for its curious absence from standard histories of the age of reform is that historians are drawn to situations of conflict . . . The women's work, while it often transformed the health and appearance of whole towns, was on the whole not controversial and only occasionally posed as a threat to existing political structures" (1992: 157–158). Municipal housekeeping that improved community health via clean water, sanitation, vaccination, and food safety campaigns, however, was no doubt fundamental to other more celebrated and publicized reforms people needed and strived for.

The Congresswomen's Caucus

After the election of President Jimmy Carter in 1976, an ad hoc coalition of women's groups, numbering more than forty, met with incoming Carter administration officials. Both the women's groups and the administration officials queried each other on women's issues and the new administration's commitments to advancing the women's agenda (Gertzog 1984: 183).[2]

Much of the increasingly feminist orientation of congresswomen after 1977 is partly attributed to the Congresswomen's Caucus formed in 1977 (Gertzog 1984: 7). Betty Dooley was the first executive director of the Congresswomen's Caucus (Gertzog 1984: 181–182). Dooley was later one of the leaders of the NCWO. Susan Scanlan was also a leader of both the Congresswomen's Caucus and the NCWO. In 1978, Scanlan also helped an offshoot of the caucus transition into the Women's Research and Educational Institute (WREI).[3]

Organizations later central to the NCWO were instrumental in the formation and shape of the Congresswomen's Caucus. The National Organization for Women (NOW), the National Women's Political Caucus (NWPC), and the Business and Professional Women's Clubs (BPWC) sought effective access to supportive members of Congress. Forming a congressional caucus was heavily urged by these outside-of-Congress group leaders who wanted formal and organized access to the House of Representatives (Gertzog 1984: 182). Activists were part and parcel of what Banaszak documented as social movement adherents existing and operating both "inside and outside of the state" (2010; see also Harrison 1998: 169–209).

Organizing around the 1977 International Women's Year Convention, in Houston, Texas, stimulated activism and coordination by groups such as the National Women's Agenda Project. After the IWY meeting, a National Women's Conference Continuing Committee worked with leadership from Sarah Harder at the University of Wisconsin—Eau Claire and Mal Johnson of Washington, DC (Harrison 2008: 42; see also Spruill 2017). Both Harder and Johnson eventually were stalwarts in the NCWO as well as their own organizations. In addition, feminist coalitions such as the Women's Action Alliance (WAA) and the National Women's Agenda were parts of the pieces of experience, networking and reform which flowed into the NCWO (see Harrison 2008: 19–47). People also traveled between and among civil rights, labor, environmental, fair housing, domestic violence, gay rights, peace, poverty, religious, reproductive rights and women's studies coalitions. The vibrant coalition of the 1960s and 1970s, the Committee for Abortion Rights and Against Sterilization Abuse (CARASA), included black, Puerto Rican, and white activists (S. Gilmore 2008a: 13).

Initially an informal group called "The Council of Presidents" started meeting in 1985. The members were presidents of a dozen major women's rights organizations in DC. A nickname for the presidents of major NGOs, labor unions, interest groups, and coalitions is "the principles." The prime emphasis for these principles in the COP was protecting reproductive choice. They met approximately once a month. Their attention was concentrated by the nomination of Judge Robert Bork to the U.S. Supreme Court and the Reagan Justice Department's undermining, and even outright hostility to maintaining the basic outlines of the *Roe v. Wade* (1973) precedent (see also Harrison 2008: 42–43).

The initial COP benefited from women leaders with stellar and diverse political and philanthropic experiences. For example, some of the energy that streamed into the COP, and then later the NCWO, came from organizational and personal experiences in the early 1970s. Many experienced bridge builders in the women of color activist community also joined the emerging coordinated effort.

Representations and Intersectionality

The American women's movement and women's social reform movements utilized various coalitions over time. Many feminists worked in overlapping movements for progressive causes, world peace and disarmament, the environment and racial justice, as well as gender justice. In *Separate Roads to Feminism*, Benita Roth explained how these memberships and interests are iterative. She asserted that we need to understand "the contradictory legacy of prior movement experiences for feminist emergence: Prior movements gift feminists with skills and contacts, while burdening them with loyalties to an existing community and potential constraints on feminist activity" (2004: 21; see also Springer 2005: 64–68). The women's movement has also benefited from the theorizing of black women concerning the intersectional nature of people's experiences and conditions and the power matrixes we all deal with (May 2015). An intersectional framework, for instance, is useful for understanding elections. While more complicated that single-axis analysis with discrete domains of politics (race politics separate from gender politics), it is "a mess worth making" in order to construct progressive, winning coalitions and more representative governments (Smooth 2006).

Social movements, S. Laurel Weldon's research showed, can be effective and inclusive avenues for marginalized groups to influence policy makers and be represented. In particular, "Women's organizations offer a site for such processes of representation—and not just for privileged women" (Weldon 2011: 147). At the same time, it is important to think about how "Change is more likely to be generated by the marginally marginalized, the most advantaged of the disadvantaged" (Clemens 1997: 92).

Most of the poor and working poor in America are women. All women (and men) face matrixes of domination from intersectional aspects of their lives lived through race, gender, social class, and sexualities. Many of the inequalities women and their families experience are imbedded firmly in the structures of our society (Roithmayr 2014; Schlozman, Verba, and Brady 2012; Walby 2015, 2009; Weber 2010). Silence about these structural power inequalities means that in America, politics often reduces discussion to individual identity (and an identity of one dimension; either/or, instead of intersectional), a single-axis worldview (May 2015). Collins pointed out, "Reducing the complexities of outsider-within social locations to questions of individual identity resonates with distinctly American beliefs that all social problems can be solved by working on oneself" (2013: 69). Recall, though, that "focusing attention on personal decisions rather than collective practices asks too much of individuals and too little of society" (Rhode 2014: 143; see also Ehrenreich 2014). Terry O'Neill (President of NOW) similarly observed that women frequently "take personal responsibility for systemic problems" (O'Neill quoted in Rhode 2014: 20).

Under many circumstances of structural inequality, social movements represented the powerless more than do elected representatives, traditional lobbying groups, voting or political parties. Recent scholarship found "that the shortage of people from the working class in American legislatures skews the policy-making process toward outcomes that are more in line with the upper class's economic interests" (Carnes 2013: 12). Weldon's research also revealed that when women of color organize separately, their influence in a large social movement like the American women's movement strengthens. At the same time, the social movement as a whole was democratically deepened, "separate organizing around social position can create more inclusive social movements and lay the groundwork for cooperation across social cleavages" (Weldon 2011: 109). The bottom line was, "Thus, despite their imperfections, women's organizations provide a critical representative function, especially for the most marginalized women" (Weldon 2011: 148; see also Freeman 1995).

Protest by groups within large, diffuse, fluid social movements also brought policy changes over time (Janeway 1981; McAdam 1982; C. Payne 2007; Rochon 1998; Shaw 2009; Weldon 2011; Woliver 2015, 1993). Critical communities worked to open up a new value context with the power of their ideas, research, narratives, and proposals (Rochon 1998: 79, 95–96; see also Klapper 2013; Hall 1979; Marilley 1996; Martin 2013; F. Mayer 2014; Neumann 2008: 113–134; Perry 2013; Wattleton 1996; Joshua Wilson 2013; Woliver 2015). Autonomous women's organizing channeled social movement political support to women policy makers, whether administrative or elective, applying the pressure needed for improvements in the status of women (Costain 1992; Weldon 2011: 40–41). The interactions meant that "autonomous women's movements and effective women's policies agencies reinforce one another in improving women's representation" (Weldon 2011: 41). Feminist organizations have been understudied: "As submerged networks of actual and potential mobilizers, the women's movement is sustained by the organizations it has produced, and these *less than totally institutionalized* organizations may be more challenging and disturbing to the status quo than some critics seem to think" (Ferree and Martin 1995a: 11, italics in original; see also Reger 2012).

Coalitions of labor unions, health organizations, law centers, and women's groups, for instance, worked for decades for family leave in the United States (the Family and Medical Leave Act). Iterations of pieces of those earlier coalitions are still active in new combined efforts to achieve paid sick leave for workers as well as paid family leave. Many citizens are already covered by private plans regarding paid family or sick leave. In these reform efforts, the point is to systematically provide paid family and sick leave for all workers, not just the lucky ones already covered (Sholar 2016).

In lobbying, advantage tracks with the civic and political capacity of the citizens that organizational advocates say they represent. However, less than one fifth of advocacy groups have state or local chapters which would indicate potential for a grass roots– and citizen-based constituency (Grossman 2012: 80). Interest groups and coalitions therein concentrate on four political venues: (1) Appearing at committee hearings in the U.S. Congress; (2) Responding to presidential announcements; (3) Monitoring administrative agency rulemaking; and (4) Tracking federal court proceedings (Grossman 2012: 89). Advocates also work on public relations and media exposure for their interests. In these endeavors, interest groups want to bear witness, lay down markers, and be visibly present, even if they are going to lose (Grossman 2012: 103). Congress, the courts, the president, and federal agencies appreciate this as it symbolizes that the government listens to everyone. The dramaturgy helps sustain myths about their impartial and democratic roles (Grossman 2012: 106).

In addition, the media rely on efficient national organizations with camera ready, accessible, and pithy spokespeople (Grossman 2012: 126–130). Institutionalization can lead to co-optation and stodginess, yet, being organized "is the crucial dynamic explaining advocacy-group success" (Grossman 2012: 100). The advocacy community disproportionately represents groups with the most political capacity, national recognition, and reputations as the "go to" expert and advocate in particular policy debates (see also Grossman 2012: 100, 171–173; Baumgartner et al. 2009).

Conservative, Neoconservative, Neoliberal Strengthening

Alongside the grassroots and institutionalized women's movement in America, conservative activism also evolved and strengthened. One aspect of conservative power in the United States is networks of conservative and libertarian think tanks which have worked assiduously to reshape the parameters of public discourse about the role of government and the rights of individuals. Donald T. Critchlow explained, "Conservatives since the New Deal had been concerned with public policy, but quite often their involvement in policy discussions was reactive and abstract. The world of the think tank, by contrast, was empirical and intended for immediate policy consumption. The result was the emergence of a form of managerial conservatism that would challenge the bureaucratic liberalism that had reigned since the turn of the 20th century" (2011: 116; see also Grossman and Hopkins 2016). The conservative and libertarian think tanks directly challenged liberal frameworks. "Conservatives believed that to achieve power the Republican Party needed to be revived ideologically and electorally" (Critchlow 2011: 127). Without political power in established institutions like the federal courts (especially the U.S. Supreme Court) and the Congress, conservatives would remain a dissenting voice among many. To help move from the periphery to the center of American politics, several conservative and libertarian think tanks were established and strengthened during this era. These include: the American Enterprise Institute (AEI) established in 1943, the Heritage Foundation in 1973, the Cato Institute in 1977 with funding from Charles G. Koch of Kansas (Critchlow 2011: 116–122). The Cato Institute is libertarian and sometimes an irritant to conservatives in the GOP because of its opposition to government regulation of social behavior such as homosexuality and legal abortion (Critchlow 2011: 122). Dark money and unfettered financial support from billionaires have also built strong conservative networks, PACs, law firms, and think tanks (J. Mayer 2017; Southworth 2008).

In addition, The Federalist Society has created a supportive network for conservative law students and professors, has nurtured and honed potential judicial candidates and has been highly successful in placing Federalist Society alumni and friends into state and federal judgeships. Their latest placement was U.S. Supreme Court Justice Neal Gorsuch in 2017 (Toobin 2017).

"A kind of 'managerial conservatism' arose, therefore, that reoriented conservative thinking on actual governance toward a more ready acceptance of the exertion of federal government power acting within the broad principles of conservatism. Neoconservatism was not welcomed in some right wing circles, but it imparted energy and expertise to the conservative movement in the 1980s" (Critchlow 2011: 105; see also Southworth 2008; Himmelstein 1990).

Contentious factions within the conservative movement proved difficult for many politicians, even Republicans. Conservatives, for example, were unhappy with President George W. Bush's support in 2003–2004 for extensions of drug coverage in Medicare. In the fall of 2015, Speaker of the U.S. House of Representatives John Boehner (R-OH), resigned in frustration over the destructive opposition (from his viewpoint) of the Freedom Caucus faction within his GOP congressional majority. The 2016 Republican presidential nomination and general campaign was also buffeted by warring conservative factions.

As discussed in subsequent chapters, a strong theme in neoconservative ideology is a rampant individualism based on the logic of free markets to efficiently fulfill human needs. One aspect of conservatism is neoliberal feminist ideology, which "undermines feminist capacities for political judgment and collective action—capacities that we need to sustain political opposition" (M. Ferguson 2017: 1). President Trump evoked neoliberal feminism when he explained that if his daughter, Ivanka, were sexually harassed at work, she could just find a new job. Free market choices deliver justice, then, one person at a time (M. Ferguson 2017). The free market, rational choice heuristic, however, is challenged by people who assert moral obligations people have to each other, communal linked fate ideas, and recent scholarship on the irrational, misbehaving, sentimental, emotional and contingent behaviors of most humans (Thaler 2015). In addition, intersectional analysis of market options highlight the constrained choices people face given matrixes of simultaneous inequalities of race, gender, social class, and sexualities. Black female state legislators, for instance, advocate for reproductive justice instead of just reproductive choice. The distinction is the difference between an attainable individual market choice for a privileged few and access for all people to the options available (Williams 2016: 292–298).

Show Up, Push Back, Move Forward, Keep the Faith

Some giant coalitions of political groups, while not necessarily fighting the status quo tooth and nail every day raise voices for the powerless. Even though the agenda and needs of groups with more resources within a coalition get a disproportionate amount of group time and energy, the coalition as a whole remembers the less endowed people in the coalition. In fact, many times large coalitions deliberately speak up for the poor, the downtrodden, and the forsaken as an aspect of their mobilization, consciousness, moral obligations, and sense of being part of a larger community. However, the advocacy for the marginalized is itself marginalized in favor of interests of the more powerful even in progressive NGOs and interest groups (Strolovitch 2007; Spalter-Roth and Schreiber 1995: 114–127; Grossman 2012: 173). Of concern, then, is whether sustained action for the poor happens.

Tactics depend on the time, place, and context for political activists. In the American south, with the end of Reconstruction following the 1876 presidential election, the disenfranchisement of black voters in the 1890s, and the use of private and state violence to suppress black people, what John Hope Franklin labeled "the nadir" of black politics, black women did seemingly unspectacular things which over time altered political assumptions. In North Carolina, for example, "It means that black women were given straw and they made bricks. Outward cooperation with an agenda designed to oppress them masked a subversive twist. Black women capitalized upon the new role of the state to capture a share of the meager resources and proceeded to effect real social change with tools designed to maintain the status quo" (G. E. Gilmore 1996: 175).

Many other women's reform efforts have over time changed the norms of political expectations and civic procedures, often to the benefit of everyone. After women secured the right to vote with the Nineteenth Amendment in 1920, many women reformed from within by tireless efforts within the major political parties, state election mechanisms, and more to require locating voting places on neutral grounds like schools and fire stations, instead of saloons or local political machine headquarters. Written ballots, procedures for counting votes and determining run-off elections and victories were often pressed by female reformers. They reformed the parties "a room at a time," incrementally with results that established norms of fair voting and elections (Freeman 2000; see also Andersen 1996; Hershey 2013; Schuyler 2006). Groups like the League of Women Voters (LWV) were part of the quiet, consistent, competent work to systematically make government more open, fair and accountable. One local grassroots LWV activist recently recounted "heartbreaking" policy setbacks on important League issues like gun control. She reflected, "However, the League excels in marathons—dogged, difficult marathons devoted to a just cause. Gun violence is just such a cause" (Hamilton 2016: 7). Routine, reliable civic engagement usually gets taken for granted especially when women are tilling and spading that ground. Chapter 3 picks up the path of women's political efforts with an overview of the origins and structure of the NCWO.

3

More Than the Sum of the Parts

NCWO History and Structure

> In contrast to optimists who dream of a revolution miraculously
> transforming all dimensions of social life, feminist activists
> construe their transformative praxis more along the lines of a slow
> boring of hard boards.
> —HAWKESWORTH, *Globalization and Feminist Activism*

Coming Together: Assembling the Council of Presidents

Close to the denouement of the ERA ratification campaign, women's rights
groups' leaders started to explore how to coordinate future projects. Initial
queries about working together carefully reassured established group leaders
and members that combined efforts would respect individual group autonomy, funding sources, and agendas. Rather than one officially combined
overarching group, an association of groups was suggested.

The Coalition of Labor Union Women (CLUW) and NOW, in 1982,
launched early forays into the cooperation and coordination of group efforts.
Molly Yard of NOW sent a memo to ERA support organizations on September 15, 1982, entitled "ERA Follow-Up" (in author files). Yard referred to a
meeting a week before on January 9, called by Joyce Miller, president of the
CLUW. Miller invited the presidents of several organizations prominent in
the ERA ratification campaign.[1] Yard explained:

> The question Joyce posed was: How can all of us who worked to-
> gether for ERA, continue to work together to advance the cause of
> women's rights? How can we take advantage of the insights and mo-
> mentum gained in the legislative battle for ERA to impact the pol-
> itical arena? Can we maximize on the existing gender gap in voting
> patterns to start to change the legislative halls of this nation so they
> become far more representative of women's concerns?

"The consensus of the meeting," Yard wrote, "was that we should work in several areas to demonstrate that the women's movement will indeed affect the politics of this nation." Yard suggested a combined effort to get out the women's vote and to target incumbents in the states (particularly Florida and Illinois) who voted against ratification of the ERA. A committee convened by Kathy Wilson, president of the National Women's Political Caucus (NWPC), had started to work on getting out women's rights voters. Yard closed by asking for help getting the word out that Eleanor Smeal, at the time the president of NOW, was putting together a meeting of ERA groups in Chicago, also to get out the women's vote. Several follow-up meetings were held in DC along the same lines. Joyce Miller of CLUW and Eleanor Smeal of NOW were instrumental in continuing discussions on possible collaborations.

1985 and 1987

Archives in the NCWO offices refer to the COP as working together in DC since 1985 ("Background on the Women's Agenda and Council of Presidents," March 21, 1989; in author files). On January 16, 1987, the COP was organized enough to jointly lobby Congress and issue a press release. The COP asserted that they represented sixteen women's groups and more than eight thousand grassroots groups of mainstream women in every national congressional district. The press release reported: "Empowered by dramatic victories in the 1986 elections, major national women's groups presented Congressional leaders Thursday with a shared agenda which seeks not only to stem the recent erosion of civil and economic rights for women, but also to press for major gains in both areas" ("Women's Groups Press National Agenda," COP News Release, January 16, 1987; in author files). Issues highlighted included pay equity, welfare reform, child and dependent care, raising the minimum wage, affordable reproductive health care for all women, and passage of the Civil Rights Restoration Act plus the Family and Medical Leave Act. The COP was represented by Sarah Harder of the AAUW, Eleanor Smeal of NOW, and Irene Natividad of the NWPC. The COP representatives "presented Congressional leaders with an agenda of economic priorities that have a strong base in civil rights and economic need, and that impact not only on women as individuals, but on the families they care for and the communities they sustain" ("Women's Groups Press National Agenda," COP News Release, January 16, 1987; in author files).

The COP continued to grow in group members and visibility. In March 1989, the COP listed forty-nine group members representing ten million women. The COP orchestrated timely action among groups who had moved beyond debating issues. "While the Council avoids loyalty oaths, all its groups support the principles in the 1977 National Plan of Action for Women. Agendas and priorities vary, but no participating organization works against any issue in that Plan. The Council promotes reciprocal support and leadership in a diverse and effective women's movement" ("Background on the Women's Agenda and Council of Presidents," March 21, 1989; in author files). The National Plan of Action was the 1977 plan adopted at the U.S. government–sponsored National Women's Conference, also known as International Women's Year (IWY), in Houston, Texas, as part of the United Nations Decade for Women.

1991

Sarah Harder of the National Women's Conference Committee (a continuing committee of the 1977 IWY) wrote a three-page profile of "The Council of Presidents of U.S. Women's Organizations" dated April 10, 1991. Harder overviewed the history and agenda of the COP. She noted, "In over-organized Washington, there was no shortage of groups coalescing, often temporarily, to lobby on specific issues, but there was no forum where leaders responsible to diverse nationwide constituencies could shape larger strategies that would build momentum and impact. There was a need to extend connections beyond largely white middle-class feminist organizations to include leaders from an increasingly diverse women's movement" (Harder 1991: 1).

In 1985, the COP concentrated on passage of the Civil Rights Restoration Act. In 1987, their next collective effort was to defeat the nomination of Judge Robert Bork to the U.S. Supreme Court. Both of these initial efforts of the COP were in close coordination with the broad civil rights community in DC and the Congressional Caucus for Women's Issues (Harder 1991: 2; and interviews).

Using the 1977 IWY National Plan of Action for the basis of the COP Women's Agenda was "a kind of chorus on a shared song sheet, which invited organizations to add their verses. It was the first time since 1977 that so many groups had signed onto a multiple issue document" (Harder 1991: 2). In January 1988 the COP cosponsored a Women's Agenda Conference in Des Moines, Iowa, attended by two thousand women and some of the 1988 presidential nomination candidates. Strategies were built on previous projects all the way back to 1982 such as the Women's Vote Project coalitions. The Women's Agenda was intended to influence state and local policy efforts as well as those at the national level (Harder 1991: 2).

While Harder characterized the COP in its seventh year as effective and successful in combined efforts with other DC coalitions such as the civil rights community, she also noted it had no governing structure, no staff, and no budget. The COP functioned under this model because supporting group members donated their resources and leadership to the coalition. They also had to maintain the groups and NGOs they principally headed or worked for.

Throughout this period, the COP letterhead listed its address as "c/o the National Committee on Pay Equity (NCPE)." It is one indication of the commitment and leadership of Susan Bianchi-Sand, chair of the COP and also president/chair of the NCPE, to the fledgling collaborative efforts.

1994/1995

In December 1994 the COP adopted an agenda for 1995 entitled "Our Pledge to the Women of America." The sheet listing policy issues spelled out the words "W O M E N V O T E" along the left-hand column. The slogan "WOMEN VOTE!" was repeated at the bottom of the page.[2]

In the mid-1990s the COP chair and Steering Committee members sought advice from the National Committee for Responsive Philanthropy on a possible federation of women's groups' models and experiences (DeRobles 1994; see also Women's Way USA 1994; in author files). There were several strategy meetings to discuss the future of the COP.

Jill Miller chaired a drafting committee for a 1995 COP Pledge to help hone the mission and focus of the COP. As a diffuse social movement coalition effort, however, including long lists of issues and policy desires was hard to avoid. As many have learned the hard way, it is difficult in a large coalition to exclude a group's or strong personality's projects from what becomes a long laundry list. Nevertheless, individuals within the emerging coalition warned about too broad of an agenda, lack of follow-through on particular issues, and risk to the credibility of women's groups if nothing is achieved (interviews; Woods 1994; Bridge 1997; K. Bonk 1996; Hartmann 1997; in author files).

1996

In late 1996, Susan Bianchi-Sand wrote to the COP Steering Committee members that "in recent months a number of different organizations (some within the COP and some others) have informally discussed the need for a more formal effective coordinating arm for the women's movement" (memo, November 14, 1996; in author files). While the council had been moving in that direction, they still needed to organize and implement a transition.

From COP to NCWO

1998

By the summer and fall of 1998 the coalition was using the moniker *National Council of Women's Organizations* (NCWO). Early NCWO letterhead noted "Formerly known as the Council of Presidents." The address listed was still "c/o the National Committee on Pay Equity."

In July 1998 several drafts of the "National Women's Equality Act for the 21st Century" circulated from Susan Bianchi-Sand to NCWO Steering Committee members. A detailed version was agreed to by members of the NCWO in early July 1998. The preamble paid homage to the work of women in American history who worked for women's rights: the 1848 Seneca Falls activists, the suffragists, and ERA supporters. The preamble concluded with the following statement:

> Women of today still have not gained full political, legal, economic, social, and educational equality. We demand that the Congress and the United States of America ensure equality for all women—regardless of race, class, sexual orientation, disability, marital status, or age—in all spheres of life, including employment, education, retirement security, health care, and care-giving and family responsibility, as well as all citizen responsibilities, benefits and privileges. To secure these rights, as we fight for a constitutional guarantee of equality for women and as we commemorate this 150th anniversary of Seneca Falls, we advance the National Women's Equality Act for the 21st Century. (In author files.)

The nine-page, single-spaced document highlighted the following guiding principles:

- Equality for Women and Girls in Education
- Equality for Women in Employment
- Equality for Women in Taxes
- Equality for Women in Retirement Security
- Equality for Women in Health Care
- Equal Access to Media for Women
- Equality for Women in the Criminal Justice System
- Equality for Women in Family Care Responsibilities

A memo to the NCWO Steering Committee from Bianchi-Sand with a copy of the new National Women's Equality Act stated that "the preponderance of work on this project was carried by the Feminist Majority, American Association of

University Women, Institute for Women's Policy Research, & Center for the Advancement of Public Policy" with recommendations from other members of the NCWO. She concluded, "Considerable thanks is owed to these organizations and their leadership. This *act* is an excellent example of substantive work which can be achieved through our coalition efforts!" (Bianchi-Sand 1998: 1, italics in original; in author files). In November 1998 an NCWO "Policy Agenda" was adopted and circulated.[3]

From periodic tallies and lists found in the NCWO office archives it is clear that the coalition under the COP and then, in 1998, the NCWO grew rapidly. As of January 1998, fifteen groups were recorded as contributing to the COP's expenses. By October 1998, ninety-four groups were doing the same for the NCWO.[4] The COP was a gathering of the big women's groups in DC. As the COP evolved into the NCWO, becoming more official and prominent, many other groups and individuals sought membership status. Heidi Hartmann explained, "Then we went through the usual period of complaints of elitism: 'What about the smaller women's groups, etc.?'" So the council established membership guidelines and expanded (Hartmann, interview, April 2, 2001).

A United Chorus: The NCWO

The NCWO positioned itself as the main voice of the American women's movement. In a 1998 grant request letter, Ms. Susan Bianchi-Sand chair of the NCWO pitched the council as "the only umbrella organization that unites the leaders of women's organizations in collective activities around issues of mutual concern. We have a history of coordinated campaigns on labor law reform, affirmative action, welfare reform, and the women's vote" (Bianchi-Sand, December 7, 1998; in author files).

Their Organizational Document explained, "NCWO is an umbrella organization that brings together national women's organizations to collaborate on public education efforts on matters of public policy affecting women" (p. 1). The council acquired 501(c)(3) status from the Internal Revenue Service in 2000. They had a website: womensorganizations.org. There was a chair and a Steering Committee of eight elected members plus the chair. In September 2000, the Steering Committee was expanded to ten members plus the chair. A vice chair position was also added in September 2000.

By 2001 the NCWO had 122 member organizations, making it one of the biggest coalitions in national politics. In statements to both the Republican and Democratic 2000 national convention platform committees, the NCWO highlighted the following out of their more than 122 group members: the AAUW, African American Women's Clergy, Black Women's

Agenda, Business and Professional Women U.S.A., Center for Advancement of Public Policy, Clearinghouse on Women's Issues, Organization of Chinese American Women, Coalition of Labor Union Women, Feminist Majority, Institute for Women's Policy Research, Jewish Women's Coalition, National Committee on Pay Equity, National Organization for Women, NOW Legal Defense and Education Fund, National Women's Conference, National Women's Law Center, National Woman's Party, National Association for Women in Education, National Convention of Commissions for Women, National Women's Political Caucus, Women's Action for New Directions, and the Older Women's League. Clearly, the list highlights racial and ethnic diversity, inclusion of union women as well as the AAUW, legal rights groups, and groups concerned with the aged and the poor.

The list did not include groups working explicitly or exclusively for gay and lesbian rights. Important to note, therefore, is that despite this official membership status of LGBTQ groups the NCWO supported the rights of sexually diverse people. The 2005 publication by the NCWO, with an introduction by Martha Burk, made common cause with gay rights in several ways. Patricia Ireland, a past NOW president and advisory board member for the Gender Public Advocacy Coalition, wrote: "Every woman who speaks up and speaks out, who is confident, competent, and ambitious, or seeks a nontraditional role is likely to be tagged a lesbian. Until the time when being identified as a lesbian, whether true or not, no longer means a woman could lose her job, custody of her children, or even her life, those threatened by our progress will continue to use this tactic to divide and weaken us" (Ireland 2005: 126). My interviews, fieldwork, and observations of events revealed the seamless incorporation of sexually diverse activists into NCWO governance and activities. As many other scholars have highlighted, lesbians in particular were and are vital to the intellectual and political strength of the women's movement. Many times it was the sexually diverse people who could be counted on to do the spade work and show up when it mattered (see, for example, Byrd, Cole, and Guy-Sheftall 2009; U. Taylor 2010: 65, 70–71; Blasius 1994; Phelan 1989, 1994). Whittier's summation succinctly states: "Lesbian feminists and lesbian communities have been central to the women's movement—radical and liberal—all along" (1995: 20). My fieldwork similarly displayed the incorporation of lesbian feminists into the leadership and membership of NCWO during the years of the study.

Membership in the NCWO was restricted to nonprofit, nonpartisan groups. Organizational members needed to be free-standing women's organizations, with their own board of directors, and leaders representing a national constituency and perspective. Organizations who sought entry into the NCWO had to be a predominantly female membership-based group, with a broad purpose that included promoting public policy and legislative strategies affecting women (Organizational Document, p. 2). In addition, the groups had to agree with the NCWO's foundational positions.

The NCWO also supported passage of the ERA, and United States ratification of the United Nations Convention on the Elimination of All Forms of Discrimination against Women (CEDAW) without Reservations, Declarations, and Understandings (RDUs) that would weaken this commitment (Statements to 2000 Republican and Democratic Platform Committees, p. 6). Reproductive rights were folded into the topic of health care equality. The NCWO was strongly pro-choice. Member groups were asked to not speak against any of the agenda items of the NCWO. If a member organization did not support one of the agenda items, they were expected to remain silent and not work or speak against the NCWO position.

The NCWO had to work a delicate balancing act. One NCWO leader explained, "The NCWO needs to be greater than the sum of the whole, but can't eclipse the parts" (Pat Reuss, interview, August 14, 2000). Its budget was often very "seat of the pants" since it "has as much resources as the volunteers manage to raise for it from foundations, organizations, soft money" (Heidi Hartmann, interview, April 2, 2001).

The NCWO at Work: Organization and Structure

The NCWO had several task forces: The Social Security Task Force, the ERA Task Force, the Affirmative Action Task Force, and the Child Care Task Force, to name a few. Member organizations paid modest dues to the NCWO. In addition, the NCWO sought overhead costs on all grants awarded under NCWO sponsorship. The Lilly Foundation (linked to the drug company of the same name), for example, substantially helped fund the Women's Health Task Force.

The NCWO benefited from many in-kind contributions from member organizations. For instance, for many years NCWO meetings were held every other month in the conference room of the NEA in DC. They also secured sponsors. Lifetime Television underwrote some of their costs. The Nonprescription Drug Manufacturers Association financially supported the publication of the 1999 NCWO Handbook. The Ford Foundation awarded the NCWO a grant to work on protecting affirmative action.

Clearly, NCWO positions were more aligned with the Democratic Party than with the Republican Party. Given that the Democratic Party had become the champion of women's rights while the Republican Party moved away from allegiances to women's equity issues (see Costain 1992; Grossmann and Hopkins 2016; Wolbrecht 2000), this made tremendous political sense. However, the leadership of the NCWO, interestingly enough, tried to communicate with and influence the Republican Party even though they found these to be futile gestures. NCWO leaders testified to the Republican as well as the Democratic platform committees at the 2000 national political conventions. Before the 2000 presidential election, the NCWO, in partnership with the National Women's Political Caucus [a NCWO member], prepared procedures and hired staff (consultants) to nominate women to the new administration. George W. Bush's administration was not as open to forays by the NCWO as the previous William J. Clinton (and hoped-for Al Gore) administration had been. Nevertheless, the NCWO gamely participated in "The Women's Appointments" project of organizing résumés, letters of reference, and background biographies of women they nominated to the Bush administration for appointive positions. Perhaps these efforts were what 2012 Republican presidential candidate Mitt Romney meant by "binders full of women."

Nonprofit 501(c)(3) Issues

Almost all of the groups who made up the NCWO, and the NCWO itself, were nonprofits. As a 501(c)(3) nonprofit organization, the NCWO carefully maintained nonpartisanship and did not officially lobby. Public education efforts on public policies are permissible for nonprofit organizations. Adversaries carefully monitor each other as well. The demise of ACORN (The Association of Community Organizations for Reform Now) through secret recordings of their activities by a conservative organization opposed to ACORN's work and access to government grants is a cautionary tale in the activist community.

Many people interviewed evoked the fate of ACORN when explaining their own negotiations of the borders between nonprofit, nonpartisanship, and public education. ACORN's "takedown," as one interviewee put it, is an urban legend. Contemporary alt-right conservative leader Andrew Breitbart, for instance, used his website to help discredit and destroy ACORN. For Breitbart himself and the conservative movement it was a badge of honor (Bruck 2017: 44).

The destruction of ACORN was swift and lethal. ACORN was formed in 1970 and dissolved in 2009–2010 after prolonged attacks by conservative activists and groups. ACORN was a grassroots organization with offices in Washington, DC. The group focused on voter registration and turnout, fair housing, and a panoply of issues related to the poor and working poor.

Republican operatives consistently alleged that ACORN engaged in voter fraud. Investigations into these allegations did not prove these broad claims. If investigations revealed that individuals within ACORN behaved unprofessionally, they were dismissed from the organization.

In 2009, two people, James O'Keefe and Hannah Giles, secretly recorded interactions they had with several ACORN housing employees in Baltimore, Washington, DC, Brooklyn, San Bernardino, and San Diego. O'Keefe dressed as a pimp and Giles as a prostitute. They asked ACORN staff for advice on their taxes and housing. Edited versions of the interactions were uploaded to O'Keefe's YouTube channel, VeritasVisuals. The videos were also promoted on Andrew Breitbart's website BigGovernment.com, now consolidated and known as Brietbart.com. The highly doctored videos appeared to show ACORN staff advising O'Keefe and Giles on how to conduct their prostitution business without getting caught by the police. Several ACORN staff, despite not giving any illegal advice to O'Keefe and Giles, were fired. Eventually, it was confirmed that the videotapes were altered and inaccurate. ACORN released full videotapes of the interactions that showed no illegal behavior by staff. Many of the videotapes instead showed ACORN staff refusing to assist the supposed pimp and prostitute, or asking O'Keefe and Giles about the prostitution details in order to alert the police. Subsequent investigations by the U.S. Government Accountability Office, the California Attorney General's Office, and the Congressional Research Service, to name a few, found no criminality or misuse of funds by ACORN.

Nevertheless, for ACORN, the damage was done. The organization lost donors, contracts, and grants. They dissolved in 2009–2010. Subsequently, O'Keefe and Giles were investigated for their deceptions and fraud and settled a lawsuit out-of-court with one of the fired staffers. The "takedown" of ACORN helped raise the stature of Breitbart.com and their leader, Steve Bannon (Gertz 2010; Proskauer, Harshbarger, and Crafts 2009; Seifter 2009; Ungar 2013; see also Southworth 2008; Sexton 2017: 209–210).

The specter of an active right wing willing to win at any cost, as ACORN experienced, influenced the caution many groups affiliated with the NCWO exercised. Several times during the years of this study concerns about edging close to violating the 501(c)(3) guidelines came up in NCWO meetings of the whole, in task force meetings, and interviews. "We get too legitimate and too 501(c)(3)," Pat Reuss explained, "So we raise money instead of causing trouble and doing good. That is my concern" (interview, August 14, 2000). Defensive carefulness, then, was not uniformly appreciated by some NCWO activists.

The FMF led efforts though the NCWO to explain the rules, reassure group members about legal advocacy boundaries, and encourage groups to set up separate entities where they could directly engage in partisan politics. Many people interviewed for this study referenced how a lot of women's groups did not fully understand IRS rules on nonprofits and that hampered their advocacy.

Chapter 5 shows that, on working the gender gap, groups were circumspect about how they were registering voters, encouraging them to vote, and educating them on issues for each election. They did not tell people which party to prefer or who to vote for or against.

Alice Cohan of the FMF explained at one NCWO meeting that groups can take positions on issues, but they cannot take a position on a candidate. So, she reassured everyone, the NCWO and groups within the council could oppose privatization plans for Social Security but not the candidates espousing those plans (NCWO meeting, May 16, 2000).

Similar concerns were raised at other NCWO meetings in 2000, and then again during the NCWO meetings leading up to the 2008 election. Each time, boundaries were explained and people reassured that they and the coalition were abiding by the nonprofit rules. At 2008 NCWO meetings (eight years later!), Alice Cohan again explained the rules and boundaries.

The Alliance for Justice announced at the May 20, 2008, NCWO meeting that they had received a grant for pro-choice issues in the 2008 election. They offered free training to groups and people working on this issue. They also offered free legal advice for how to engage in election activities as a nonprofit and not break the law. The Alliance for Justice wanted 501(c)(3)s to be as powerful as possible in the national and state election season while remaining within the law.

At this juncture, Alice Cohan suggested that the NCWO as a whole should have an agenda item for training about 501(c)(3)s at the next meeting. Cohan said she noticed during meetings that many group members said first of all "[our group] is non-partisan, BUT . . ."; then the person explained how they agreed with an issue or were dismayed by a policy proposal. Cohan pointed out that most women's organizations are 501(c)(3)s and that "limits us in our ability to be active and effective in politics." The FMF, for instance, Cohan explained, is a (c)(3) but also has a separate (c)(4) and a PAC because the FMF did not want to be limited. NCWO chair Susan Scanlan responded that an agenda item of training at the next meeting was a good idea. Scanlan asked if the Alliance for Justice could give a fifteen-minute talk on this at the next council meeting. An Alliance for Justice staff person readily agreed.

Speakers from the Alliance for Justice presented a short training at the September 16, 2008, council meeting. However, some groups were slow to change. At the January 19, 2010, NCWO meeting, Alice Cohan of the FMF, while discussing the prospects for the ACA to include reproductive health care (see Chapter 7 for more on the ACA and the NCWO), reported that the U.S. Catholic bishops were very involved in trying to thwart inclusion of reproductive health care in the ACA. Cohan then referenced the special election in Massachusetts for the U.S. Senate seat vacated by the death of Democratic senator Ted Kennedy. Cohan stated, "Many of you don't have PACs or C4s. This is an opportunity for me to remind you that we all are watching the election in Massachusetts. If Coakley [the Democratic candidate] loses, it really messes up health care [reform]. There would only be 59 votes [for health care reform]. This election is affecting everyone in the country. This is an opportunity for me to say again that women's groups must develop C4s and PACs, otherwise, we are just sitting back and watching. And, having no impact on the results" (NCWO meeting notes, January 19, 2010).

In July 2010 Alice Cohan explained that over time many women's groups collapsed their C4s and their PACs and were only organized as C3s. Many groups did this because they relied on grant funding from foundations. Cohan saw this as crippling the feminist movement, limiting direct action and political election work, and thus hindering the impact of the groups (interview, July 13, 2010).

Funding and Funders

A sticky wicket for cooperative efforts is how to raise money without competing for the same resources with members of your coalition. The NCWO was not immune to these frictions. The NCWO waxed and waned in terms of budget and personnel resources. Securing grants, sponsorships, and in-kind contributions, to name a few, is how the NCWO, like many nonprofits, floated (or sank).

The 2008 financial crisis had a devastating effect on many groups in DC. The wealth of patrons and donors was diminished, foundation endowments shrank, and corporations pulled back from many philanthropic and nonprofit projects. Several groups that were members of the NCWO folded up and closed their doors as funding dried up. Chapter 8 discusses foundations and money further in terms of global feminist issues, many of which the NCWO dealt with as well.

Much of the money nonprofits and advocacy groups depend on comes from corporations. The NCWO secured several outside funders.[5] Informants for this research mentioned funding problems frequently. The NCWO's acceptance of "big pharma" [pharmaceutical corporations] money was brought up without prompting many times. Leaders of the NCWO were aware that some members of the coalition or other social justice groups not in the NCWO raised their eyebrows about nonprofits that took big pharma money. For the NCWO, which represented hundreds of groups and millions of women, it made sense that many business entities would be interested in making a friendly relationship with that potential market and respected organization.

Social justice operatives are fully aware of the delicacy of these issues. Kim Otis explained, "The money [available] is corporate or corporate philanthropies. Groups have to engage with them. An example: Walmart. They would be very interested in funding women's groups because women make 80 percent of the consumer decisions in a family. How to work with that and how to change that [work with the corporations and change the corporations]? Groups do not want to take corporate money and then whitewash those donor reputations because of the funding" (Otis, interview, September 4, 2014). At the same time, NGOs that accept corporate money might find their integrity tainted in the eyes of some activists.

Funders can influence a group's agenda. When vaccines to prevent cervical cancer (linked to the human papillomavirus [HPV]) were introduced, several groups within the NCWO received funding from the drug companies coming out with the shots. The shots were derided by some conservative groups as leading to increased sexual activity among youths. Women's groups and public health groups countered this with admonitions of support for a vaccine that can effectively prevent a cancer. At several NCWO meetings, drug companies and public health entities had agenda time to inform the coalition about the shots and their benefits, costs, and availability. While this was informative, and the NCWO as a whole felt the new drug was very beneficial to women, there were critics. One informant quipped to me, "If that group wasn't receiving the drug money, we wouldn't even be having this conversation [about Gardasil at NCWO meetings]" (interview). To their credit, leaders of the NCWO did not raid other group's funding sources or accept corporate money indiscriminately. While admiring the honesty of the NCWO, informants also mentioned these ethics as a reason the coalition was sometimes strapped for funds.

Bundled Up for Strength

Political organizers tell the story of how a single stick can be easily snapped in two. A bundle of sticks, however, is stronger and cannot be easily broken. The concept echoes in the chant heard at many marches, "The people, united, can never be defeated." Knowing the logic of this and achieving it with large numbers of people, however, are two different ball games.

There are both strengths and weaknesses in large interest group coalitions (Costain 1982, 1980; Hula 1999, 1995; Shaiko 1999; M. Smith 2000; Woliver 1998a, 1998b, 1993). One strength is an amplified voice derived from

a large, combined membership total. A further strength is the diverse expertise and lobbying strategies different groups bring into a coalition. Moderate
groups within the coalition, for example, can play on "the radical flank effect"
offered by more radical groups within the coalition and movement (Whittier
1995: 75).

There are even successful coalitions of coalitions. After the U.S. Supreme
Court weakened key aspects of Title IX in the 1984 *Grove City College* decision, civil rights and women's rights coalitions coordinated their efforts to
pass the Civil Rights Restoration Act in 1988. Their mobilization was strong
enough to also override President Ronald Reagan's veto of the Restoration
Act. NOW was instrumental in this coalition of coalitions (Clark 2016: 37).
NOW, under the leadership of Eleanor Smeal, was also a major force for
formation of the COP and then the NCWO.

The size of large coalitions, however, also includes weaknesses. In order
to keep the various groups within a coalition and not defecting, compromises
might have to be made on issue positions, lobbying tactics, and more. The
media pays attention when a large coalition claiming to speak for millions
of members holds a press conference, testifies at a congressional hearing, or
issues a press release. Coalition leaders know, however, that the media also
love fights and conflicts, especially among women. If members of a coalition
loudly and publicly exit the fold, the resulting media coverage of disagree-
ments can be damaging.

In addition to race, social class, gender, and sexuality, when someone is
politicized to a social movement, their political generation, also matters. "In
other words," Whittier explained, "coming of political age at different times
gives people different perspectives" (1995: 15). Generations within a movement are regenerative yet can also cause tensions among microcohorts who
define their feminism and choose tactics and alliances in ways different than
the "old guard" (Whittier 1995: 57, 78).

Differences, however, are smaller than commonalities and the need to
stay together, especially if politics is hostile to feminism. Women's networks
often are described as fictive kin, chosen families, or chosen kinship networks
(Whittier 1995: 112). For women's communities the "reality check" is an
important contribution to women's well-being while challenging the status
quo. Other women in feminist networks provide reminders "that, despite
opposition and sometimes invisibility, feminists are neither crazy nor alone"
(Whittier 1995: 113).

Many groups pushed back against neoliberal agendas of individualized
and market-based politics and rights concomitant with blueprints for limited
government. As Chapter 4 explores, the women's movement's cultural and

political aspects came together in a 2003 skirmish about the all-male membership policy of the Augusta (Georgia) National Golf Club. The NCWO challenged the practice as not just a game but a given, "neutral" heritage of not taking women seriously nor including them in the larger concept of players in politics and society. As subsequent chapters show, the NCWO amplified this message: countering neoliberal antigovernment, anticollective, anticommunity, and antigroup policies.

4

Master Narratives While the Masters Golf

Happily serving men *and* women in clubhouses everywhere.
—Amstel Light Beer Advertisement, *Sports Illustrated*

The Master's Tools Will Never Dismantle the Master's House.
—Lorde, *Sister Outsider*

I n 2003, NCWO leaders questioned the male-only membership policy of the Augusta National Golf Club. Before and during the aptly named "Masters Golf Tournament," one of the tournaments in the PGA Tour, played at the Augusta National Golf Club, NCWO chair Dr. Martha Burk and others pressured club leaders, members, and corporate sponsors about the membership policy that excluded women. The NCWO and allies asked why women were so blithely and unceremoniously unequal in this PGA event while corporate powers and decisions about participation and financial support of the male-only practices went largely unexamined. Chapter 4 explores this highly publicized and bitterly fought action by NCWO leaders who questioned women's exclusion from the Masters Golf Tournament. I argue that the skirmish was not just about rich men playing golf but whether women count as full citizens. Gender justice should incorporate the view that gender discrimination would be beyond the pale, bad for businesses, political parties, or candidates. To prevent these problems to begin with requires systematic change.

My analysis theorizes whether this (in)famous incident in our gendered/raced/classed culture wars was a distraction for the NCWO or a timely challenge to the larger systematic metanarratives of power that keep the masters golfing as masters. I theorize how an issue of gender dominance, male cultural hegemony, and large metanarratives about corporations and sports and politics, was reduced to a domestic spat between one man and one woman. The effect on the power and reputation of the NCWO is also explored.

Internal movement dissent regarding NCWO leadership's attention to the male-only golf tournament, coalition activists realized, would be delectable media candy handily verifying two subtexts about women and politics: (1) The feminist movement is elite and out of touch; and (2) Women cannot get along with each other (interviews and fieldwork; in author's files). Even without overt dissent within the coalition, and in the face of a politically united front, however, the NCWO actions regarding the Masters Golf Tournament were molded into a dominant metanarrative script that, in the short run, did not disturb male privileges and the status quo. The long run, however, was a different story.

Events began in the fall of 2002 when Martha Burk, chair of the NCWO at the time, sent a letter to Mr. William W. ("Hootie") Johnson, chair of the Augusta National Golf Club asking him about the club's exclusively male membership rules, which also governed play at the Masters Golf Tournament. Mr. Johnson called a press conference and said he and his club would not be threatened at the end of a sword. A media frenzy ensued in domestic and international print, television, radio, cable networks, and social media. Files in the NCWO office contained several hundred media stories and press clippings from around the world on this controversy. The coverage of the golf debate far exceeded the coverage of any other action the NCWO took during the period of my research.

The NCWO tried to focus on the corporations and CEOs who were members of the exclusive and private club, sponsored club events, attended events, or entertained clients and business associates at events. Club defenders and much media coverage demonized the person, Martha Burk. The issue was reframed in he said/she said terms of "Hootie vs. Martha."

In April 2003, when the Masters Golf Tournament was played in Augusta, the NCWO was there protesting. I attended the protest as a participant observer. The protest grounds were relegated to a muddy spot far away from the golf course entranceway and the golf crowds. Town and citizen hostility to the NCWO protest were palpable. Prominent also was the NCWO's critique of corporations, which relied on women's work, business, and money, yet participated in a gender-segregated event. Also, the solidarity displayed at the protest by Rainbow Coalition activists from Atlanta was important to NCWO activists. Yet, the support and participation by the Rainbow Coalition was not covered much by the media, if at all.

CBS news decided to broadcast the Masters Tournament as planned. The club announced it would not have corporate sponsors during the network television coverage of play. Within two years, corporate sponsors were again sponsoring the broadcast of subsequent Masters Tournaments. Martha Burk stayed involved in the NCWO and headed up its Corporate Accountability

Task Force. The club did not change at that time, the NCWO soldiered on, attention died down, and the masters are still pretty much masters at "The Masters."

Linked Fates and the 99 Percent

Important in the context of these events are also the following: (1) This took place during the George W. Bush administration, a time when women's rights adherents felt challenge and backlash from many sides; (2) during this time Tiger Woods was still an untarnished golf star; and (3) this was before the corporate meltdowns and government bailouts of 2008 and 2009. There was little critique of corporations at the time in mainstream (male stream) media and politics.

The NCWO was challenged during this action as addressing an issue far removed from the lives of most families, women, and girls. Whether or not women could be members of the Augusta National Golf Club and play at "the Masters" Tournament was widely ballyhooed as irrelevant to many of the millions of women the NCWO claimed to speak for. In American culture, sports play a huge role in the entertainment industry, corporate advertising, collegiate communities, and more. In the past, segregation by race in sports was framed as barriers to opportunity, leadership, and creation of role models and heroes, among many attributes. The media and the public pay a lot of attention to what is going on in the world of sports. Until recently there has largely been a lack of critique of gender segregation and inequalities in sports. Intersectional matrixes of domination are also acutely played out in sports.

When Don Imus, a talk radio celebrity, for example, said in 2007 that the award-winning Rutgers University women's basketball team were just "nappy headed hoes," the NCWO and dozens of other civil rights, sports, education, and women's rights groups sprang into action. The women in the NCWO spoke up to support the Rutgers athletes. They also spoke up because comments like that were about all women, all people of color, and, of course, all women of color. Linked fate was part of the outrage and action. Imus's comments did not matter only to student athletes playing Division I college basketball. After all, how many American women would qualify to be on such high-level basketball teams? The mobilization sought to support the students on the Rutgers team, and challenge Imus's insults as degrading to all women and people of color. The Masters Golf issues were similarly related to many macro- and microaggressions against people. When excluded and degraded people push back against such statements and practices, they are often told they will ruin a beautiful tradition that "everyone" reveres with their nasty, negative, and thin-skinned activist attitudes.

Regarding the Masters Golf Tournament, the NCWO tried to focus on the large issues of corporate accountability and legal exclusions/inclusions that have political and economic effects on all of us. The minutes for the September 16, 2003, NCWO meeting note discussion of a Moloney/Sherman Tax Bill (by Representatives Carolyn Moloney, D-NY, and Brad Sherman, D-CA). The minutes establish that their proposed "Ending the Tax Breaks for Discrimination Act" would eliminate tax deductions for membership in clubs that discriminate and require such clubs to print NOT TAX DEDUCTIBLE on their receipts. Over a ten-year period, these discriminatory clubs cost tax payers $52 million (NCWO meeting minutes, September 16, 2003; in author files).

Critique of the skirmish over the Masters Golf Tournament also focused on whether those who golf in Augusta matter to American women. It was cast as an elite woman's issue, after all most women might not aspire to golf at a place like Augusta National Golf Club. But many movements have fought for the right of people (black people, Native Americans, Jewish people, women) to be equal members in public and private clubs, public and private political parties, and public and private associations.

Even a very problematic popular book on the incident paid passing homage to the money and power aspects of membership in the Augusta National Golf Club. Although full of ad hominem comments on women's groups, leaders, and supporters, and with a golf sports writer's defensiveness and awe for the Augusta National Golf Club's leadership, members, and traditions, the author noted the links (in several paragraphs) to the business connections, networks, and privileges derived from membership in this all-male club (Shipnuck 2004: 92–93). The author also quoted several people, like the Reverend Jesse Jackson, who discussed the linked issues of race and gender prejudice and exclusion in white-only/male-only traditions (Shipnuck 2004: 185). Yet these messengers trying to explain that the tradition of the club was "of a piece" with the linked fate of many intersectionally positioned and marginalized groups were brushed aside and described as shrill, strident, off base, reaching, or worse. Understanding the issues in terms of power writ large did not gain traction or play well. Instead, "Hootie vs. Martha" was a more salable story line.

Standpoints, Personal Stories, Metanarratives

Many groups of people tell their stories in personal terms, but it is difficult, complicated, and rare for individual stories, those of the hardships of growing up poor in America for instance, to be theorized into larger narratives that systematically critique dominant ideologies (Snyder 2008). Periodically we see this played out when an advocacy group asks about social and economic inequality in America, and politicians and media pundits respond, "We are not engaging in class warfare discussions with you." What is left unsaid is that the given normal in the culture is or is not "class warfare."

Similarly, the housing market failures and high number of foreclosures since 2008 were often framed in terms of individual families who bought too much house or did not understand mortgage contracts and complex financial matters. Those who ventured to suggest the complicity of corporations and predatory lending throughout (see A. Hill 2011) were dismissed as stirring up social discontent to deflect from individual responsibilities. Recently, however, more evidence of larger nefarious systemic, institutional corporate practices, coupled with social forces constructing the financial and housing crisis, have been documented (Gogoi and Pickler 2011; A. Hill 2011). Not far afield from this is the "Masters" golf game, but especially the politics and controversy surrounding it in 2002–2003, the master narrative of who gets to define normal, abnormal, strident, disruptive, and ridiculous was played out in the engagement between the NCWO and the Augusta National Golf Club.

Questioning a dominant cultural icon like the Masters Golf Tournament casts the interlocutor as nonobjective while the status quo is defended with many points, including "tradition," that are presented as unbiased. Feminist and critical race theory has long troubled the water of dominant discourses of knowledge, justice, objectivity, and given traditions and social norms (Woliver 2015; C. Dolan, Ledford, and Woliver 2001). Universal assertions by presumed and concealed masculine subjects are a foundation of much objective knowledge. Women's movement, queer, and critical race theorists have critiqued the purity of these knowledge claims through standpoints that refuse separations of body and mind (D. Smith 2007). From this starting point evolved deep critiques of objectivity and ostensibly neutral social norms and heritages.

The cultural scripts for being a feminist mean, "We think of ourselves as generating meaning through our language use, rather than language generating us" (McCann and Kim 2010: 308; Rich 1979). Our language includes a symbol system we learn from birth so that "the meaning of words and gestures are already defined in discourses before we give them voice" (McCann and Kim 2010: 308; Rich 1979). One script is the "he said/she said" duality of two personalities individually fighting over a benefit presented as a zero-sum game. The "cat fight" and/or "gender wars" trope of "politically correct" politics systematically trivializes deep structural issues of equal opportunity, privileges, racism, heteronormativity, masculine privilege, and misogyny. Media often focuses societal attention on individuals who are fighting, personalizing disputes between characters rather than larger critiques of dominant systems of power.

So, in 2003, the issue of patriarchal privilege as exemplified by the Augusta National Golf Club's all-male policy became a fight between a male/female couple called "Hootie and Martha" or, better yet, "Hootie versus Martha." Like Shakespeare's *The Taming of the Shrew* it became a drama to be watched to see which person wins and which is subdued. Part of the power of this is the media's idiosyncratic framing of politics into news about individuals and their situations, rather than larger social forces (Iyengar 1994).

Addressing larger social forces such as American corporations' blithe participation in events that officially and without apology exclude women is a tough playbook to challenge. For ten years I supervised the Women's and Gender Studies internship class at the University of South Carolina. The class is required of our undergraduate Women's and Gender Studies majors. Students choose their internship placements with faculty supervision. They did noble work and useful projects: working in sexual trauma services, homeless shelters, battered-women refuges, illiteracy, hunger, and poverty abatement endeavors, to name a few. Many made several semester commitments to train and then serve as *guardians ad litem* for children in the city and county court systems. The students were wonderful ambassadors for our program and university in the community. They helped many people and NGOs. They learned and grew and so did I.

In required reading for the internship class we read studies of people making a difference, the value of social capital, and the way that a community can be more than the sum of its parts. We also discussed an African parable about people saving children from drowning in a river. In the parable people did this over and over and over again until finally one person said, "I am going upstream to see who is throwing our children into this river."

In *The Soul of a Citizen* the same parable was invoked by Greg Ricks, a former director of Boston's City Year program. Ricks "compared the situation of community service volunteers to people trying to pull an endless sequence of drowning children out of a river. Of course we must address the immediate crisis, and try to rescue the children. But we also need to find out why they're falling into the river—because no matter how hard we try, we lack the resources, strength, and stamina to save them all. So we must go upstream to fix the broken bridge, stop the people who are pushing the children in, or do whatever else will prevent the victims from ending up in the water to begin with" (Loeb 1999: 209). The upstream intervention, the catch is, required addressing the source of the problem and trying to fix it, to prevent the crises in the first place. Change upstream was essential.

The upstream nature of cultural givens was similarly missed when a question to corporations that benefit from women's purchases, business, and labor, that might take their travel and entertainment expenses off their corporate taxes and unhesitatingly attend a golf tournament year after year after year that bars women as members, was dismissed as silly. Twenty years before the NCWO's query to the Masters Golf Tournament, Gloria Steinem recounted her initial doubts about 1960s' feminist demonstrations against swanky New York City hotels and restaurants that discriminated against women as customers. Steinem initially thought these actions were irrelevant to all women and only important to wealthy women able to patronize those establishments. On further reflection, Steinem believed that the protests were actually part of an ethos that the world (even the New York Park Plaza Hotel) should operate "*as if women mattered*" (1992: 25, italics in original). Steinem wondered whether the media had a single key on their typewriters/keyboards when reporting stories on feminist activism: "whitemiddleclass" (1992: 24). Rather than being frivolous, the efforts made important points and had contagious effects. Perhaps Gloria Steinem watched the NCWO's Masters Golf Tournament controversy from a similar perspective. In an accompanying voice, Cynthia Enloe asked what difference it would make if women were treated seriously, with gravitas, in every aspect of life, as a matter of course (2013).

In some areas, it is still okay to discriminate, hurt, harm, belittle, or exclude some people. In 2000, with Chris Dolan and Angela Ledford, I studied the social movements engaged in the Confederate flag debates at the South Carolina state capital (see C. Dolan, Ledford, and Woliver 2001). In the summer of 2015, the Confederate flag debate flared up again in South Carolina. One triggering event was the massacre of nine African American citizens in their Wednesday night Bible study class in Charleston, South Carolina, by an avowed white racist. The shooter evoked the Confederate flag as part of his ethos, standpoint, and identity. The Confederate flag issue was dismissed both times as not important, as if the status quo (of the flag being on the capitol dome in 2000 or on the front lawn of the capitol in 2015) was simply local culture and tradition. Framing "the way it has always been" as politically neutral, "just simply the way it is," conjures a "view from nowhere" explanation of "how life is around here." Counterdiscourses and many people speaking and pushing back about the sources of community harm when people are excluded, slighted, insulted, and abused by the old traditions chipped away at the "givens" and brought about change. In the late summer of 2015, the confederate flag flying on the lawn of the South Carolina State capitol was lowered, furled, and stored for eventual display in a museum.

Given that the Augusta National Golf Club in the fall of 2012 invited two women to join (Darla Moore and Condoleezza Rice), the ruckus stirred up by the NCWO and affiliated groups might have had a long-term impact. In 2012, Martha Burk and the NCWO celebrated this long awaited partial victory. On November 14, 2014, a third woman was named a new member of the Augusta National Golf Club. Officials for the Masters underscored throughout who was still in charge: they did this on their own terms, in their own time, with their own judgment. The Masters' officials carefully framed the change as a seamless process of their heritage of membership selection by merit. The implication was that, in their past or present practices and traditions, not a trace of gender injustice could be found.

As the beer advertisement at the beginning of this chapter highlighted, a characteristic that matters in many transactions today is green: the color of money. As long as you hold enough green money where you are on the gender spectrum eventually might not matter. Yet, it was gender, per se, that mattered to the Masters. Free market liberalism did not operate at the Augusta National Golf Club. No matter how much money you had, gender discrimination per se had been keeping people out of the game.

Perhaps Martha Burk's challenge to Hootie Johnson, or more accurately, the women's movement members organized into the NCWO's challenge to male exclusivity as exemplified in the Augusta National Golf Club and similar institutions, if we look deeper, was not just a personal story of Martha getting on Hootie's nerves and trying to ruin the fun. It also exemplified postmodern subjectivity troubling the Masters' master narrative and hoping to destabilize dominant discourses. The Masters Golf Tournament is not just a golf game. Hegemonic masculine privilege as a cultural given functions as more than a cultural text, it does real harm as it creates and re-creates social norms about who is in control (Hawkesworth 2006; MacKinnon 1993). In other words, who is the master, and who is not.

Edward Said's *Orientalism* (1978) helps us understand these power structures. When one group of people sections themselves off as eligible to be "the masters" while others are placed beyond the pale as "natives," "dependents," or second-tier people in a colonial regime, one powerful metaphor for this hegemony is the plantation. People can admire the masters/Masters and defend them from criticism and demands for change, while the structures that people live and work in are colonial and abuse their labor, loyalties, and affections. One political slogan puts it this way, "Remove the plantation from your mind."

Glimmers of linked fate, however, pop up in our culture and politics in encouraging ways. In March 2016 the state of North Carolina enacted a law called H.B. 2. It mandated that people use bathrooms that matched the sex assigned to them on their birth certificates. The law was aimed at sexually diverse people, especially transgender citizens and children. Quickly, major sports associations announced they would boycott the state of North Carolina if the bill was not repealed. Boycotters included the NCAA, the NBA, businesses, convention organizers, professional associations, and more. North

Carolina lost millions of dollars in business because of H.B. 2. Among many consequences, in November 2016 the incumbent Republican governor of North Carolina Pat McCrory who signed and defended H.B. 2 was narrowly defeated for reelection by a Democratic challenger, Roy Cooper. People in North Carolina and all over the country stood up for their fellow citizens, surprising the ruling politicians in North Carolina with their solidarity.

The Corporate Accountability Task Force

A result of the Masters Golf Tournament showdown was a new NCWO task force chaired by Martha Burk, the Corporate Accountability Task Force. Burk was knowledgeable about corporate behavior. For instance, her husband was an accounting professor and his nonprofit, Stake Holder Alliance, was engaged in corporate accountability (Burk, interview, September 1, 2000). Burk's nonprofit, Center for Advancement of Public Policy, was also involved in business and politics issues. During the extensive publicity over the 2003 Masters' Golf issues, the NCWO received many emails, phone messages, and other communications from women working in corporations who wanted advice on how to deal with discrimination. Having inadvertently become famous from the Masters' publicity, and as chair of the NCWO, Burk could apply pressure on businesses to "put their money where their mouth was," as the old saying goes.

Burk and the task force carried on the work regarding exclusionary and discriminatory corporate policies and practices. They made examples of corporate CEOs who were members of the Augusta National membership and who refused to resign when invited to do so by Burk and the NCWO. Many of them were flagged as corporate hypocrites since their membership seemed to contradict their company statements about fairness and diversity. Burk explained,

> Our comments were simple and to the point: Regardless of company rhetoric, CEO membership in a club where high-level business is done and where women are kept out makes a clear statement about how they, and by extension their companies, really value women. We always added another simple truth—if the issue were race they would not maintain the memberships nor the stone wall of solidarity in refusing to resign or even to speak out against the discriminatory policies. (Burk 2005a: 106)

The NCWO partnered with the law firm of Mehri and Skalet to investigate and litigate sex discrimination at financial firms (Burk 2005a: 131).

Burk and the law firm put together class action lawsuits with various results: judgments against the companies, settlements out of court, or dismissals. Burk attended dozens of shareholder meetings and asked about gender discriminatory practices by the companies. Up to 2010, she gave regular updates to the NCWO meetings about her activities.

Martha Burk retired to New Mexico and worked with Governor Bill Richardson on gender equity issues in state government and with businesses the state contracted with for supplies and services. From New Mexico she regularly traveled to DC to attend NCWO meetings and other DC events. The issues raised by the Hootie vs. Martha episode are important aspects of women's second sex status and display the hard work of many groups, people, and entities like the NCWO to make sure women are treated fairly and with gravitas.

Spectacular, Yet Undervalued

My undergraduate students working in Women's and Gender Studies internships were encouraged to strive for systematic advocacy changes related to their particular placements. We discussed how to metaphorically walk upriver to find the problem headwaters that they addressed downstream as interns. One theme that emerged from students' written reflections and group discussions was how daunting systematic reforms and possible solutions would be. The students said it would require a large social movement, organized into an alliance, with the people working together to demand change, justice, equality, and not just symbolic language or weapons of mass distraction. After all, there are "many words that succeed, and policies that fail" (Edelman 1977). Large, messy, zigzagging coalitions like the NCWO seemed to be what the students had in mind.

Coalitions between feminists in different parts of the social hierarchy are difficult to sustain and need individuals and organizations to act as bridge builders across race/ethnicity, sexuality, and especially social class divides. "Continuing inequality between groups of feminists, then, makes coalition making both necessary and difficult; inclusive solidarity is only possible when partners at once take notice of inequality and strive not to reproduce dominance. That kind of process takes time and energy, and it is somewhat fragile, as it is hard to battle oppressions while fighting internal conflicts generated by those same injustices" (Roth 2004: 223).

My fieldwork with the NCWO reveals similar patterns. One strength is the diverse expertise and lobbying strategies that different groups bring to an effort. The coalition as a whole made sure to speak for the poor, the unorganized, and the voiceless. Feminist pioneer Pauli Murray described the process, "Like-minded women found one another, bonds developed through working together, and an informal feminist network emerged to act as leaven in the broader movement that followed" (Murray quoted in Kessler-Harris 2001: 234).

With the actions surrounding the Masters Golf Tournament in 2002/2003, the NCWO had spectacular media attention, vociferous blowback and opposition, and dissent from within and without. In the fullness of time, some change occurred in the Masters' membership. Many of the advocacy points here were also spectacular but undervalued by the media and the larger public.

Chapter 5 explores how the NCWO worked the gender gap in elections. The NCWO like most social movement coalitions and clusters of interest groups depended on electoral outcomes to advance their agendas. Elections shape whether coalitions like the NCWO play offense, defense, or at all. While the NCWO, like almost all organizations and coalitions with established presences in the national capital, looked white, well-educated, connected, and networked within the Washington progressive establishment, it nevertheless spoke up for the larger community. The NCWO's activism concerning the Masters Golf Tournament illustrated broad accountability issues surrounding who plays golf at Augusta National Golf Club in the spring and who can be categorically excluded.

5

Working the Gender Gap

The NCWO and Voter Engagement, 2006–2014

Chapter coauthored with
ANNIE BOITER-JOLLEY

> In DC you are either at the table or on the menu. DC is where the
> pie gets sliced.
> —SUSAN SCANLAN, WESCAD conference

> We need to ask our students, "Who benefits from your rejection of
> the term 'feminism'? Who benefits when you claim black feminism
> and its main ideas?"
> —COLLINS, *On Intellectual Activism*

Women make a difference in the electorate. As part of a recognized gender gap, women voters are highly valued by political operatives. In the U.S. Senate, one study demonstrates, "the competition between the parties to reach women voters creates opportunities for policy leadership and party messaging among women senators. Indeed, women senators act as ambassadors to women voters, promoting how the party's policies help women. This is particularly true for Democratic women as female voters more strongly favor the Democratic Party" (Swers 2013: 16). Concerns over the gender gap also have potential power for Republican women. In this chapter, the NCWO's voter turnout and engagement efforts are discussed. The NCWO devoted resources during the 2006, 2008, 2010, 2012, and 2014 elections as seen in interviews and fieldwork. One effort, "The Church Ladies Project," is examined in detail in this chapter. An NCWO activist and Church Ladies Project ringleader admonished us, "I want to be sure the Church Ladies themselves get the credit for this" (René Redwood, interview, 2010). In addition to fieldwork, we interviewed key activists and consultants related to the Get Out the Vote (GOTV) or Get Out Her Vote (GOHV) projects.

Advocating Turnout

Many national interest groups and coalitions focus considerable resources and energy on increasing voter turnout every election cycle. Women's movement organizations in Washington, DC, are now central to this effort. Formalizing activism is "a major characteristic of the U.S. women's movement at the beginning of the new millennium" (Burrell 2010: 211; see also Swers 2013: 27).

The "gender gap" phrase was coined in the early 1980s during Eleanor Smeal's presidency of NOW. The concept was used to gain support for the ERA and to encourage Democratic presidential nominee Walter Mondale to select a woman as his running mate (K. Bonk 1988). There are many moving parts to the dynamics of the gender gap. For instance, Emily's List (not an NCWO member as it is partisan) also encourages women to register and vote (Pimlott 2010: 34). Currently, Emily's List is more than a PAC. Emily's List is a multipronged influence and campaign organization, and an adjunct to the Democratic Party (Pimlott 2010: 148). The League of Women Voters (LWV), an NCWO member, also emphasizes voting and works at the grassroots level to get out the vote. Unlike Emily's List, the LWV is devotedly nonpartisan.

Attracting Women's Votes

The gender gap is located between different statistics depending on who defines the term. One definition is that the gap is "the difference in the proportion of women and the proportion of men voting for any given candidate" (Whitaker 2008: 1). Another measurement uses the difference in votes for the winning candidate in a presidential election (CAWP 2012). Other scholars focus on the gap in votes for Democratic presidential candidates (J. Dolan, Deckman, and Swers 2007; Huddy, Cassese, and Lizotte 2008). One broad conceptualization of the gap is "the difference in the proportion of women and the proportion of men who support a particular politician, party, or policy position" (Carroll 2010: 117). A further expansion also includes "differences between men and women in their political attitudes, beliefs, values, policy preferences, issue agendas, political party affiliation, and voting" (Conway, Steuernagel, and Ahern 2005: 37).

The two following chapters, Chapter 6 on social security and gender and Chapter 7 on health care reform and the NCWO, discuss an additional aspect of the gender gap: how public policies make citizens. There is a feedback effect of political learning as public policies shape citizen attitudes (McDonagh 2009: chapter 3). In turn, NGOs like the NCWO work the citizen attitudes and the gender gap on issues like protecting Social Security and providing access to health care for more Americans.

Whether the gender gap is caused by women leaving the Republican Party to join the Democratic Party or men leaving the Democratic Party for the Republican Party remains unsettled (Whitaker 2008; Huddy, Cassese, and Lizotte 2008; Carroll 2010; Norrander 2008; J. Dolan, Deckman, and Swers 2007; Polsby and Wildavsky 2004). Whatever the cause, women tend to be more liberal than men, encouraging them to favor Democrats (CAWP 2012; Norrander 2008; Whitaker 2008; Huddy, Cassese, and Lizotte 2008; Carroll 2010; J. Dolan, Deckman, and Swers 2007; Polsby and Wildavsky 2004). In part, the gender gap is rooted in women's and men's different attitudes toward "women's issues" such as reproductive rights, equal pay, and gender discrimination (Norrander 2008, 10). However, the partisan nature of the gender gap is influenced primarily by the difference in women's and men's aggregate opinions and beliefs concerning domestic and international use of force, "compassion" issues relating to the size and role of the government (particularly in respect to welfare and other "safety-net" features of government), and economic issues based on individuals' concerns about their own financial status (including women's economic vulnerabilities) (Norrander 2008; J. Dolan, Deckman, and Swers 2007; McDonagh 2009; Carroll 2010; Norris 2003). Agenda outcomes for groups like the NCWO rise or fall based on elections partially shaped by the gender gap.

Since 1980, the gender gap (measured here as the difference between women's and men's support for the winning presidential candidate) has ranged from a low of 4 percent in 1992 to a high of 11 percent in 1996, most often falling somewhere around 7 percent (CAWP 2012; Carroll 2010: 126). Since 1992, women have voted overwhelmingly for the Democratic presidential candidates. The exception is 2004, when Kerry beat Bush by only 3 percent of the women's vote yet still lost the election. Ten percent more women voted for Kerry than did men (CAWP 2012).

In 2012, Barack Obama benefited from a 10-point gender gap (55 to 45 percent of the vote), the largest gap since 1996. Measured differently—using a formula that takes into account women's larger percentage of the voting population—the gender gap increased from 12 to 18 percent between 2008 and 2012, with 55 percent of women voting for Obama, compared to only 45 percent of men (in 2012, women made up 54 percent of the electorate, according to CNN exit polls) (Bassett 2012). The gap particularly helped Obama in battleground states.

Voter turnout since 1980 shows women outvoting men each election. In 2008, men's turnout rates actually *decreased*, leading to an even larger discrepancy in turnout rates (S. MacManus 2010: 94). Furthermore, from election to election, women make up the majority of "undecided voters" (S. MacManus 2006: 374). Thus, not only do more women vote than men but more women's votes are up in the air: ripe targets for persuasion.

If current trends continue and women turn out at ever-increasing rates, the gap should grow. However, the Democratic Party cannot take women's votes for granted—as was demonstrated in 2004, 2010, and 2014. A majority of white women did not vote for the Democratic presidential candidate Hillary Rodham Clinton in 2016. In contrast, more than 90 percent of black women voted for Hillary Clinton in 2016. Throughout the years of this study, the NCWO has lent its heft and might to education and turnout projects, improvising on standard tactics and deploying inventive maneuvers.

The 2004 and 2006 elections proved problematic to many progressive groups because of low voting participation rates by young women, single mothers, and those living in poverty and near poverty. A concerted effort was launched by various coalitions to increase the vote in 2008, and this continued in 2012. Groups of women were pinpointedly targeted to register to vote, vote early, and be prepared to defend their registrations and votes. Groups with 501(c)(3) status negotiate the boundaries between education, advocacy, and partisanship with alacrity. Activities of partisan political organizations, like Emily's List, ran parallel to many of the NCWO and affiliated efforts but did not overlap or cross 501(c)(3) rules.

The gender aspects of both the 2008 and 2012 presidential elections were often compounded by the elections' racial aspects (S. MacManus 2010, 80; Whitby 2014). There is an important, and nuanced, racial element that plays into the gender gap (Conway 2008). The "race gap" between black and white voters is both larger and more predictable than the gender gap (Huddy, Cassese, and Lizotte 2008). Full understanding of the gender gap requires acceptance of intersectionality, valuing the messiness of overlapping domains of race politics and gender politics. One scholar predicted, "We can look back to the 2004 elections and look ahead to 2008 to see that the fate of progressive politics may depend upon the degree to which those at the intersections—women of color—are made visible during elections" (Smooth 2006: 403). Black women account for the predominance of black voters. "Yet despite this ardent support, African-American women's voting patterns are largely dismissed by political party strategists and subsumed in scholarly discussions of the gender gap" (Smooth 2006: 407). Black women's support of Democratic presidential candidates, for instance, is greater than white women's support. Waning white women's support for the Democratic Party was evident as early as the 1990s. "In all of these constructions of so-called women voters, the silence around the intersection of race and gender is deafening" (Smooth 2006: 407). Care must be taken not to reduce the complexities of women's votes into "essentialist fanfare" (Smooth 2006: 409).

Women are not homogeneous voters. The gender gap is built on intersectional matrixes to include race and social class. The base supporters for progressive politics, then, are women of color. Intersectional analysis of elections requires that "the differences among the women generating the gender gap in politics are recognized, exalted, celebrated, and, most of all, given serious scholarly attention" (Smooth 2006: 410).

While the gap persists across race lines, black women and white men tend to lie at the respective left and right extremes. This will be considered further in the discussion of microtargeting and party attempts to snag atypical voters.

Traditional GOTV

GOTV traditionally conjures up labor union telephone banks, knocking on doors, organizing rides to the polls on Election Day, and "walking around money" for preachers and neighborhood leaders to encourage voting. Christian Coalition election flyers on car windshields in church parking lots are also an iconic image from GOTV efforts. Today's ubiquitous campaign text messages, tweets, and emails are twenty-first-century versions of these tactics. Microtargeting, which goes beyond gender and partisan affiliation, was employed in 2000, gained prominence in 2004, and by 2008 had become a new norm in the GOTV arsenal (Burbank and Goldsmith 2010; S. MacManus 2010). Microtargeting techniques have also proven invaluable in the quest for women's votes.

The authors of *Get Out the Vote: How to Increase Voter Turnout* found that merely "reminding [voters] that Election Day is near" is not sufficient, even when they are reminded in person (Green and Gerber 2008: 137). Additionally, simply giving voters information about the election (whether in the form of flyers, voting guides, or messages delivered in person) does not increase turnout. Even when canvassers, callers, or mailers tell people which candidate or party they should vote for, turnout does not increase. Rather, potential voters need to feel engaged by the party or campaign. Voters need to "feel wanted at the polls," as if they've been invited "to a social occasion." Increased turnout is best achieved through personal contact and conversations (Green and Gerber 2008: 137).

Many studies also show that repeated contact is extremely influential, a finding echoed in Engaging Women project reports (Mulhauser and Redwood 2008b). As René Redwood told the NCWO, "Remember, as Kathy Bonk said, 'These are the women who waited to be asked to dance.' And, they waited to be asked to run for office and everything else. They must be outreached to individually, personally, not by a T.V., an ad, a web page, a flyer. They are key to the election" (Woliver, notes from NCWO meeting, September 16, 2008).

Awareness that other people are paying attention to whether or not you vote motivates turnout. Green and Gerber suggest that these turnout behaviors are linked by social environment (2008: 137). Delivering voters can go a step further, our study reveals, because successful GOTV tactics are enhanced when there is a high degree of voter *engagement*. Potential voters cannot simply be "talked at" or informed, they should be conversed with, tailored to, and involved. The NCWO helped engage women with these tactics as will be explained.

Although the gender dynamics may have been less overt during the 2012 presidential election (all presidential and vice presidential candidates in 2012 were male) there were gender-related issues that highlighted party and candidate differences. Debates were heated over the ACA, particularly related to contraception and reproductive health care (see Chapter 7 for more on this). Gaffes also grabbed headlines: (1) Republican Senate candidates' comments about "legitimate rape"; (2) Republicans doubting that pregnancies could result from rape; (3) Romney's promise to defund Planned Parenthood; and (4) Romney's clumsy stance on equal pay (he said he had "binders full of women" for possible jobs). Gender-related issues were front and center in the 2012 election. These issues only increased the already heightened focus on women's votes, ultimately proving the most helpful to Democratic candidates.

Targeting and the NCWO

Engaging Women, 2006

Launched in advance of the 2006 midterm elections, and originally intended to be a six-year project, Engaging Women (EW) was a coalition organization headed by political consultants and activists Karen Mulhauser and René Redwood and eventually included in the larger NCWO umbrella. The first phase of the project operated in three states and targeted seventy thousand coalition members, thirty-three chapters, twenty campus groups, twenty-nine women's centers/women's studies departments, 145 faculty members, plus several staff and statewide coalitions ("Engaging Women: Concept Paper" 2006). An early memo noted "our democracy is in trouble . . . Because of women's influence on their friends, families and cultures, increasing their participation is the fastest way to boost participation across the board and rescue our faltering democracy" ("Engaging Women: Concept Paper" 2006: 1). The plan was that through the efforts of the project, "the voter power of those who have historically been left out of the American political process will be enhanced." The National Council of Negro Women was also key to the Women's Vote Project. Mary Butler of the NCNW coordinated with others and the NCWO on voter turnout efforts.

Designed to facilitate voter registration, education, and turn out among the members of partner organizations, one of EW's most important functions was as a sort of "list cleaning" service. Coalition partners—such feminist 501(c)(3)s as the NCWO, NOW Foundation, FMF (including *Ms.* Magazine and the *Ms.* Community), Women's Action for New Directions Education Fund/Women Legislators' Lobby (WAND/WILL), the Dolores Huerta Foundation and Organizer Institute, National Congress of Black Women, the Women's E-Media Network, and the AAUW—collaborated by providing EW with lists of their contacts, donors, members, and potential donors, which EW then compiled into a common database.

EW helped community groups with their microtargeting. Using a list management company called Target Smart, EW ran this combined list against commercial files, postal records, death records, voter files, and itself, adding and cleaning up mailing addresses, email addresses, telephone numbers, and voting history. When EW returned these "enhanced" lists to the coalition partners, the organizations could tell who on their lists were registered, how often they voted, and who drop-off voters were (people who only vote in presidential elections). While organizations only had access to their own lists, they benefited from the information included in other lists concerning their members. Armed with these new and improved lists and $2,500 to put toward voter engagement efforts, EW coalition partners developed tailored messages based on the organization's mission, member demographics, and priorities. Since 2006 was a midterm year, messages often stressed the importance of Congress in policy making.

In addition to the lists and funding, EW held regular meetings with designated women from each coalition partner and contacted leaders in states targeted for their critical mass of members in partner organizations. Mulhauser suspects that much of the organizations' enthusiastic participation in the project came from their ability to maintain control over their own messages. In addition, there was virtually no fund-raising involved for the individual groups. The organizations were "thrilled" to receive their enhanced lists (Karen Mulhauser, interview, July 21, 2010). Many organizations, assuming that most of their members regularly voted, were stunned when they learned that, in some cases, fewer than 70 percent were even registered to vote. Further, according to Target Smart's reports, there was much less of a membership overlap between the organizations than leaders and organizers had imagined (Redwood, interview, July 19, 2010; Mulhauser, interview, July 21, 2010).

The first phase of the EW project also offered an opportunity to test the "trusted source" model of voter engagement. Results (see below) show that EW, largely because of its use of trusted sources, had higher success rates than similar organizations that used different tactics for voter engagement and much higher rates than the population at large. Based on our fieldwork we have started to identify a long-term "trusted source" community network–based voter registration and turnout effort from the women's community, both secular and religious. Organizers assert, "Every time we reach out to engage a woman, we touch far more than one person. For every American woman who becomes an advocate voter, a whole community follows her example" ("Engaging Women: Concept Paper" 2006: 2). Consultants connected to the NCWO worked with "Hollywood donors," the Hip-Hop Caucus, Rock the Vote, environmentalists, the NEA, and more to build a trusted community network of sources to emphasize the value of registering and voting (Redwood, interview, July 19, 2010; Mulhauser, interview, July 21, 2010).

The Church Ladies Project, 2008

A major focus of Phase II of the Engaging Women project, one key GOHV project the NCWO supported with in-kind resources and as fiscal sponsor in 2008, was "The Church Ladies Project." The Church Ladies Project was part of a "ground war" focus on the grass roots and key states by the NCWO and its affiliates (other large national coalitions of labor unions, civil rights organizations, and progressive groups like MoveOn.org, to name a few) to generate increased voter registration, to encourage and deliver early voting, and to increase voter turnout generally. The National Conference of Black Women, an NCWO member, was a key partner in the Church Ladies Project (Woliver, notes from NCWO meeting, September 16, 2008). Black sororities were also instrumental in the Church Ladies Project work (Liz Anderson, interview, June 17, 2009). In the words of one interviewee, the project worked "to ensure an honest, effective vote."

NCWO concentrated these efforts on African American church ladies because of their connection to traditionally undertargeted populations but also in part because of their legacy of power and influence in the black community. "The church ladies," one memo claims, "have created an environment where the church is a place for worship, fellowship and education . . . Sunday school [has been] used as a tool by Black women . . . to inform the congregants to learn the latest issues of the day." Traditionally, these women have "created an alternative space that simultaneously provide[s] service to black communities while giving black churchwomen an arena to perfect their leadership skills" ("Letter to Interested Parties," April 3, 2008; in author files).

Invoking black women's leadership in the antilynching and women's movements, Church Ladies Project literature references the historic position of women as the "backbone in their community," noting that they derive a strength from their roles as "breadwinner, family counselor, mother and spiritual advisor of their flock" to inspire civic activism ("The Church Ladies Project—Leadership by Women of Faith," n.d.; in author files). Religion is so embedded in many communities that one scholar reflected on her research about black female activists: "The religious experience was such a taken-for-granted aspect of their lives that the women usually did not mention it. They assumed, since I was a black woman, that I did not need to be told about the importance of religious experience in the context of their oral histories" (Gilkes 2001: 5).

Being the backbone in the community is almost a trope for African American women. When used in terms of black churches, the "backbone" can evoke women's lack of access to the pulpit and expectations of female silence and subservience (Gilkes 2001: 9–10; see also Stout 2010: 197; Billingsley 1999; Harris 1999; Joshua Wilson 2013). A close study of black women in the church offers an expanded view of the image. "However," Cheryl Townsend Gilkes writes, "central to the African American experience is its religious history and black women's activities and commitments form the backbone or indispensable central framework on which every expression of black religion survives" (2001: 10).

In this spirit, a Church Ladies document highlights, "The walk of faith for black women continues not only for personal salvation, but also for social justice and political empowerment of the community through the church" ("The Church Ladies Project—Leadership by Women of Faith," n.d.; in author files). Other documents invoked women's roles in passage of the Voting Rights Act of 1965 and the temperance movement. Leaders such as Fannie Lou Hamer, Ella Baker, Sojourner Truth, Rosa Parks, Coretta Scott King, C. Delores Tucker, and others were invoked as well ("Letter to Interested Parties," April 3, 2008; in author files).

The project targeted key states with the acronym: W O M A N. These were "select W-O-M-A-N states (WA, WI, OH, OR, MD, MA, MI, MN, MS, AZ, AR, NV, NJ, NM and NC)" targeted for increasing voter participation through a trusted source method ("The Church Ladies Project—Leadership by Women of Faith," n.d.; in author files). Activists and consultants interviewed were particularly proud of the Church Ladies work in the state of North Carolina in 2008. They noted that the grassroots nature of this effort was essential given that most black churches have less than one hundred members and are often rural.

Early voting was emphasized in the 2008 elections, especially by the Democratic Party, the Obama campaign, and the NCWO. For the women's groups, early voting was framed in a gendered manner: these voters have children to pick up at day care, they cannot wait in a long line on Election

Day; or, these older people (a lot of them women) cannot stand in that line on Election Day. Page Gardner, an indefatigable voter turnout strategist, concomitantly worked on "Women's Voices, Women's Vote," particularly targeting single women (Woliver, notes from NCWO meeting, September 16, 2008; Jan Ericson, interview, July 19, 2010). In the Church Ladies Project, therefore, one of the key goals was to encourage, explain, and facilitate early voting with money for church vans, gasoline, drivers, and bottles of water for early voters.

A major tactic the Church Ladies Project used was the creation and dissemination of voter guides. The guides were based on the 2004 NCWO *Voter Guide to Women's Issues* and *The 2006 ABCs of Women's Issues*. Guides were distilled and specifically targeted to the African American community. Each guide could be customized by location and congregation. On seven designated Sundays, these guides were placed inside church bulletins. The seven weekly inserts highlighted themes identified by NCWO partner organizations and members of participating churches. The themes were:

1. Economic security (pay inequality and poverty)
2. Housing (affordable housing and homelessness)
3. Health care (specifically dealing with HIV/AIDS and equal access to health care)
4. Education (focusing on improving public education, the burden of student debt, and presenting education as a "path toward . . . economic security")
5. Violence prevention (especially domestic violence)
6. Environment (including the "unequal distribution of environmental hazards" and the "unequal enforcement of environmental laws and regulations")
7. Faith and well-being (to include weight/health issues, depression, and using faith to help manage these challenges)

Each insert incorporated Scripture verses relevant to the highlighted issues. The selected scripture "conveyed faith-filled reasons on why voting for policy solutions was (and is) particularly crucial for African-American women at [that] moment in time" ("Letter to Interested Parties," April 3, 2008; in author files).

Importantly, the inserts did not merely report on the issues but invited readers to fully *engage* in the process, providing issue overviews (complete with facts and statistics) contextualized in the unique experiences of African American women. A section entitled, "Your Answer Is in Your Vote—Ask the Candidates!" provided a list of questions that voters who cared about an issue should ask political candidates. A "Vote For" section, offering a list of endorsed policy positions, helped voters identify candidates who best addressed these questions.

In addition to illustrating why church members *needed* to vote (and making the issues personal), the inserts also contained information about where and when to register and vote. A key aspect of the flyer detailed steps members could take to protect their votes. The last page of every bulletin was the same, with sections detailing where to get further information about voter registration requirements by state with cites to www.Vote411.org and 1-866-OUR-VOTE for help before and on Election Day. A section called "Know Your Rights" included information about voter identification requirements; provisional, conditional, and challenge ballots; and assistance available for blind, disabled, or non-English-reading/writing voters. Continuing the theme of engagement beyond voting, a section called "You Can Do More Than Just Vote" included information about becoming an Election Judge and helping others register to vote. A line of text at the bottom of the page again tied together faith and political engagement: "The Church Ladies tithe with their time, talent, and treasure," followed by the NCWO website address.

These grassroots Church Ladies Project efforts displayed a nimble adaptation of hybrid frames (Goss and Heaney 2010) and organizations coming together for the 2008 vote. The Hip-Hop Caucus and the Church Ladies engaged in pragmatic cooperation in turning out the vote in 2008. Whereas less technologically adept Church Ladies forwarded neatly alphabetized rolodexes of their member/voter lists to the DC offices of the Church Ladies Project, leaders of the Hip-Hop Caucus used Twitter and Facebook to remind followers and friends to register, to vote early, if possible, but, especially, to vote. Lil Kim, T. I., Queen Latifah, and others mobilized their fans and listeners through existing electronic social networks, once again using "underutilized infrastructures" to appeal to undertargeted groups of voters. With hundreds of thousands of recipients, these tweets had enormous impact (Redwood, interview, July 19, 2010).

Because organizers were familiar with the wide range of capabilities the diverse pool of participating churches, auxiliaries, and other organizations would have at their disposal, they carefully designed Church Ladies Project materials to be tailored to specific communities. Bulletins were available as downloads from the Church Ladies Project website, in emailed form, or even as hard copies mailed to churches with limited technological resources. Additionally, participating auxiliaries were encouraged to engage young people in the project and "tap the youth ministries" for technological assistance ("Letter to Interested Parties," April 3, 2008; in author files). Each issue bulletin was developed as a customizable template available online so that churches and auxiliaries could "download and *own* the document with the organization's name and contact information" (emphasis ours) ("Letter to Interested Parties," April 3, 2008; in author files).

By far the largest budgeted expense (an anticipated $288,000 for 1.6 million pieces for bulletins or mail), the Church Ladies Project sought out in-kind donations to minimize printing costs ("Letter to Interested Parties," April 3, 2008; in author files). Among other organizations, the Church Ladies Project sought $100,000 of in-kind printing from Women's Voices, Women's Vote (which focuses on single women voters). This illustrates another aspect of coalition work: the involvement of ready-made partners in organizations with similar goals who can step up to meet the needs of organizations whose goals align with their own ("Letter to Interested Parties," April 3, 2008; in author files).

The Church Ladies Project, similar to labor unions, Rock the Vote, MoveOn.org, and others, also "lawyered up" for the election. They had hotlines set up for any problem with voter registration, lack of ballots, broken voting machines, poll worker issues, and language or literacy barriers. Among other popular media outlets and figures, the widely syndicated radio host Tom Joyner was an early advocate. Joyner promoted the hotlines for months before the election entreating his predominantly African American radio listeners to remember and use the hotlines (Redwood, interview, July 19, 2010). Much of this careful preparation derives from the hard lessons of the 2000 presidential election. Our informants noted explicitly that in North Carolina the Church Ladies Project was instrumental in delivering the vote for Obama, and electing a slate of women Democrats up and down the ticket in 2008.

Get Out Her Vote, 2000–2012

Since 1980, women have led men in both registration numbers and turnout rates among the voting eligible population (Center for American Women and Politics [CAWP] 2012; S. MacManus 2010: 88). However, while this trend has generally been increasing among younger (under forty-five) women since the 1970s, older women (over sixty-five) are increasingly falling behind men in both registration and turnout (CAWP 2012; S. MacManus 2010: 88). It was this inconsistency, as well as the generally low turnout rates among young people and attention paid to groups of women typically overlooked by traditional, party- and candidate-led GOTV efforts, that led women's organizations to begin specifically targeting subsegments of women voters and potential voters, not only to get them registered but even more importantly to get them to turn out to vote (CAWP 2012; S. MacManus 2010).

Dating back to 2000, "Get Out Her Vote" (GOHV), a grassroots initiative led by the FMF, worked to register, engage, and turn out young women on college and university campuses around the country. The GOHV campaign specifically targeted campuses in states where ballot initiatives and referenda related to FMF's mission (reproductive rights, affirmative action, etc.) appeared. The GOHV effort sent national campus organizers to targeted schools. Organizers identified existing Feminist Majority Leadership Alliances (FMF's student-led, campus-based affiliates), other feminist-oriented student organizations, interested students, and faculty, and put the GOHV tools in students' hands. FMF hired students part-time to organize GOHV activities on their campuses with the guidance and support of the national campus organizers. By primarily relying on student-led organizations, GOHV tapped into existing networks as well as students' knowledge of their campus and community. GOHV saved national organizers the time and effort of building a local base of student support and researching available and optimal resources. Campus directors were trained in both the process and the issue sides of the campaign. They used toolkits provided by FMF to distribute literature, conduct registration drives in student unions and commons, hold rallies, and encourage (and sometimes escort students to) early voting where available. FMF affiliates hosted film screenings and turned out the vote on Election Day. Throughout the process, organizers and directors emphasized that "voting is a way to give voices to traditionally oppressed people—women, minorities, poor people, students—that it's the most fundamental way to have a voice" (Beth Kadar, interview, July 23, 2010).

Literature from the 2012 GOHV campaign encouraged young women to "VOTE AS IF YOUR LIFE DEPENDS ON IT!" and highlighted the fact that the 112th Congress was "the first time in 30 years the number of women represented . . . had declined" (feministcampus.org). One pamphlet stressed the importance of the mobilization of "young feminist women," and encouraged students to build upon the momentum achieved during the 2008 election.

AAUW's "My Vote 2012"

Capitalizing on successful projects and initiatives from previous years, many organizations continued working to get out women's votes in 2012. One was the AAUW's "My Vote 2012" campaign. Conducted through the organization's Action Fund, the program, formally titled "It's My Vote: I Will Be Heard," focused on turnout, education, and resource dissemination. Geared especially toward college age women and "millennials," the program pushed voter registration through events and reminder postcards sent to potential voters in the weeks before their state's voter registration deadlines. Similar to the GOHV initiative, Engaging Women, and the Church Ladies Project, the program was designed to put the necessary tools into participants' hands and take advantage of existing infrastructures. The parent organization even made funds available in some states for advertising in college newspapers.

A major component of the project was the "Woman-to-Woman Voter Turnout Manual," which included information about voter turnout techniques, planning strategies, volunteer recruitment tools, coalition building techniques, targeting strategies and messages, voter education guides, and many other tools designed to facilitate trusted source registration and engagement. Mirroring the philosophy and findings of similar groups, the project description reads, "Women who don't already have the voting habit must be urged to vote through a personal appeal. The more personal the contact with a voter, the more likely she is to vote" (aauw.org). Embracing this idea, the My Vote 2012 webpage stressed that voting is a habit where social networks of voters are important. AAUW branches, therefore, should increase women's voting turnout woman by woman (aauw.org; accessed January 3, 2013).

Again bringing GOTV into the twenty-first century, My Vote 2012 got its message out even further through Twitter, Tumblr, the blogosphere, and regular email campaign updates. NCWO council meetings of the whole received regular updates on all of these projects. The NCWO was kept informed on the projects' formative stages, implementation, and voter turnout impact.

Patterns: Registration, Early Voting, and Turnout

The efforts of the NCWO and many other groups paid off. Studies conducted in six states showed that the aggregate rate of new voter registration in 2008 increased 89 percent for women and only 74 percent for men (S. MacManus 2010: 92). This gender discrepancy showed up in turnout rates as well. The increase resulted from targeting traditionally lower-turnout populations, especially young black women and Latinas (S. MacManus 2010: 93). Overall, 131.1 million people turned out in 2008, and while the turnout rate was slightly lower than the turnout rate in 2004, over five million more voters actually voted in 2008—the highest total number of votes cast in history (S. MacManus 2010: 92). Early voting also seems to have played a major role in the 2008 election's historic turnout levels. According to the National Annenberg Election Survey, 34.3 percent of voters voted early in 2008, as opposed to 20 percent in 2004 and only 14 percent in 2000 (Kenski, Hardy, and Jamieson 2010: 255).

In addition to record-breaking registration levels, early voting, and overall voter turnout across the gender board, studies indicate that the unique approaches to GOTV/GOHV and voter engagement adopted by women's organizations and coalitions in the 2006 and 2008 elections especially succeeded in turning out women previously overlooked by traditional GOTV efforts. In 2006, follow-up reports on the EW project showed that members of the coalition partner organizations voted "at a higher percentage than the population at large" and indicated that the more often those members were contacted by their organization about turning out, the more likely they were to actually go vote.

Even among drop-off voters who tend to vote only in presidential election years, contacted members were more than 15 percent more likely to vote than noncontacted members. Contacted drop-off voters were 8.5 percent more likely to vote than their noncontacted counterparts. Although the dataset was fairly small for this category, the results showed that repeated contacts dramatically improved the turnout rate, in some cases by more than 10 percentage points for each additional contact ("Engaging Women 2006: Summary of Impact on Elections"). In Michigan, Washington, and Arizona, where extensive data were collected for the project, the targeted members of the coalition partner organizations turned out at 72.94 percent, more than twenty points higher than the aggregate rate of 52.89 percent ("Engaging Women 2006: Summary of Impact on Elections").

Although the extensive postelection data gathering of the first phase of the Engaging Women project was not a component of the Church Ladies Project (due in part to the grassroots nature of the campaign, and in part to funding issues), the campaign blueprint and methods to engage and turn women out to vote were nearly identical to those used by EW. These tactics included list enhancement, individually adapted and targeted messages, and particularly the use of trusted sources. We infer that the project was similarly successful—especially when coupled with the registration and turnout increases attributed to the nature of the 2008 presidential election.

Not only did the participants in the project self-report higher turnout rates and general successes but a similar project headed by EW's Karen Mulhauser, geared toward propeace and antiwar organizations, "Peace Impact," adopted EW's methods, including the extensive postelection data gathering. "Peace Impact" reported successes that mirrored those in 2006, including a coalition turnout rate of 74.2 percent against a general population turnout rate of 61.7 percent, according to "Peace Impact: Engaging an Under-Utilized Infrastructure for Electoral Impact: A Report for 2008a."

Higher registration rates are not enough, however—what really counts is getting people out to the polls on Election Day. Further, it is not enough for women to out-vote men at the polls. Women voters have outpaced men since 1980. To really see an increase in effectively working the gender gap to win women's votes, an increase in women's already superior turnout rates is needed. In 2008, women did just that: women turned out at a rate of 60.4 percent, as opposed to men's 55.7 percent—an increase of 0.3 percent for women and a *decrease* of 0.6 percent for men from 2004 rates (S. MacManus 2010: 93). In raw numbers, women outvoted men by about 9.7 million votes nationally (Carroll 2010, 140; Center for American Women and Politics).

The persistence of the gender gap in favor of the Obama/Biden ticket (seven points in 2008, based on the difference between women's support for the winning candidate and women's support for the losing candidate, and ten points in 2012) indicates that the Democratic Party, the Obama campaign, and fellow travelers in a nonpartisan, advocacy-oriented tract, like the NCWO, were successful in woman-targeted registration and GOTV/GOHV efforts. This is in sharp contrast to the 2004 presidential election, when Republicans turned out more targeted women (S. MacManus 2006: 378).[1] Future research should look more closely at the differences in both parties' GOTV and targeting strategies from 2004 to 2016. Scholars should also give credit where credit is due, especially to efforts like the 2008 Church Ladies Project.

The severe economic collapse of summer and fall 2008 undoubtedly helped Democratic candidates. The financial crisis, depth of the recession, and levels of unemployment set many mainstream free market economists on their heels (Madrick 2014: 8). One pundit ironically reflects, "Were it not for the social programs started in the New Deal of the 1930s and expanded in the 1960s, including Social Security, unemployment insurance, and Medicare, and those adopted later, including the earned income tax credit and food stamps—the great embrace of government, not its denigration—the nation would likely have entered a full-fledged depression by 2009" (Madrick 2014: 8). Many women realize that these programs help them and their extended families stay above the water economically. The aggressive federal government rescue efforts beginning in 2008 helped matters not get worse. In other words, "non-laissez-faire economics saved the day" (Madrick 2014: 8).

In 2012, both campaigns actively targeted women voters, through both messages and participation (which may be key to actually *engaging* women in the process and ensuring their turnout) (Riccardi 2012). While Democratic candidates tended to focus targeted messages on reproductive rights, health care, and equal pay issues, Republican candidates focused on less overtly gender-specific issues such as jobs and the economy. The 2012 elections had the largest gender gap in U.S. history: a 20 percentage point gap in favor of reelecting President Obama.

Activists and consultants noted that even though these projects were very successful, and they were ready to reprise them in subsequent elections, they were not funded (Mulhauser, interview, and others, 2014). The 2015 and 2016 presidential campaign by Hillary Clinton had a strong gravitational pull absorbing a lot of the resources that might previously have been used for the efforts of NCWO and affiliates.

From Retail Activism to Feminist Majorities

Our sources referred to political epiphanies they had after the 2000 presidential election debacle. They realized that who secretaries of state were (think: Katherine Harris of Florida in 2000) mattered a lot. These S.O.S. (secretaries of state), the consultants believed, could be effectively positioned by just a few PAC contributions and targeted primary campaigns. Future researchers should explore the secretary of state issue more.

As many scholars have shown (Andersen 1996; Barakso 2004; Freeman 2000; Wolbrecht 2000; Costain 1992), the American women's movement has often worked within the two established political parties to achieve gender representation and gender-based social policies. The Church Ladies Project, we find, is part and parcel of the national women's movement's efforts to shape national politics through strategic alliances with labor, civil rights, and other progressive groups. The project echoes the roots of many women's groups (Beckwith 1986; Evans 1979; Freedman 2002; Katzenstein 1998; C. Payne 2007; Tarrow 1998) in labor, civil rights, and social justice politics. In a largely secular modern women's movement, the Church Ladies Project worked between the sustaining powers of religion and community ties (Horton 1990; Woliver 1993) to affect the 2008 elections. If sustained over time, such coalitions of coalitions strengthen the national women's movement organizations within the larger progressive and social justice communities, both secular and religious.

Though gender-related challenges were perhaps less overt in 2012 and 2014 than in 2008 or even 2010, women remained the essential targets of political parties' attempts to work the gender gap to their advantage. Will public education efforts of 501(c)(3)s and NGOs like the NCWO remain central to election outcomes? Certainly, legacies of these coalitions of coalitions will persist into future elections. Activists will continue to strengthen national women's movement organizations in part by expanding their political reach through voter turnout and party engagement.

Move Forward: Hopeful Signs

Many leaders of the NCWO emphatically mentioned in interviews or in meetings the devastating sexist treatment Senator Hillary R. Clinton (D-NY) endured during the 2007–2008 presidential nomination campaign. Scholarship and pundit analysis almost uniformly agrees with this assessment. In *Notes from the Cracked Ceiling*, Washington Post reporter Anne E. Kornblut asserts that gender is an inescapable factor in assessments of women candidates—including Sarah Palin as well as Hillary Clinton (2010; see also Traister 2010).

Recent research has found that gender stereotypes about women political candidates might be fading. The research published by Deborah Jordan Brooks sketches the following scenario for female politicians in the United States: "Over time, each [woman candidate] helped to overcome the token status of women politicians, becoming part of a larger and much more powerful sisterhood. In the process, it seems that candidate gender has become yet another characteristic that brings diverse ideas to the political arena rather than the all-important road block on the campaign trail that it was once believed to be" (2013: 175). Brooks, therefore, asks academics and media to encourage women to run and temper the old double standard narrative about female candidates. Brooks's work is based on carefully examined experiments. She notes both the strengths and the weaknesses in this experimental method but convincingly displays the moderation of gendered double standards.

A study based on interviews with campaign consultants and candidates negotiating gender campaigns finds "women's electoral success may be a result of *adaptation to* instead of *triumph over* gender barriers" (Dittmar 2015: 10, italics in original). For consultants, gender was part of the picture of 2010 campaigns to the point where ignoring gender would be professional malpractice (Dittmar 2015: 48). Campaigns are gendered institutions "whereby gender not only is embedded in expectations for and behavior of candidates but also influences the psyche and strategic consideration of all those involved" (Dittmar 2015: 4). These are the premises the NCWO and allies work on in getting out her vote, engaging women, and mobilizing trusted sources.

Given the strength of the gender gap and women's groups, along with political party officials and individual candidate consultant attempts to benefit from the gender gap and increase women's voting turnout, if more women eventually ran for office, the two trends combined would affect public policy. Many scholars have documented "the difference women make" in political discussions, agenda making, and legislative outcomes (N. Brown 2014b; S. Thomas 1994; Karpowitz and Mendelberg, 2014; Swers 2002). Brooks's research also reveals that voters want leaders, not ladies, as political representatives. Female candidates benefit, for example, by toughness. However, women candidates still must demonstrate strength without being strong (Deborah Jordan Brooks 2013: 111). Nadia Brown points out as well that black women state legislators in the United States feel that they represent intersectional viewpoints and communities. Brown writes that black female state legislators' standpoint is complicated and, "although there are many consistencies in Black political identities, they are also more fluid and dynamic than widely acknowledged" (2014b: 117). Black women legislators "may in fact build bridges between essentialist and nonessentialist forms of Black politics" (2014b: 118).

Yet another encouraging sign for gender in elections is that many female candidates balance their images with competence, knowledge of issues, and hard work on the campaign trail. If sexist attacks occur in a campaign, publicly identifying and critiquing them eliminates their effectiveness (Deborah Jordan Brooks 2013: 154). As Deborah Jordan Brooks wrote, "Looking forward, I concur with those who argue that women have a very promising future in American politics" (2013: 14). Brooks continued, "The very good news from my study is that we do not somehow have to figure out how to change the views or reactions of the general public in order to give women a fighting chance in politics" (2013: 162). New theoretical frames highlighting the overrepresentation of men in political representation, like powerful poetry, shape ways for us to imagine new futures (see, for example, Murray 2014).

When more women and feminist or progressive men run, they will be campaigning in terrains where many people, including unspectacular spadework done in EW and the Church Ladies Project, will shape their campaigns and chances for nomination and election. As learned from years of effort to get out her vote, trusted sources need to "touch" each voter sometimes four, five, or six times to deliver the vote.

Collective efforts around the women's vote were rooted in a sense of linked fate and communal efforts to address social problems. Their critique of neoliberalism includes the point that millions of Americans actually benefit from collective, communal government programs such as Social Security (see, for example, Schwarz 1988; Moyers 2003). Social Security, their position is, needs more communal buy-in, not less. Particularly anathema would be gambling with Social Security via Wall Street's markets. Women are often the most likely to be harmed by neoliberal, market-based policies, the NCWO consistently pointed out. The next chapter details these themes with close study of the NCWO's push back against privatizing Social Security.

ANNIE BOITER-JOLLEY is a Ph.D. candidate in Political Science at the University of South Carolina. She holds an MA in Political Science from the University of South Carolina and a BA in Political Science and Women's and Gender Studies from the University of South Carolina Honors College. In addition to academic work and political activism, she serves as a founding director of the Deckle Edge Literary Festival in Columbia, South Carolina.

6

Gender and Safety Nets

Reforming and Saving Social Security

> The face of Social Security has a uniquely woman's profile.
> —Chair Susan Bianchi-Sand, "Statement at 12/2/98 NCWO Social Security Press Conference"

> There is a pernicious wage gap that exists over a woman's working life that ends up hitting women the hardest in retirement. That's because the gap shrinks the three main sources of income for senior citizens: personal savings, pensions, and Social Security benefits.
> —Representative Carolyn B. Maloney, "Falling into Poverty: The Gender Gap is Perilous for Women in Their 'Golden Years'"

Illuminating the Female Face of Social Security

When working-class and poor people's economic situation is discussed in the United States, some politicians and pundits fear that "class warfare" is about to erupt. It depends on the framing, as the following parable explains: "Wars and elections seem to trigger the psychopathology of projection. When one party (whom we shall call party A, for purposes of identification) grants huge tax cuts, mainly to the superrich, and the opposing party (here called party B) points out the unfairness of this measure, how does party A respond? By passionately and fervently crying, 'Party B is igniting class warfare!'" (Cathcart and Klein 2007: 89). Tax breaks for the rich are not called "entitlements" or "welfare" and relieving poverty is not called a "benefit" or "stimulus." How policies are framed, who they are intended for, and how they are administered and funded shape public reaction to those policies and the sense of citizenship that recipients derive from being part of a program.

In 2012, when Republican presidential candidate Mitt Romney told a luncheon audience that 47 percent of Americans believe they are victims who the government must support, he did not mention the billions of dollars in corporate support the government routinely doles out. One business journalist noted, "Romney may say that he wants small government, but what he's pushing for is a government that's small when it comes to helping people and big when it comes to helping business" (Surowiecki 2012: 42; see also Carnes 2013; Thorpe 2014).

One strength of left, progressive lobby groups is their reliance on solid, timely research to help make their points (Berry 1999: 21, 155–156; Jones 2000). In *Creating a Female Dominion in American Reform, 1890–1935*, Robyn Muncy found, for instance: "Since the New Deal, progressives' enthusiasm for what appeared to be powerless, data-gathering agencies has seemed a bit naïve. But as it turns out, some progressives saw those little, fact-finding government agencies not as isolated entities in a growing government but as integral parts of a closely knit community of organizations, and as part of that nexus, small government bureaus actually did act as significant agents of reform" (1991: 62). Feminist groups within the NCWO were deft and hardworking practitioners of the adage "knowledge is power." They added to their research, data, and statistical studies a female face that would suffer the consequences of misguided, gender-insensitive policy making.

Parables and stories flesh out data and statistics. "When despair is the disease one hopes to remedy, anecdotes can be antidotes" (Stout 2010: 283). In somber U.S. congressional hearings, "witnesses make little use of evidence based on research to support their arguments, and even less use of comparisons to other issues or political units; anecdotes are by far the favorite kind of evidence" (Burstein 2014: 158).

Being able to tell your narrative, and have it heard by others, bestows respect. For instance, U.S. Supreme Court justice Ruth Bader Ginsburg ensured that court records reflect the stories of girls' and women's lives. One scholar highlighted Justice Ginsburg's notorious dissents ("no truth without Ruth" one saying goes), as in the Lilly Ledbetter pay inequity case (2007), and explained, "Being now the only one of the Court with the experience of growing up being a woman, she felt obliged to speak her truth" (Hirshman 2015: 275). "Her truth" included Justice Ginsburg's own experiences in the legal profession. Justice Ginsburg's scholarship and jurisprudence meant "she was there to represent their [girls and women's] existence" (Hirshman 2015: 300). Justice Ginsburg's written opinions incorporate women's narratives.

Gender wage discrimination is rampant and the predominant factor in economic inequalities (IWPR 2010). Women's precarious economic positions are exacerbated by lack of private pensions for women compared to men, the gender discriminatory manner in which private pensions are paid out, and the echoes within pensions of women's employment patterns, unequal pay, promotion disadvantages, gendered structuring of jobs (pink and blue collar), discrimination, and much more (see, for instance, Conway, Ahern, Steuernagel 1999, especially chapter 5; Correspondents of *The New York Times* 2005; Patterson 1996; Hounsell 1996; Ehrenreich 2001; R. Payne 2005). More than half of American women employed full-time outside the home work for employers who do not provide retirement benefits (Patterson 1996: 156). Of course, women working part-time or temporarily are in similar dire straits. Women working where retirement plans are offered (less than half of the women working full-time) have a more difficult time vesting in the plan given their higher probability than male workers to take time off to care for family or change jobs before vesting.

The feminization of poverty has many aspects to it. One is that more women than men are likely to end their lives in poverty (Hounsell 1996: 166). In addition, the United States population is aging and an aging society is an increasingly female society (Lynch 2011: 168). Never forget, also, that every step in these life patterns is harder and less equitable for women of color (A. Hacker 1992; Hine and Thompson 1998; Triece 2013).

Policies Shape Citizens

Two distinct types of New Deal social policies sorted American citizens. The first covered white men who were endowed with national citizenship. White men were incorporated into policies centrally administered in a unitary manner (by the federal government) through standardized, routinized procedures. The second ("othered") set of Americans were women and minority men. They were considered state citizens and were therefore subject to policies that were shaped and hindered by federalism and local control. Those policies were administered with state and local discretion and variability (Mettler 1998: xi, 5; see also Schneider and Ingram 1997; Campbell 2014).

A third set of people should be added to this analysis: those excluded completely because of their sexual orientation. During the rollout of Social Security in 1935, for example, explicit steps were taken to exclude homosexuals. Similar exclusions of LGBTQ people were manifest in welfare policies, aid to families, and more (Canaday 2009). Policies can exclude citizens, then, as well as make them.

The national citizens were rights-bearers. The othered citizens were ruled in nonliberal patterns based in relational, role-oriented, or difference-based terms. Differences of women and people of color were defined as inequalities, and their benefits were charities instead of rights. The circle of power and right remained unbroken as the two sets of citizens developed different kinds of political participation expectations and roles (Mettler 1998: xi–xii). Economically fragile and poor women, then, were "pitied but not entitled" (Gordon 1994). The development paths of these social systems were locked in "through their sedimentation in institutions" (Walby 2015: 30).

Social Security and Medicare programs have facilitated the proud mobilization of senior citizens to engage in politics to protect "their" benefits. In fact, interest in Social Security is greater among lower-income seniors who are more dependent on the program. The programs have boosted political participation of low-income seniors above expectations for people of such low socioeconomic status (Campbell 2003: 11).

Social stigma concerning bankruptcy also silences financially fragile people while institutions preying on desperate people solidify their political acumen (Warren 2014: 53–56, 128; A. Hill 2011). Who is politically active, then, is in part a legacy of existing government programs (Campbell 2003). Policies and institutions shape citizenship.

Within these social programs and policies, also, is the given of "normative masculinity" (Kessler-Harris 2001: 178). The tax code, for example, reflected dominate ideas about normative families and gender fairness so "the law became an instrument as well for endorsing certain kinds of gender roles, influencing personal behavior, and encouraging particular forms of activity" (Kessler-Harris 2001: 196).

Federal legislation in response to the Great Depression and the end of World War II reinscribed gender, race, and class inequalities in their policies and procedures. Fair labor laws, including minimum wages, exempted small ("mom and pop") employers, farm workers, and domestic workers. As a result, "ninety percent of black working women received no benefits from the new laws providing for a minimum wage, maximum hours, and assistance for the unemployed and elderly. By leaving out these workers, New Deal legislation actually ensured that, relative to other workers, African American women particularly, and domestic and agricultural workers generally, would be worse off than before" (Fredrickson 2015: 35). Race and gender were factors that "carefully calibrated the value of the return" of American social policies (Kessler-Harris 2001: 161). It was work (defined as outside the home, in an establishment with more than fifty full-time employees and not agricultural) that shaped these social programs, not citizenship (Kessler-Harris 2001: 120). Many of these exclusions still stand today.

At the end of World War II in the United States, the GI Bill's education and training provision had a positive effect on male citizen civic involvement for decades thereafter (Mettler 2005: 9; Hartmann and Burk 2012: 11). Veterans were treated with respect and were proud of receiving benefits. The GI Bill was fundamentally inclusive, magnanimous, and life-transforming for male veterans (Mettler 2005: 10). The inclusivity had limits, however, as civilian defense plant workers like "Rosie the Riveter" were not covered. The GI Bill "widened the gender divide in educational attainment. In turn, the incorporation of a generation of men into the polity exacerbated the gender gap in active citizenship, highlighting the power of government programs to stimulate the participation of some groups relative to others" (Mettler 2005: 11; see also 144–162).

Families: Divorce, Death, Disabilities, Diversities

Part of the misinformation about Social Security rests on the idea that people paid in and should get back what they already paid for. Social Security is an insurance program based on spreading out economic risk to the whole public. It is not an investment account. While initially presented to the public as an annuity program, early amendments to the Social Security Act, which added dependent wives and aged widows to the benefits, broke that frame. Those two groups had not paid into the system. Important to remember was that "no charitable impulse toward women motivated this act; no concern for their poverty inspired it. Rather, Congress added dependent wives and aged widows in order to shore up the legitimacy of a system in trouble" (Kessler-Harris 2001: 132). A masculine and heterosexual marriage ethos infused the policy: "As long as she remained dependent on him, the level of the surviving widow's benefits, like the level of children's benefits, would be tied to the earnings of the deceased male, feeding the illusion that families deprived of a father or husband would nevertheless conceive him in the abstract as a continuing provider" (Kessler-Harris 2001: 136).

Spouses who did not work outside of the home were eligible for benefits equal to 50 percent of their working spouses' Social Security benefits. A married couple with one spouse working at home, then, received 150 percent of the benefits earned by the wage worker. Private accounts would not include these stay-at-home wives (or partners) spousal benefits as they depend on individual wage earnings, not the work of maintaining a home and raising a family. Concern that the remaining spouse after a wage worker died would be without benefits was forcefully presented in Social Security reform debates. Annuities that a wage worker purchased for retirement might expire at his or her death, leaving the surviving spouse without income.

The special needs of women also include what happens to a couple's assets (if any) and pensions after a divorce. People married for at least ten years have a right to monthly benefits calculated from a former spouse's earnings. These payments are not deducted from the spouse's Social Security retirement benefits. Divorced partners (particularly women who do most of the care work in a family and earn less pay than male spouses) would be harmed financially by changes in Social Security that did not incorporate the gender and social class aspects of divorce and widowhood (Kirchhoff 1998).

The disability program aspect of Social Security "is also the nation's single largest provider of life and disability insurance benefits, delivering such relief to more than 13 million Americans [in 1997]" (Kirchhoff 1998: 1044). Supplemental Security Income (SSI), funded through general revenues instead of payroll taxes, aided another six million poor, disabled, and elderly workers, and about $56 billion to more than seven million widows and widowers in 1999 (Kirchhoff 1998).

In addition, Jacob Hacker explained, "[Social Security] offers a guaranteed benefit in retirement that is more generous to families with low lifetime incomes, whose heads are disabled or pass away, and who have the good fortune to live a long time after retirement (elderly widows are the chief example). The program protects families not just against these risks but also against the risk of large drops in their assets due to stock-market or housing-price instability as well as the risk of unexpected inflation, which can devastate families on fixed incomes" (2008: 132). For many observers, then, "Social Security—because it pools risk across millions of citizens and uses the power of government to guarantee against the major threats to family income during (and, in some cases, before) retirement—simply does not have the kind of inherent uncertainly built into it that private accounts would" (J. Hacker. 2008: 133).

An additional issue raised at the NCWO 1999 Working Conference concerned lesbians and their families. The draft report documented that

> some participants noted that lesbian couples and single women (including single mothers) cannot take advantage of spousal benefits and hence do not receive any recognition of their unpaid care-taking work in the current Social Security system. While the Family Service Credits discussed above would provide care-giving credits to single mothers and lesbians, spouses in lesbian couples would still not have access to spousal benefits, and single, never-married women, whose earnings are often low because of sex discrimination in the labor market, would receive no credits to boost their benefits (unless they had some significant care-giving years). Eleanor Smeal [President of FMF] suggested that never married women (including those not married long enough to be eligible for spousal benefits) receive a 15 percent premium on their benefits (up to some benefit threshold) to compensate them for their artificially low earnings. (Task force, draft report: November 16, 1999: 18; in author files)

Speaking up for lesbian families in Social Security reform reports during the Bush administration in 1999 displayed some of the grit and reach of the NCWO.

Free Markets, Private Citizens

Economic inequalities have increased during a time when our democracy has weakened. Citizens struggle to maintain public goods under constant attack by free market adherents. Neoliberalism, sometimes called "the Washington consensus," neoconservativism, or neoclassical economics, advocates free trade, deregulation, privatization, more reliance on markets than government, and more concern for efficiency than equity (Reich 2007: 10; see also Barker and Feiner 2004). At the same time as the rise of neoliberalism, "As inequality has widened, the means America once had to temper it—progressive income taxes, good public schools, trade unions that bargain for higher wages—have eroded" (Reich 2007: 4). The denouement: consumers and investors, as rational individuals, gain power, while citizens and the public good lose strength (Reich 2007: 56). A consistent message many Americans hear, including the very fragile and the vulnerable middle class, is "they alone are the ones responsible for their successes and failures" (J. Hacker 2008: xii, 6).

The reframing has been labeled "The Great Risk Shift," wherein more and more economic responsibility is off-loaded by government and corporations onto economically fragile workers and their families. It is a fundamental transformation of our social contracts from a sense of shared fate to one of individual gain (J. Hacker 2008: xv, 66). In the name of personal responsibility, "proponents of these changes speak of a nirvana of individual economic management—a society of empowered 'owners,' in which Americans are free to choose. What these advocates are helping to create, however, is very different: a harsh new world of economic insecurity, in which far too many Americans are free to lose" (J. Hacker 2008: 6).

One aspect of corporate political power and the tsunami of corporate and private wealth in politics is the predominance of corporate hired "experts" in policy making. In these policy experts' models, public or common goods are absent from their calculations (Reich 2007: 158–161). Heidi Hartmann of IWPR, for instance, repeatedly warned attendees at NCWO meetings about the Peterson Foundation in this regard.[1] Corporate public relations includes charitable giving and cosponsorship of public events, NGO projects, and publications. Reich sums up the situation: "Making companies more 'socially' responsible is a worthy goal, but [the country] would be better served by making democracy work better" (2007: 182).

Neoliberalism eschews an ethos of linked fate. The shift includes a decline in the all-in-one-boat philosophy of shared risk to go-it-alone personal responsibility (J. Hacker 2008: 35–60). Two pieces of seemingly low-hanging fruit, fat public programs that could ostensibly be managed better privately and within the free market system, led to the new frontiers of transforming Medicare and Social Security. Reformers proposed switching from guaranteed benefits defined by law to individualized private accounts. Private accounts, however, left workers and families shouldering more and more of the risks that public programs once covered (J. Hacker 2008: 8).

Softening up the public regarding changes to Social Security has been decades in the making. President Clinton, interestingly, helped out with his announcements in 1998 that he was launching a yearlong effort to "save Social Security." The rhetoric of this matched some neoconservative and libertarian pundits at the time. Indeed, "A couple of years ago the idea of a semiprivate Social Security system seemed unlikely, pushed only by the Cato Institute, a libertarian think tank, and a few other groups" (Kirchhoff 1998: 1041). The mix also included the record-setting pace of the stock market, a trend by private corporations moving to 401(k) savings accounts and away from defined-benefit pensions, "making many more comfortable with the notion of managing their money" (Kirchhoff 1998: 1041). Citizens no longer could depend on pooled risk and common safety nets. Shafted were workers, "civic society, and the spirit of *E Pluribus Unum*" [from many, one] (Lynch 2011: 49).

Push Back

From NCWO records gathered, meetings and events attended, and interviews conducted, it is clear that the coalition was active on protecting and even trying to enhance Social Security since at least 1998. A timeline of events is included at the end of this chapter.[2] At a 1998 press conference, the chair of the NCWO stressed that Social Security reform is a critical issue for the NCWO given women's financial circumstances and economic vulnerabilities (Bianchi-Sand, "Statement of at 12/2/98 NCWO Social Security Press Conference"). The NCWO's concerns were "not only the adequacy but the equity of Social Security" (Bianchi-Sand, "Statement of at 12/2/98 NCWO Social Security Press Conference"). The NCWO members worked separately and together on the issue.

Nuanced, gender-sensitive research found "women's movements are important advocates for economic justice for women" (Weldon 2011: 108). Unions are also central for worker protections and rights (Schlozman, Verba, and Brady 2012; Mosle 1996). In the long campaign by the NCWO and others to protect Social Security, the coalition was aided by research and expertise from member groups, political heat fanned up from voices of the aged and disabled, advocates for families writ large, and friends in the labor movement, to name a few.

First, displaying the female face of Social Security was emphasized. "Social Security *is* women's security," Susan Bianchi-Sand, NCWO chair, succinctly put it, "We want to ensure that any proposal that compromises these protections is off the table and that women are at the table when decisions about reform are made" (Press Release, NCWO, December 2, 1998; italic in original). In a 1998 grant request letter the chair of the NCWO put it this way: "Women are all too frequently left out of the national debate on reforming Social Security. Through our coalition efforts, we can bring critical information to thousands of activist women, thereby engaging them in the important decisions which are likely to take place in the next several years" (Bianchi-Sand, December 7; in author files).

Second, the extent that women and disabled family members depend on Social Security was highlighted. At press conferences and briefings, the women's groups often had "real women" speak about their lives as widows, retired workers without pensions, mothers of disabled children, and more who could only (if barely) make ends meet because of the constancy and stability of Social Security benefits. An NCWO slogan in the 1998 flare up over reform asked "the President and Congress to keep the heart in Social Security by strengthening and preserving the valuable protections for women under the Social Security system" (Press Release, NCWO, December 2, 1998).

Third, Social Security benefits were linked to the economic, reproductive, and caring histories of women's lives. Social Security reflected these life patterns in earned benefits calculations often to the detriment of women and caregivers. Forty prominent political women, for example, signed a letter to Vice President Al Gore in 1998 urging him and the president "to address the issues facing women" in their discussions of Social Security's future. They stated, "Women retiring in the next 20 years will have less than one-third the income necessary to retire comfortably, a situation that is greatly exacerbated for women of color. Several Social Security proposals under consideration would only make this situation worse" (Thurman et al. 1998). They added that three out of five women worked in low-wage jobs that offered few benefits, or pension plans. Many women worked in part-time and contingent jobs as well.

Although many commentators pointed out that Social Security was intended to be part of a "'three-legged' retirement stool that also include pensions and private savings" (Kirchhoff 1998: 1042), economic and behavior realities were that many people, particularly women, did not have savings or pensions and relied on Social Security exclusively when retired, disabled, or caring for disabled people in their families. As one 1998 Executive Summary document in the NCWO files on Social Security put it, "you can't save what you don't earn."

On top of this, most women took time out of the workforce (11.5 years on average) to raise children or provide care for ailing parents or spouses. When out of the formal workforce and doing care work, women (and a few men) received no Social Security account work credits, which lowers their benefit amounts when they were eligible for Social Security.

The NCWO and allies also noted that women live longer than men by an average of seven years and are twice as likely to be poor than men. They pointed out, "Women often become poor for the first time on the day their husbands die. In fact, the fastest growing group in poverty are single women and widows over the age of 65" (Thurman et al. 1998: 2).

Fourth, private accounts invested in the stock market were warned against. A 1998 article on possible reform of Social Security noted "advocates of private savings argue that, overall, both men and women would be far better off investing in the stock market, which is expected to return an average of 7 percent annually over the next 75 years, compared with less than 3 percent return on government bonds used to finance Social Security" (Kirchhoff 1998: 1043). As for the start-up costs of administering these new accounts and procedures, a Cato Institute cochair told *CQ Weekly* that transition costs were not an insurmountable barrier. Cato officials asserted that instead of raising taxes, the government could borrow to finance transition expenses. Illuminated were "the possible pitfalls of transforming Social Security from a system based on shared pooling of risk to one that allows personal risk-taking" (Kirchhoff 1998: 1038).

Fifth, the campaign critiqued dominant budget items and the impact of tax cuts on the overall federal budget. Particularly mentioned were the Bush tax cuts for wealthy Americans. Many (but not all) groups explicitly mentioned the effect of waging two long, costly wars in the Middle East and Afghanistan without paying for them.

Sixth, were proposals to strengthen Social Security particularly as it impacts women. In the same 1998 grant request letter referenced above, the NCWO chair wrote, "Further, we believe now is the time to bring the persistent inadequacies for women in the Social Security system to the attention of policy makers" (Bianchi-Sand, December 7; in author files).

To "Keep the Heart in Social Security" reforms should:

- "continue to help those with lower lifetime earnings, who are disproportionally women;
- maintain full cost of living adjustments;
- protect and strengthen benefits for wives, widows, and divorced women;
- preserve disability and survivor benefits;
- protect the most disadvantaged workers from 'across the board' benefit cuts;
- ensure that women's guaranteed benefits are not reduced by individual account plans that are subject to the uncertainties of the stock market;
- address the care-giving and labor force experiences of women; and
- further reduce the number of elderly women living in poverty." (Press Release, NCWO, December 2, 1998).

The NCWO statement concluded, "Proposals to divert workers' current payments from the Social Security system into individually held, private accounts, whose returns would be dependent on volatile investment markets and would not be guaranteed to keep pace with inflation nor provide spousal benefits (including benefits to widows and divorced women), would reduce the retirement income of many women" (Press Release, December 2, 1998).

Women's advocates raised these basic points over the next two decades to spotlight the female face of Social Security. They closed with a mantra frequently repeated during the years of struggle over Social Security reform: "If Social Security does not effectively serve women, it will not effectively serve anyone" (Thurman et al. 1998).

Chorus Mobilization

Women more than men, the NCWO asserted, "are willing to make sacrifices to guarantee that SS [Social Security] remains a lifeline of retirement security. Fully 42 percent of women expect SS to be [a] major source of their retirement income. Indeed[,] women's lives depend on it" (Bianchi-Sand, Susan. "Statement at 12/2/98 NCWO Social Security Press Conference"). The NCWO had many allies in efforts to derail the Social Security reform train. The NCWO message on behalf of the women's community was like preaching to the choir in many DC communities. Labor unions, women and family law centers, liberal and progressive think tanks, civil rights organizations, and advocates for the disabled, the aged, the poor, and the orphaned all lent their political skills to the effort. In turn, the NCWO bolstered individual members of the mobilized chorus in their activism as well.

There were, however, exceptions. In my participant observations at NCWO-affiliated events and meetings, and during my interviews, I noticed the distrust and the dismissiveness that activists and policy analysts expressed toward the AARP (American Association of Retired People; not a member of the NCWO). I assumed the AARP was like one of the big banks "too big to fail" but in this case the AARP was "too big to critique." The AARP was seen by many activists and scholars in this study as "nothing more than an insurance company" with big conflicts of interest concerning the politics of Social Security, Medicare, and Medicaid (interviews; see also Lynch 2011: 140–145). Fodder for the AARP criticism included their support for the Medicare Prescription Drug and Modernization Act in 2003 without the government's ability to purchase medicines wholesale. In addition, the AARP did not support a single-payer system during the 2009 and 2010 debates over the ACA. During the Obama administration, the NCWO and others opposed efforts to extend the age when people would be eligible for Social Security. At one NCWO meeting, Heidi Hartmann confronted a group of

AARP speakers on this issue. She and the NCWO saw extending the age of eligibility as benefit cuts and harmful to many people who work on their feet, outside, and/or in demanding jobs (Woliver notes, NCWO meeting, November 16, 2010).

The NCWO sought to counter the neoliberal agenda regarding Social Security. Getting the word out was one important part of the NCWO's efforts. "What Every Woman Should Know about Social Security" was a segment of the 1999 Teleconferences "Americans Discuss Social Security." For the "What Every Woman" segment, First Lady Hillary Rodham Clinton was the chair and Rep. Jennifer Dunn the cochair. In the spring of 1999 Susan Bianchi-Sand, NCWO chair, approached the editors of the *Ladies Home Journal* and *Good Housekeeping* to discuss the importance of Social Security reform for women. She offered to provide briefings to the magazine staff on the issues and to provide data and research as needed (Bianchi-Sand 1999; in author files). The NCWO throughout this era also testified to congressional committees, congressional staff briefings, and administration officials.

NCWO leaders and individual groups together met with administration officials throughout the era examined. In 1999, leaders from the National Women's Law Center, the Institute for Women's Policy Research, and the Task Force on Social Security of the NCWO (led by Heidi Hartmann) met with Gene Sperling, assistant to the president for Economic Policy and director, National Economic Council. They discussed President Clinton's proposals involving Social Security, Medicare, and the USA Accounts. In a subsequent follow-up letter to Sperling, the group reminded him women are more likely to have lower earnings than men and take time out of the labor force for care work. Therefore, problematic to them were individual retirement savings plans that primarily benefit higher earners. They urged that there be progressive government matches to the accounts and that the equity issues within families be incorporated into any reforms. They advocated earnings sharing and spousal protections as well (Entmacher, Campbell, and Hartmann 1999; see also Hartmann and Fierst [and twenty-six signatories] 1999; in author files).

A June 24, 1999, NCWO letter to Gene Sperling made four recommendations to improve the adequacy of Social Security benefits for women. The first recommended raising elderly poor women's benefits, especially the largest group thereof who were widows. The group of signatories also pointed out to Sperling and to the administration that the life paths of elderly women were diverse, with some eligible for survivor benefits while others were not. They wrote, "It is equally important to help elderly women who are not entitled to survivor benefits because they did not marry or were divorced after a marriage of less than ten years. Not only do single and divorced women have a higher poverty rate than do widows, their numbers are increasing, especially among African-American women." The second recommendation was to increase benefits to the lowest earners. Third was that any package of changes to SSI (Supplemental Security Income) should "help the poorest recipients and ensure that the package does not leave SSI recipients no better, and perhaps worse, off." Fourth was a proposal to reduce or eliminate the earnings limit for retirees below the normal retirement age since they believed it would detrimentally impact women. If workers were encouraged to begin to collect benefits at age sixty-two, their lifelong benefits would decrease, throwing older retirees and their wives and widows into poverty (Hartmann and Fierst [and twenty-six signatories] 1999; in author files).

Minutes from 1999 meetings of the Technical Subcommittee of the Task Force on Social Security of the NCWO document detailed analysis and study of every aspect of the reforms the Clinton administration proposed. In addition, they started to assess the reforms Republican presidential candidate George W. Bush was promoting. The minutes display the amount of attention the group was paying to the plights of economically vulnerable people, especially women and children, under the proposals. The context of women's lives in an economy still infused with gender wage discrimination, lack of credits to women's caregiving work, and more were central to the meetings. One strong recommendation was that women's child care work be given credit within the Social Security benefit system. Unintended consequences from a change in one policy to eligibility for another program were also considered. Participants were concerned, for example, that raises to Social Security benefits not remove people from Medicaid (Fierst 1999a–1999c; in author files).

In this political chess game with many moving pieces, possible tax cuts were also opposed by the same groups. They foresaw pressures down the road to cut social programs or to not enact prescription drug coverage under Medicare given revenue shortfalls (Bland-Watson 1999; in author files).

Leaders in the NCWO Task Force on Social Security emphasized to funders: "It is critical that women's organizations take the lead in the debate on Social Security reform and that the Task Force continue to provide a strong voice for women, working to protect their benefits and strengthen the system. By creating a Women's Plan to Strengthen Social Security, and working over the following months (or years) to build support for it, the Task Force has an opportunity to make a difference in the lives of all women" (Hartmann 1999c; in author files).

Through the work of Heidi Hartmann (director and president IWPR and a key NCWO leader) and others, the MacArthur Foundation in 1999 awarded a two-year $250,000 grant to the NCWO's Task Force on Social Security. The goal was to preserve and improve Social Security as it provides economic security for women. They hired a full-time director for the Task Force on Social Security of the NCWO, Christopher Turman.

On September 21, 1999, the Task Force on Women and Social Security's Policy Initiatives presented to the general NCWO meeting their recommendations.[3] The report was based on the Working Conference on Women and Social Security held July 19–22, 1999, in Virginia. Points were summarized in "NCWO's Checklist to Ensure That Social Security Reform Works for Women." The eight items on the checklist were:

1. Reduce the number of elderly women living in poverty.
2. Continue to help those with lower lifetime earnings, who are disproportionately women.
3. Maintain full cost of living adjustments.
4. Strengthen benefits for wives, widows, and divorced women.
5. Preserve disability and survivor benefits.
6. Protect the most disadvantaged workers from across-the-board benefit cuts.
7. Ensure that women's guaranteed benefits are not reduced by individual account plans that are subject to the uncertainties of the stock market.
8. Address the caregiving and labor force experiences of women (Task Force, September 21, 1999a; in author files).

They listed four short-term policy initiatives, five reforms to strengthen social security for women, and three solvency recommendations.[4]

The NCWO draft task force report on the Working Conference on Women and Social Security, prepared by the IWPR, noted that all members of the NCWO coalition might not be in agreement on a single set of reform proposals given the different political strategies NCWO groups adhere to. Cogently, the draft report posed, "Speaking with a single voice is preferable, but a well-orchestrated chorus can be effective as well" (1999: 5).

The March 2000 publication by Heidi Hartmann and Catherine Hill of the IWPR entitled *Strengthening Social Security for Women* provided the framework, data, and analysis of problems. Published under the auspices of the Task Force on Women and Social Security of the NCWO, the report was widely publicized. The report's main point was that privatizing Social Security would not solve any problems for women but would, instead, exacerbate them. Public education and media publicity campaigns in the fall of 2000 included dissemination of more than one hundred thousand copies of the NCWO Women and Social Security Project brochure to women across the country.

On February 25, 2000, the IWPR in partnership with the NCWO Task Force on Women and Social Security released the report "Why Privatizing Social Security Would Hurt Women: A Response to the Cato Institute's Proposal for Individual Accounts." The IWPR report explicitly refuted the Cato Institute contention that individual private accounts invested in the stock market could simultaneously raise benefits and solve the system's long-term financial problems. IWPR highlighted four central mistakes in the Cato analysis: "the failure to account for the transition for a 'pay as you go' system to a pre-funded program, an overly optimistic view of future economic growth, the failure to account for administrative costs, and the failure to account for the high cost of replacing the disability and life insurance provided to American workers by Social Security" (C. Hill 2000b; NCWO 2000a; in author files). They cautioned that stock market prowess could wane and that the elderly could not depend on the growth projections for investments that private account advocates presented.

The 2000 IWPR and NCWO report ended with an explication of the harm the individual private accounts would have on women. They noted, "For example, women tend to live longer, and unless sex discrimination in insurance were eliminated, would have to pay more for annuities (guaranteed monthly income) in a privatized system. Because many women earn less than men, they benefit from the current system because it provides proportionately higher benefits to lower earners. This feature would be lost in a privatized system, leaving millions of women facing poverty. Since women tend to have smaller accounts, it is likely that the yield on their accounts would be below average, as women would (appropriately) avoid risk" (IWPR 2000; in author files).

The task force held a Women and Social Security Summit in February 2001, which was well attended and received good media coverage. The task force put on its website (www.women4socialsecurity.org) a "Social Security Calculator" where people could project their Social Security benefits under various scenarios. Based on "well documented assumptions about economic growth, administrative costs, and the significant burden of switching from a pay as you go to a pre-funded system" the calculator also illustrated "the benefit cuts facing workers under Governor Bush's plan to partially privatize Social Security" (C. Hill 2000a). The press release included an endorsement from Martha Burk, then chair of the NCWO. Burk stated, "The majority of the more than 100 organizations in NCWO are extremely concerned about Social Security privatization" and that the calculator presented "an easy way for women to see what they will lose under such proposals" (C. Hill 2000a).

The combined voices offered by the NCWO's concerns, studies, and critiques of possible Social Security reforms seemed to have an added legitimacy. For instance, after the Task Force on Social Security of the NCWO came out with its report, both Martha Burk and Heidi Hartmann were interviewed by many major media. In addition, they debated proprivatization adherents on various talk shows. Heidi Hartmann, for instance, debated a person from the Cato Institute on the CBS *This Morning* news show. The segment earned the "Hess Award" from the Brookings Institution for good media coverage of a public policy issue.

NOW Fanning the Heat

NOW president Patricia Ireland issued a strong press release on February 25, 2000, warning of dire consequences to women from the "shell game called 'privatization'" that politicians are playing with "our Social Security tax dollars." NOW, a steadfast NCWO member, listed many of the same issues and ideas from the 2000 IWPR and NCWO report. NOW was more political in its analysis. NOW called out conservative small government politicians and their Wall Street friends for a manufactured crisis and self-serving solution. "The greatest menace to Social Security is not a crisis in funding," NOW noted, "but cynical politicians who are more interested in kowtowing to big money interests than they are in safeguarding the elderly, people with disabilities, widows, widowers and their dependent children." Tearing holes in the social safety net would result (NOW 2000: 3; in author files). NOW vowed they would not fall for the shell game of quick fixes and would hold politicians accountable on Election Day.

A panic atmosphere created by financial industry lobbying for privatization of Social Security was a scam for Wall Street moguls to use to line their pockets, the NOW message continued. Details NOW provided noted how the Social Security system took in $1.5 billion a day, so the possible fees financial managers could reap from even a small fraction of that amount are quite an incentive for their campaign (NOW 2000; in author files). Of the many points NOW made about dangers from private accounts they also warned, "Hard as it may be to remember during this boom, the market lost 45 percent of its value between 1965 and 1978. Seniors need a steady income they can count on, not the booms and busts of the market" (NOW 2000: 3; in author files).

"Young people," NOW president Ireland asserted, "also should beware. Seniors aren't the only ones who benefit from Social Security. Three million children and their sole caretaker parents depend on Social Security's death and disability benefits to survive. Indeed, Social Security's safety net is wide; without it, vulnerable people of all ages will suffer" (NOW 2000: 3; in author files).

The double-teaming of IWPR and NCWO with NOW's message was an instance of the national groups in DC speaking together and apart on an issue important to women and their families. In the next few months AAUW, the National Women's Law Center, the Institute for America's Future, the FMF, and the National Committee to Preserve Social Security and Medicare, to name a few, joined in with strong press releases and well-documented position papers taking on the private account juggernaut.

Labor unions also stood up to the private account reform momentum. The American Federation of Labor and Congress of Industrial Organizations (AFL-CIO) in February 2001 released a position statement and fact sheet entitled, "Breaking the Covenant with America's Working Families: Bush Plan to Privatize Social Security Imperils Future Retirement Security for Millions." One section highlighted how privatization would disproportionately hurt women and people of color (AFL-CIO 2001a; in author files).[5] Many coalitions the NCWO cooperated with also aided the effort, such as Social Security Works and Save Social Security (Jan Ericson, interview, July 19, 2010).

In the spring and summer of 2000, news outlets such as *Business Week*, *Newsweek*, *Washington Post*, and many more, covered the concerns of the IWPR and NCWO's reports. The coverage linked Social Security to potential gender gap issues in future elections.

The Bush Years

Presidential candidate George W. Bush was candid about his intent to set up private accounts and save Social Security with free market efficiencies and profits. Task force research, conference proceedings, and NCWO with IWPR reports on women and Social Security conducted, published, publicized, and discussed in 2000 served as credible materials for groups within and without the NCWO who sought to preserve all or parts of Social Security.

Reports were in anticipation of the 2000 presidential election. The analysis provided talking points for candidates or groups wanting to defend Social Security. Task force publications also provided questions citizens could ask politicians at town meetings, fund-raisers, or visits back home in the districts about how private accounts would work and how they would affect widows, the disabled, low-income workers, part-time workers, and women who work at home. Through grant money, the task force was able to send out more than one hundred thousand copies of its brochures and reports on Social Security. They developed a symbol for their campaign: a dollar bill folded into the shape of a ribbon lapel pin.[6]

Many NCWO groups continued to emphasize the disproportionate impact changes in Social Security would have on women. They were often strong allies within the NCWO yet also worked solo on the mission. For instance, an OWL (Older Women's League) brochure admonished readers, "Retirement planning must include looking at how much you will depend on Social Security for your income. Women tend to rely on Social Security for a greater share of their retirement income and as a result, they have a special stake in any discussion about changing Social Security" (OWL n.d.). OWL explained that 90 percent of retirement income for almost half of all older women is from Social Security. Reasons included women's lower wages since "over a lifetime in an average-wage job, this wage gap adds up to about $250,000 less in earnings that we [women] could save or invest for retirement" (OWL n.d.). Another reason is women continuing to provide care for babies, children, sick family members, the elderly, and the dying. The OWL pamphlet pointed out, "Women average 11.5 years out of the paid workforce because of these caregiving responsibilities" (OWL n.d.). OWL utilized the NCWO tag line, "Remember, if Social Security reform doesn't work for women, it just doesn't work" (OWL n.d.).

After the U.S. Supreme Court decision in *Bush v. Gore* (2000) put an end to ballot recounts in the contested 2000 presidential election, a very disappointed and worried NCWO membership prepared to push back on the new Bush administration's highly anticipated reforms of Social Security. The AAUW (an important NCWO member), for example, greeted the new Bush administration in January 2001 with a fact sheet entitled "Social Security: AAUW Principles for Reform" (in author files). Like female U.S. senators, the AAUW played both defense and offense. The AAUW listed five items they insisted be in any reform:

1. Guaranteed benefits on which women and families depend.
2. The system should not be replaced by individual retirement accounts.
3. Budget surpluses must be used to extend the solvency of Social Security well into the twenty-first century.
4. Women's retirement security must not only be maintained but also improved.
5. Changes to Social Security must be considered in tandem with changes to Medicare (in author files).

The AAUW also spoke to the issue of the female face of the program: "Social Security is especially important for women because nearly two-thirds of women 65 and over receive a majority of their income from Social Security and one-third rely on Social Security for 90 percent or more of their income. Without Social Security, over half of all elderly women would be living in poverty" (2001a).

A Women and Social Security Summit was planned for February 7–10, 2001. Conveners were the NCWO Women and Social Security Project, IWPR, BPW/USA, OWL, the National Council of Negro Women, and the AAUW.

On May 2, 2001, President George W. Bush appointed a commission to study how to reform Social Security. Immediately, NCWO members noted that the commission members already favored individual retirement accounts. The AAUW characterized the problems of private Social Security accounts for women as "threaten(ing) essential protections for women and families including: full cost-of-living adjustments; compensation for women with lower lifetime earnings; spouse and widow benefits; and disability and survivor benefits" (AAUW 2001a). A fax alert from the AAUW (2001b) highlighted two issues:

1. Women have more to lose if individual retirement accounts replace Social Security.
2. Benefits will not be guaranteed under the private accounts reforms.

A skirmish developed in early September 2001 when President Bush's Commission to Strengthen Social Security was called out by many for only inviting one women's group critical of privatization to testify to the Commission: OWL. No labor, African American, Latino/Hispanic, or church groups were invited. Roger Hickey, codirector of the Institute for America's Future and director of the New Century Alliance for Social Security, wrote in an opinion piece printed in *The San Diego Union-Tribune* about these absences from the hearings. Hickey specified, "But where are the leaders of any other women's groups—NOW, the National Women's Law Center, Business and Professional Women, the Feminist Majority, the Institute for Women's Policy Research, and the many other groups, who joined under the auspices of the National Council of Women's Organizations to warn that privatization represents a bad deal for women?" (Hickey 2001).

The 9/11 Attacks and Systemic, Communal Help

It became clear while reviewing all of this and documenting the moves and countermoves of the groups and interests in August and early September 2001 that, as we know, this whole context gets turned upside down by the 9/11 attacks. At the first NCWO meeting after the attacks, November 13, 2001, the coalition issued an "NCWO Statement on Domestic Priorities." The one-page document began:

> The National Council of Women's Organizations, the nations' largest and oldest umbrella coalition of 152 women's organizations stands

in support of the international fight to end terrorism. We honor the courageous men and women dedicating their lives to our freedom and security. The recent terrorist attacks have ushered the United States into a critical period internationally—but they have also intensified the challenges we face at home. While we clearly need to allocate national resources for rescue, medical treatment and rebuilding as well as military action against terrorism, we cannot sacrifice domestic priorities in the process. Our national security and unity depend upon a strong economy, a strong social infrastructure, aid for the victims of the September 11th attacks and support for U.S. families. (NCWO 2001a; in author files)

In responding to the 9/11 attacks, the statement continued, "This is a time for all of us to share the economic sacrifice and not put the greatest burden on the most vulnerable among us" (NCWO 2001a; in author files). Noted were the impending national security costs and the tumbling stock market. Steps Congress should take, the NCWO memo continued, include fair taxes, no cuts in domestic spending that would jeopardize the social safety net, expedition of unemployment claims and ending biases against part-time workers (many of them women and minorities), raising the minimum wage, and ending the five-year welfare clock. The "NCWO Statement on Domestic Priorities" concluded, "Over 3,000 survivors have applied for Social Security as a result of the events of September 11. In addition to retirement benefits, Social Security provides long-term, inflation-protected income for children and widowed spouses of deceased workers. This important safety net must be protected against privatization proposals that jeopardize the revenue needed to pay these benefits by diverting designated payroll taxes into individual accounts" (NCWO 2001; in author files). In these statements, the NCWO noted the relevance of linked fate social programs like Social Security and its Survivor Benefits as central to the national ability to systematically and reliably assist many survivors and their families harmed by the 9/11 attacks.

The military response to 9/11 was costly in American blood and treasure. Groups focused on social programs linked the costs to thrusts against programs like Social Security. The Center for Economic and Policy Research issued a report entitled, "The Cost of the War on Terrorism and the Cost of Social Security," which honed the point. Comparing the two expenditures is useful, they asserted, since, "clearly the expenditures associated with the war on terrorism are not trivial. They will impose a burden on the budget. However, this spending has not been associated with the sort of apocalyptic adjectives which often [have] been used to describe the burden that Social Security will impose on the nation" (Baker 2002: 2). National security, the NCWO explains, includes family and domestic well-being (see also Enloe 2013, 2007).

One Voice

In a united voice the NCWO on April 8, 2002, urged Congress to reject private Social Security account proposals. Their news release called on the House and Senate "to clarify their position on Social Security private account plans. NCWO rejects current proposals in Congress and the three recommendations of President Bush's Social Security Commission to create so-called voluntary private accounts" (Turman 2002; in author files). Harms to women and families were recounted. The release ended by pointing out that small but prudent minor changes could shore up Social Security's finances and that even after 2041 the program could meet 73 percent of current obligations (Turman 2002; in author files).

Throughout 2002 a wide-ranging print and media conflict was waged by adherents of private accounts and the NCWO and allies pushing back (see, for example, Hartmann and Turman 2002a–2002c; in author files). NCWO files included an August 26, 2002, memo from the National Republican Campaign Committee communications director to "GOP Incumbents and Candidates," which advised that "Words Matter in the Social Security Debate." Recommended was emphasis on "saving" Social Security rather than "changing" or "reforming" it. GOP politicians were also reminded that personal accounts are not the same as privatization (Schmidt and Forti 2002; in author files). The RNC memo indicated that the campaign by progressives and the women's community against "privatization" was ruffling some feathers.

The Women's Equality Summit, Congressional Action Day (WESCAD) was funded, organized, and led by NCWO people in the springs of 1999, 2001, 2002, and again in 2007 and 2008. Each gathering emphasized that women's economic security includes welfare reform. Sample letters that attendees of the 2002 WESCAD could sign and send to their members of Congress first threw down a marker: "I am a constituent from your state and I am in Washington, DC today attending the Women's Equality Summit & Congressional Action Day sponsored by more than 70 member organizations within the National Council of Women's Organizations (NCWO)" (WESCAD 2002; in author files). The letter continued, "Women live longer than men, earn less, and are more likely to be dependent on the social safety net throughout their lives. Thus, women have a unique stake and significant interest in the budget priorities and domestic policy options currently being considered" (WESCAD 2002; in author files).

Proposals to change welfare concerned the letter author(s) and potential signers. The sample letter suggested, "First and foremost, Congress must invest in programs that improve education and training opportunities for poor mothers allowing more flexibility in time limits and work requirements. Successful policies must include support such as child care, anti-violence initiatives, housing assistance, healthcare coverage, and transportation" (WESCAD 2002; in author files). Protecting reproductive rights, preserving Social Security, and helping women in Afghanistan were also included. The letter was holistic and aimed at structural issues shaping women's economic chances. The authors were fully cognizant of the plight of poor and downtrodden people, most of them women and children, and the central role a solid safety net has for their prospects.

Throughout the Bush administration the NCWO and allies pushed back on neoliberal reforms to Social Security by continuing to highlight the female face of the program and the fragile economic condition of many older Americans, especially women. Overlapping coalitions like the Leadership Council of Aging Organizations also participated in the effort and lent their voice to the chorus (Leadership Council of Aging Organizations 2004; in author files). Large advocacy groups like the National Partnership for Women and Families, the National Women's Law Center, the Feminist Majority, and NOW seconded the NCWO theme of a false crisis and sham fix for Social Security. Materials from NCWO during the period warned, "Without Social Security, the poverty rate for women over 65 would have been an astonishing 52.9 percent!" (NCWO, Women and Social Security Project, n.d.; in author files). In 2004 the Office of House Democratic Leader Nancy Pelosi (CA) issued statements asserting that the Republican proposal would cut benefits (January 24, 2004).

Economic Meltdown of 2008

The housing bubble burst, the foreclosure tsunami, and the financial crisis of 2008 all had a particularly devastating effect on women. Women's groups held briefings on "The Female Face of Foreclosure" (July 25, 2008). Wider Opportunities for Women (WOW) released data on the impact of questionable and predatory house loans for women of color and older women. WOW's research documented, "The cumulative effects of pay inequity, occupational segregation in low-wage jobs, and workplace policies that do not honor or acknowledge caregiving responsibilities, find old women with fewer resources upon retirement. This has made older women, particularly women of color, more susceptible to the predatory practices of the subprime mortgage lenders" (Wider Opportunities for Women, n.d.; in author files). The Women's Institute for a Secure Retirement (WISER) issued a report corroborating many of the points other groups were making about the gender inequalities in the social safety net and the exacerbating effect the 2008 economic crisis was further imposing on women (Hounsell 2008).

IWPR published a detailed study by Heidi Hartmann, Jeff Hayes, and Robert Drago entitled, "Social Security: Especially Vital to Women and

People of Color, Men Increasingly Reliant" (2011). The Executive Summary began "Social Security is the bedrock of retirement income for older Americans" (2011: i). They noted that it is also "our most effective anti-poverty program, lifting more than 14 million men and women aged 65 years and older above the poverty line in 2009" (2011: i). The data seemed incontrovertible. The charts and summary statements broke down the essential aspects of Social Security by gender, race, ethnicity, income, ability/disability, and family events such as divorce and death. A separate fact sheet from the IWPR in April 2011 detailed more fully the situation of "Latinas and Social Security" (Hayes, Yi, and Berg 2011).

The most recent NCWO-affiliated research report covering the period of this fieldwork came out in June 2014. Authored by Heidi Hartmann of IWPR, "Enhancing Social Security for Women and Other Vulnerable Americans: What the Experts Say" was based on interviews with five Congress members, ten staff, two former members of Congress, five senior leaders of the SSA and the Executive Branch and eight think tank, advocacy, and academic leaders. Hartmann found support for future consideration of more adequate benefits for the poor, credits for care givers (mostly women), and modernizing the system to account for changes in women's lives. Every respondent who had worked at the Social Security Administration and several other policy experts pointed out that Social Security was no longer viewed as having an independent policy voice. There was, then, "no longer a voice for the poor when changes to Social Security are debated within the Administration" (Hartmann 2014: 25). Rather, Social Security policy changes originated from the White House, with advice and assistance by the Department of Treasury. These shifts reflected how Social Security became a tool of macroeconomic policy (Hartmann 2014: 25). Many respondents, independent of partisan affiliations or ideology, "suggested that the most politically viable outcome of Congress tackling changes to Social Security's solvency and adequacy would be a mixture of benefit cuts, modest benefit increases for low earners, and revenue increases. The failure of that middle road to date suggests that Social Security remains a third rail in American politics" (Hartmann 2014: 29).

Within the context of women's groups pressuring for equity in national politics, it should be noted that the NCWO and members of the coalition were dealing at the same time with numerous skirmishes in Congress, the Executive Branch, the courts, and elsewhere. One example was their successful protest against changes planned for the Women's Bureau in the Department of Labor (NCWO and fifty-one separate group signatories, August 3, 2006; in author files). A 2005 request for public comment on discontinuing the Women Workers Series (WWS) from the Current Employment Series

(CES) survey by the Bureau of Labor Statistics elicited at least three letters from NCWO to various officials. Getting right to the point the letters read, "On behalf of these ten million women [collectively represented in the NCWO], NCWO requests that you continue to collect data on women workers in the CES Program" (Burk, interviews, February 18 and May 13, 2005; in author files; see also Hartmann and Burk 2012: 16).

Pushing back on Social Security privatization relied heavily on data separated by gender. Researchers could then illustrate women's dire economic vulnerabilities and the hardships possible without the steady, systematic, and routinized (yet not perfect) benefits of a program like Social Security. Countering an almost under-the-radar government proposal to change routine data gathering was unspectacular yet essential work by the NCWO.

Inside and Outside the State

At the same time, Democratic Party officials and congresspeople and their staffs were composing opposition statements against the privatization push. In their litany of concerns, many of these documents mentioned how the changes would hurt women in particular (see, for example, Democratic Staff 2001a, 2001b; Matsui 2002; in author files). Lionesses and lions in the U.S. House and Senate also included Ted Kennedy, Barbara Murkowski, Barbara Boxer, Nancy Pelosi, Carolyn Mahoney, and Henry Waxman. Their allegiance was steadfast.

Push back on privatization of Social Security was also aided by the coordinated messaging of female Democratic U.S. Senators who "generally emphasize a woman's perspective, often the perspective of a mother trying to take care of her family, on a party priority" (Swers 2013: 70). On these caucus priorities the female Senators deliberately pushed the woman's point of view. As a Democratic staffer explained, regarding President Bush's privatization of Social Security efforts, "[T]he women were the in-house experts on fighting Social Security privatization and how bad this would be for women. Talking about the fact that women live longer and women's history in the workforce" (Swers 2013: 70). Indeed, Swers found, "Women [in the U.S. Senate] are particularly active on those issues that have a direct connection to consequences for women as a group" (2013: 95). Republican and Democratic women senators drew on their moral authority as women to gain media attention and build legislative support for their issues.

Part of their strength, as Heidi Hartmann explained, included, "Congresswomen really need to know that the women's movement is still out there" (interview, September 22, 2010). Female senators, for example, participated in coalition-building efforts and made women's issues legislative priorities.

"Gender differences in legislative behavior are even more pronounced on feminist issues that tap questions of women's rights and are most easily connected to consequences for women as a group" (Swers 2013: 97). These senators drew on their personal experiences as women and "their greater connection to and understanding of the patterns of women's lives" (Swers 2013: 97). Their efforts helped illuminate the female face of Social Security as they played both offense and defense on women's rights (Swers 2013: 97–101). Heidi Hartmann and many other interviewees underscored that the friends of the women's movement in the Congress and White House really need the data from the women's community to be able to do the right thing.

While the NCWO was able to highlight the gender impact of Social Security reforms, and the problems for working poor people (predominantly female) contained within a private accounts model, many women's activists interviewed felt, at the time, that the private accounts juggernaut would be difficult to halt. The makeup of the Bush Reform Commission was one indication of how the deck seemed stacked (from the NCWO member's point of view) in favor of the private investment accounts.

With Friends Like These: Obama Administration Skirmish

The November 2008 election of Barack Obama and Joseph Biden was widely celebrated in the women's rights community (see also Chapter 5 on working the gender gap in 2008 for more details). While relieved and enthusiastic about the Democratic presidential victory, several women's leaders interviewed for this study went out of their way to explain that their role was not to be Obama administration acolytes or partisans. One powerful president of a national women's group, also central to the workings of the NCWO, stated, "My cheerleader uniform is still at the cleaners. We cannot be cheerleaders for the Obama Administration, we are an advocacy group. President Obama can govern and be President, he does that well. We will advocate for women's rights" (Terry O'Neill, NOW president, interview, September 16, 2009). In other words, a president's role is to make compromises and govern, whereas NOW's role is to insist on no compromises on fundamental issues.

By 2010 the national debt was again a hot issue. The insurgent Tea Party movement within the Republican Party strongly critiqued "entitlements," the deficit, and a perceived overreaching federal government. In early 2010 the Obama administration formed a deficit reduction study commission. Named the National Commission on Fiscal Responsibility and Reform, it was chaired by two fiscal conservatives, Erskine Bowles and former Republican Senator Alan Simpson. Concerns about budget deficits were fanned by billionaire investment banker Pete Peterson, the Concord Coalition, and the

Committee for a Responsible Federal Budget (Madrick 2014: 69–70). The Bowles-Simpson commission called for federal spending to be no higher than 21 percent of GDP, which was the average in the 1970s. The economic ideology behind it was that deficits had to be cut sooner rather than later. But to achieve the targeted 21 percent would require sharp social spending cuts, including Social Security and Medicare (Madrick 2014: 70). The commission's emphasis, during a Democratic presidency, showed the sedimentation of the neoliberal project in parties of the center-left as well as the right (Walby 2015: 124). Women's leaders quickly posted up to defend social programs that appeared to be some of the most vulnerable to cuts from deficit hawks given the sanctity of other items in the budget like the military and the nearly impossible chances to effect tax reforms.

In 2010 labor unions again were central components of a large coalition called "Strengthen Social Security," which NCWO also belonged to. The labor unions I observed at the July 29 event organized a well-attended press conference at the National Press Club announcing the new combined campaign. Their united message strongly stated that Social Security should not be cut but rather strengthened.

The NCWO, via its Older Women's Economic Security Task Force, took on their erstwhile friends in the Obama White House with their April 14, 2011, "Statement of Terry O'Neil and Heidi Hartmann, Co-Chairs, on the President's Plan to Reduce the Deficit" (O'Neill and Hartmann 2011; in author files). The report began with all the points President Obama had made that resonated with their own analysis: the budget should not be balanced on the backs of seniors and low- and middle-class Americans, and the real cause of the short-term deficit was two unpaid-for wars, an unpaid-for prescription drug program, the worst recession since the Great Depression of the 1930s, and the tax cuts for the wealthiest Americans. However, they noted, a White House fact sheet raised questions for them. The president's framework for reducing the deficit, the fact sheet stated, was to reduce with "*three dollars of spending cuts and interest savings for every one dollar from tax reform that contributes to deficit reduction*,' an approach that will almost certainly put too much burden on those who depend the most on federal programs, often women, children, and seniors" (O'Neill and Hartmann 2011, italics in original; in author files).

They also sounded the alarm about plans to chisel cost savings from Medicare. They "ask the President to make clear that Social Security will not be discussed as part of the budget deficit negotiations, since as the President noted, it has played no part in the growing deficit" (O'Neill and Hartmann 2011). They urged him to focus on controlling health care costs throughout the economy, not only in Medicare, and to maintain Medicaid programs.

Finally, they insisted that the well-off should pay their fair share of taxes (O'Neill and Hartmann 2011).

In a collective report, *Breaking the Social Security Glass Ceiling*, researchers highlighted again how all the differences and disparities of women's lives layer and accumulate to the detriment of women when they are older (Estes, O'Neill, and Hartmann 2012). The report was a combined effort of IWPR, the National Committee to Preserve Social Security and Medicare Foundation (NCPSSM), and the NOW Foundation.

Compassionate Communities, Dispassionate Rational Actors

Throughout the Social Security saga these frames overlapped with skepticism and caution about the impetus for the proposed changes in Social Security. Deficit reduction goals energized some of the Social Security reformers or privatizers. The NCWO joined many groups in questioning the need to reduce the deficits with cuts to important social programs and safety nets. In doing so, the tax cuts to wealthy Americans and the wars paid on credit were presented as bigger causes of the deficit. Some groups asserted also that cutting the deficit was an excuse since the deficit was a small percentage of the federal budget and was part of the landscape for a large government like the United States. The icing on the cake for protectors of Social Security was that the program was not part of the deficit at all.

Intertwined with all these elements of the issue was a strong critique of the impetus for the privatization of Social Security campaign. Wall Street, neoliberals, free market theorists, and small government ideology were presented as behind the privatization movement. The bottom line for the coalition was that Social Security worked, Social Security was not the problem, and the programs should be enhanced and expanded to more accurately reflect how, where, and when many women worked.

Volatility in the stock market bolstered their message. Acutely painful to neoliberal arguments for less government regulation was the 2008 bursting of the housing bubble, the domino effect of the housing foreclosure crisis, the failure of many financial institutions, and the need for the federal government to bail out banks and corporations deemed "too big to fail."

Targeting cuts to social services, however, seemed ineluctable given how beliefs in inherent free market efficiency and fair outcomes were presented:

> This is at least partly because the narration of the crisis as a fiscal rather than financial crisis has become hegemonic, thereby allowing the marginalization of this test of theories about markets. Narrating the crisis as if it were primarily a fiscal rather than a financial crisis

enables the construction of the most relevant political debate as one centered on the level of public expenditure rather than on the regulation of finance. It facilitates the side-stepping of the real causes of the crisis, found in the failure to regulate finance, and thus of the examination of the potential policies which would prevent it from happening again. (Walby 2015: 165)

Move Forward

Against the political odds, many scholars, pundits, and advocates have re-invigorated economic equality, or, at the least, fairness proposals. As Neera Tanden prefaces the 2014 *Shriver Report*, "Endemic economic insecurity is not inevitable" (viii). Rather it builds from social choices that can be discussed and amended. "It's time to revive the notion of a collective national responsibility to the poorest among us," Ehrenreich writes, "who are disproportionately women and especially women of color. Until that happens, we need to wake up to the fact that the underpaid women who clean our homes and offices, prepare and serve our meals, and care for our elderly—earning wages that do not provide enough to live on—are the true philanthropists of our society" (2014: 39).

Reframing working poor women or women on the brink, Galinsky, Bond, and Tahmincioglu wrote: "We must find ways to support the low-wage women who support our economy" (2014: 314). A move forward in the politics of Social Security was the highlighting of the years of caregiving women often perform (Eisler and Otis 2014: 67–68). The Social Security Act's calculation of work leading to retirement benefits does not include caregiving as work. Momentum has built to provide credit for caregiving as in the Social Security Caregiver Credit Act. The NCWO was a leader in those efforts.

Many scholars have underscored the increasing income and political power inequities in America. Modern "supercapitalism" has shredded many safety nets once taken for granted (Reich 2007; Lynch 2011: 44–65). Educated, professional, and managerial Americans in the upper middle class and the superrich (the 1 percent) face different prospects in their old age or if disabled than do the middle class, working poor, and poor. "Those further down the economic ladder faced increasingly competitive labor markets in which idealism quickly gave way to pragmatic realism regarding rising economic instability and survival in a world dominated by global supercapitalism" (Lynch 2011: 30, see also 195). Indeed, the double inequities in wealth and political voice worked together to almost ineluctably reinscribe themselves (American Political Science Association 2004; Morgan and Skelton 2014; Schlozman, Verba, Brady 2012; Walby 2009).

Some company policies maneuver job classifications to contract work, temporary work, salaried work, or part-time work in order to get around minimum wage, overtime requirements, and benefit provisions such as family and medical leave, health insurance, pensions, and earned sick and vacation days. "Like squeezing a balloon, if we fix only one issue, such as the loophole for temps or independent contractors, part-time workers or employees of small, exempt establishments, the problems will just bulge out somewhere else" (Fredrickson 2015: 145). Many scholars agreed with the author of *Under the Bus* that "it is clear that the best and only way to ensure low-wage women and those with little bargaining power an end to excessively long workdays, denial of overtime, chaotic scheduling, and lack of benefits is to provide universal programs, like Medicare, available to all. Only when all Americans are equally entitled will we see the day when employers are not constantly searching for the regulatory exit door" (Fredrickson 2015: 127).

Another move forward was the Department of Labor regulatory change announced in 2013 to include in-home direct care workers under the minimum wage and overtime rules of the Fair Labor Standards Act. The change started in January 2015.

Essential, Yet Unspectacular

The push back against privatizing Social Security was a huge mobilization and accomplishment. Both sides learned from the skirmish. Neoliberals realized that frontal assaults on social programs such as Social Security did not work and harmed Republicans electorally. So more subtle "stealth strategies" emerged wherein neoliberals stated they were not eliminating protections altogether but only changing the *form* of the programs in order to save them (J. Hacker 2008: 58–60, italics in original; see also 130–134). Many of these reforms, such as the private retirement accounts called 401(k)s were heavily subsidized with public funds. These private options for retirement and medical insurance, beginning in the 1980s during President Ronald Reagan's administration, had many results including: (1) decreasing tax revenues for government programs; and (2) peeling off voters for a new conservative government coalition (J. Hacker 2008: 38, 121).

Social Security and Medicare seemed to still hold the specter of "the third rail in politics" (touch it and you die). However, free market advocacy continued to challenge some of the ideology behind even stalwart programs like Social Security and Medicare. One study concluded, "In short, Social Security helped create a constituency to be reckoned with, a group willing, able, and primed to participate at high-rates, capable of defeating objectionable policy change" (Campbell 2003: 3). Veterans benefit recipients have similar, but not as powerful, political credibility and participation. Welfare recipients were not as fortunate: their benefits were stigmatized, and payments were so sparse that people could not elevate out of poverty. The poor and working class also have little to no disposable income or time to devote to politics. For the poor, the coup de grace is that accessing programs was demeaning, contingent, and dispiriting (Campbell 2003: 136; Campbell 2014; Hancock 2004). Nevertheless, even in these abject and hopeless conditions, poor women, especially black women in groups such as the National Welfare Rights Organization, demanded respect, viable benefits and conditions, and a voice in policy implementation (U. Taylor 2010: 67–68; Piven and Cloward 1977). They talked back and dissented from the complacent status quo in order to set society straight concerning their plight and value as contributing and active citizens (Triece 2013).

The structure of policies can exacerbate rather than ameliorate existing inequalities of participation. The loop closes when inequalities of participation, in turn, shape the fortune of government policies. Privatization of Social Security, therefore, "could break the back of the senior lobby" (Campbell 2003: 2). The impact of social program design on democratic citizenship should be considered in policy analysis. Programs like Social Security and Medicare and Veterans benefits has positive effects on recipients who exercised their citizenship rights more fully. "Without voice such clients become victims of a democratic system in which the vocal and the organized prevail" as seen in programs for the poor (Campbell 2003: 137).

Senator Elizabeth Warren (D-MA) pondered, "How do we build a future? I made the case for what I believe: We are stronger and wealthier because of the things we build together. We are more secure when we create a foundation that allows each of us to have a decent chance to build something on our own. We are better off when we invest in one another. It's economics and values, tied tightly together" (2014: 216).

During the years examined in this chapter, Social Security was not "reformed" or privatized. In a 2000 interview, Gail Shaffer, president of Business and Professional Women's International, highlighted how the mobilization worked:

> Each of us have our own little niche. Business and Professional Women is the spearhead on pay equity, maybe, and we will ask for some help. If it is a domestic violence issue, NOW will give us a "heads up" and we will get our members to add their voices to that issue. For example, the collaboration on Social Security has meant we have had far more impact going to the White House, the Congress, than any single group would have had. By combining our voices we have had a big impact. (Shaffer, interview, September 5, 2000)

Regarding the 2010 dustup, Heidi Hartmann reflected, "The Democratic wing of the Democratic Party finally convinced Obama to stop saying he would cut Social Security" (interview, September 19, 2014). A dogged, informed, and persistent aspect of the years of push back, it should be noted, came from the NCWO and allied feminist and progressive groups and coalitions. However, as Yogi Berra once quipped, "It ain't over, till it's over." In politics, issues such as the future of Social Security and fighting about health care reform are never over.

The following chapter on health care reform and gender politics echoes many of these points. In both Social Security and health care reform, efforts to build and maintain citizen-based programs to alleviate economic hardships were possible when activists played the game for the long haul.

7

Health Care Reform

Being a Woman Is Not a Preexisting Condition

> Keep your government hands off my Medicare.
> —Citizen's sign at South Carolina town hall meeting with Rep.
> Bob Inglis (R-SC)

W hen Congress drafted the ACA, provisions included many policies important to women's health. These were part of a campaign centered on the slogan, "Being a Woman Is Not a Preexisting Condition." The NCWO was an important player in health care reform. Public opinion polls revealed that women believed more than men in the need for health care reform and were concerned about rising health care costs and the fragileness of health care coverage (Goss and Skocpol 2006: 329, 336).

My analysis focuses on the reproductive politics provisions of the ACA. The NCWO evolved from a constellation of pro-choice groups. The NCWO keenly wanted national health care reform. As the chapter explains, however, the coalition had to "stand down" on comprehensive reproductive rights in order to see the ACA pass. Many leaders of the NCWO and affiliated groups lamented that the ACA was passed at the expense of women's full reproductive rights. As many people told me, the ACA was passed "on the backs of women."

Birth control was included as preventive health in the ACA. Some draft versions of the ACA provided coverage for legal abortions. For decades, abortion has been a condensation symbol and lightening rod for many interest groups and politicians (Ainsworth and Hall 2011). It did not go unnoticed that funding for legal abortions was included in early markups for the ACA.

Advocates for the poor and working class, reproductive rights adherents, and many more were optimistic yet nervous about the abortion provision. The thinking was that with a popular Democratic president, Democratic control of both chambers of Congress, and a strong feminist Speaker of the

House, Nancy Pelosi (D-CA), the provision had a chance. As a condensation symbol, though, "abortion is a handy public-policy hand grenade to be tossed in the middle of any legislative battle by those whose goal is to blow things up" (Marcus 2009: 48). Chapter 8 discusses that ratification of international treaties is also buffeted by the abortion condensation symbol.

Big policy changes like comprehensive health care reform required a large mobilization of general interest and civic-minded groups. But many women's groups were niche positioned. Consequently, general interest groups, particularly those regarding gender issues, were waning in strength and membership (Goss and Skocpol 2006: 329; Goss 2013).

In addition to the fieldwork and archives used throughout this study, my analysis of the NCWO during health care reform efforts in 2009–2010 is based on participant observations at several events focused on the U.S. Congress. For instance, on November 18, 2009, the Planned Parenthood Federation of America, with the NCWO as a cosponsor, and several related health care organizations and providers organized and coordinated a one-day U.S. Senate "Stop Stupak" lobbying day. I attended the daylong event. At the end of the day, I shadowed pro-choice activists as they visited individual Senator's offices to advocate for full access to reproductive rights in the ACA. Part of my examination of the NCWO and health care reform also assesses how reproductive politics was framed by national interest groups and coalitions.

Introduction: The Women's Movement and Health Care Reform

Health care and women's bodily agency issues have been central to the women's rights community. NOW, for instance, has backed a single-payer system since 1993 (Jan Ericson, June 16, 2009, interview). Some background and context regarding women's health issues included women slighted by cardiologists (Bor 1991), by medical research (Ames 1990; Rosser 1994, 1991), by medical routines ("Factors Help Avoid Hysterectomy" 1994; Lore 1994; "Mammograms for Women in Their 40s Contested" 1995), and by many male MDs ("Going to a Female Doc" 1993; "Study: Female Doctors More Likely to Give Pap Smears, Mammograms" 1993). Women were overmedicated and overmedicalized during pregnancy and birth. The high Cesarean section rate in the United States was also concerning (Gawande 2006). Women's choices regarding their reproductive lives were constantly under siege (Adcox 2007; Brinson 1992; "Challenges to Abortion" 2006; Crary 2006; "Study: More Women Need Birth Control to Save Lives" 1993; Gorney 1998; Hansen 2007; Herbert 1998a; Rosenberg 2005; Sheinin 2007; Sinderbrand 2005; Slevin 2009; Toobin 2005; Woliver 2002b). An additional issue has been the punitive monitoring of pregnant women, particularly poor women and women of color ("Women on Drug Charges Fill Jails" 1992; Herbert 1998b; C. Reid 2007; Woliver 2002b). In short, mainstream medicine and science was seen by feminist scholars as often male-streamed (Begley 1999; Clarke 1998). For women's groups reproductive politics involved "undivided rights" at the intersections of gender, race, class, and sexualities (Silliman et al. 2004).

Books such as *Our Bodies, Ourselves* (first published in 1970), written by upstart women who were not medical professionals, were important aspects of the women's health movement (Alvarado 1992; see also Morgen 2002; Ruzek and Becker 1999). When the fourth edition of *Our Bodies, Ourselves* was coming out one reporter noted, "one thing about the book has remained the same: its sassy, pugnacious attitude that women know best—especially when it comes to their own bodies" (Alvarado 1992; see also Traister 2015).

Leaders such as Senator Barbara A. Mikulski (D-MD) and Representative Patricia Schroeder (D-CO) pushed for equity in research and clinical trials for women's health. Mikulski wrote a legislative provision requiring the NIH to establish an Office of Women's Health Research, and to take steps to include women and minorities in clinical research trials (Monroe 1992). The Women's Health Initiative was founded in NIH and funded as well (Rubin 1993). The Congressional Caucus for Women's Issues (CCWI, discussed in Chapter 2) provided crucial impetus to these reforms. The CCWI in 1985, for instance, released a General Accounting Office audit showing that $7 billion a year in federal dollars were spent on health care research that largely ignored women (Monroe 1992; see also Women's Health Research Coalition 2000). Problems exclusive to or predominantly experienced by women were woefully underfunded as well. Sometimes leaving women out of studies and clinical trials was justified because if the woman became pregnant, there could be harm to the fetus. Patricia Ireland, NOW president at the time, commented that sometimes fetal health is of more concern than women's (Monroe 1992).

One long-standing victory for antichoice adherents is the Hyde Amendment. First passed in 1974 the Hyde Amendment prohibited Medicaid funds to be used to pay for legal abortions. Additional prohibitions have been made for U.S. military health care services at home and abroad. The Hyde Amendment was upheld by the U.S. Supreme Court in *Harris v. McRae* (1980). Upholding the Hyde Amendment coupled with legal abortion funding bans in the 2010 ACA help ensure that impoverished reproductive choices remain part of American poverty (Erdreich 2013: 128).

Antecedent: Clinton Health Care Reform, 1993

The Clinton administration's health care overhaul efforts in 1993 have been carefully analyzed by media and scholars (see Eleanor Clift 1993; J. Klein

1993; Morgenthau and Hager 1993; R. Thomas 1993; Samuelson 1993; Skocpol 1997, to name a few). After the failure of health care reform in 1993 the hardships many families experienced when uninsured or underinsured continued and often worsened (Cowley 1993; Johnson 1993). Many groups published extensive and thoughtful position papers, policy recommendations, and background discussion materials regarding the fragile American health care system and possible reforms (see, for example, IWPR Research by: Hegewisch and Zhang 2013–2014; Williams and Gault 2014; Yi 2013; League of Women Voters Education Foundation 2000; Fried 2003; Towey, Poggi, and Roth 2005; Pollitt 2007).

The specter of what went wrong or right in 1990s reform proposals foreshadowed the 2009–2010 efforts. In 1993–1994 reform efforts women's groups and advocates were concerned about lack of coverage for women's reproductive health including legal abortion coverage (Hasson 1994; Cohn 1992). More than twenty years later, similar issues were raised about women's health coverage in the ACA.

Health care, like many social programs, was woven within a dominating "gendered imagination," which was heavily racialized. The resulting programs framed what was possible, and bound up what was considered just, fair, normal, and politically plausible (Kessler-Harris 2001: 5–6). New Deal social policies, labor laws, and distribution of national resources for economic development incorporated gender and race as "a crucial measure of fairness and served a powerful mediating role" (Kessler-Harris 2001: 6). One result meant "appeals to gender could enhance the public appetite for some policies and silence resistance to others. They legitimized, rationalized, and justified policies that could and did serve many other ends, including maintaining a stratified and racialized social order and undercutting radical threats" (Kessler-Harris 2001: 6). Gendered and raced worldviews remained in many people's thinking about what was "natural" and described how "traditional habits of mind have become embedded in our legislature, judicial, and policy-making apparatus" making redefining social policies well-nigh impossible. Citizens, then, faced constrained choices that "suggest the complicated ways that informal as well as formal rules constrain options in tension with a historical process that has yet to reach its conclusion" (Kessler-Harris 2001: 295–296).

The NCWO, allied groups, and experts monitored federal policy and court proceedings with regard to women's health throughout the 1990s and up to passage of the ACA.[1] The 2006 and 2008 elections helped set the stage for viable national health care reform. As Baumgartner et al. found in their study *Lobbying and Policy Change* (2009), the status quo is usually decisive in national politics, except when there is huge change. As they explained, social cascades sweep forward large policy changes and national group lobbyists realize a policy train has left the station. Activists realized they better get on the train or get run over. When they hopped the train, however, they kept up their work to amend the new policy to their interests.

In addition, women's roles in the U.S. Congress made a difference. To avoid threats to the ACA by abortion politics machinations, "politically charged negotiations like these require the vigorous advocacy of senators with a personal commitment to the issue" (Swers 2013: 42). Indeed, Democratic female U.S. senators ramped up efforts to protect feminist causes from the Republican Party's conservative agenda (Swers 2013: 55, 109).

Regarding interest group politics writ large, the skirmish illustrated that part of the given of the status quo in our politics of paltry social safety nets is the neoliberal norms of McDonagh's points in *The Motherless State* (2009). The Hyde Amendment achieved a "new normal" frame that only radical and fringe groups would want to change.

Abortion politics also reflected a shift in the center of our politics, what Naomi Klein has called *The Shock Doctrine* (2008). Antichoice interests have softened up the entire discourse on abortion to their benefit. The activists I shadowed were working from a center that had moved rightward and a status quo that framed them (pro-choice, fair access, public funding for abortions adherents) as fringe, problems, and potential spoilers for health care reform. One activist commented at the time, "It is so ironic that we are now essentially defending the Hyde Amendment" because we say "we accept the Hyde restrictions" in health care reform.

Confronting a "New Normal" Antichoice Status Quo

In reproductive politics, the large coalition represented by the NCWO and Planned Parenthood stood fast for health care reform knowing that *Now Is the Time* as Todd Shaw (2009) characterized social change efforts. While not wanting to obstruct health care reform over issues like abortion they were also caught in a dilemma of not wanting to accept health care reform "on the backs of women." As a coalition aware of the large numbers of women and families without health insurance, the progress possible in eliminating gender ratings in insurance policies, and inclusion of routine preventive health screenings for many of the illnesses that plague women (breast and cervical cancer, to name two), they felt obligated to tacitly accept a new status quo of not just the Hyde Amendment but potentially an expansion of Hyde through the Stupak amendments and then further blocking proposals by Senator Ben Nelson of Nebraska (a Democrat).

A Democratic from Michigan, Representative Bart Stupak led the efforts in the House to make sure the ACA did not cover funds for legal abortion (see Ainsworth and Hall 2011: 60–64). Representative Stupak was cochair of the Congressional Pro-Life Caucus. The Stupak Amendments were discussed as a huge expansion of the impact of Hyde because the Stupak policy would restrict exchanges from funding abortion if they received federal subsidies for individual or family premiums. The catch was that health care reform as proposed had generous subsidies for premiums. Some estimates included family incomes of up to $80,000, which was great for expanding coverage and affordability, but which meant that almost all the exchanges would receive federal money and thus would be barred (per Stupak provisions) from allowing abortion coverage.

Another pro-choice frame utilized was that this amounted to a further loss to women and families because some private health insurance plans covered legal abortion. So, contrary to the Obama administration promise that people would not be losing anything in health care reform (oft-repeated was candidate Barack Obama's phrase, "If you like the health coverage you have now, you will not be losing anything in the new reforms"), many would lose abortion coverage because of Stupak's and others' efforts. Many activists interviewed for this study believed this was progress made at the expense of women.

The Affordable Care Act and Women

The health care debate laid bare some hard truths for supporters of legal abortion, "that a Democratic president, Democratic Senate, and Democratic House do not add up to a pro-choice outcome. A victory on health care for abortion-rights supporters will consist, at best, of maintaining the status quo" (Marcus 2009: 48; see also Kirkpatrick and Pear 2009; Tomasky 2009).

Ruth Marcus of *The Washington Post* and *Newsweek* reported, "Democratic leaders urged the abortion-rights crowd to stand down on health care" (2009: 49; see also Jackson 2009). The leader of the pro-choice congressional caucus, Rep. Diana DeGette (D-CO) and forty or more supporters threatened to sink health care reform if the Stupak amendments were included. DeGette explained to Marcus, "We don't want to kill health-care reform. We think it is a massive expansion of health care for women. But you can't have a devil's bargain of reducing their access to abortion at the same time. That's a devil's bargain nobody should have to make" (2009: 50).

At the end of July 2009, the NOW National Action Center reported that House Speaker Nancy Pelosi (D-CA) met with several antichoice Democrats to assuage their concerns about federal money being spent through health care exchanges for legal abortions. NOW warned that private health insurance plans that cover legal abortions might become future targets for antichoice prohibitions. If so, the memo stated, millions of women would be affected (NOW National Action Center 2009a: 2–3; in author files).

A September 2009 sign-on letter circulated to NCWO members urged the Congress to pass health care reform in the context of women's unequal wages, benefits, assets, and wealth. The chair of the NCWO set the context: "More than half of women have forgone necessary care because of cost, and one-third have made a difficult trade-off, such as giving up basic necessities, to get health care. In total, *seven in ten* women are either uninsured or under-insured (i.e., they have coverage but still spend more than they can afford on health care); struggling to pay a medical bill; or are experiencing another cost-related problem in accessing needed care" (Scanlan 2009a, italics in original; in author files). Points made included how women utilize health care more than men and therefore need insurers to stop imposing annual or lifetime benefit caps. Given many women's financial precariousness, copayments and premium costs should be considered in calculations on affordability. Reforms should also limit or eliminate "cost-sharing for preventive and screening services, including pregnancy prevention." The overall theme of the letter, and many more from the NCWO and partners, stressed the need for health care to be affordable and accessible to women.

The Planned Parenthood Federation of America repeatedly pointed out that 98 percent of American women use birth control at some point in their lives. So, reproductive health care was basic health care. "Bold action is needed to address the health care crisis," Scanlan asserted. "To do anything else is morally and fiscally irresponsible." The letter ended with the promise, "The National Council of Women's Organizations stands ready to work with you to realize the ultimate promise of health care reform" (Scanlan 2009a; in author files).

However, women in general, working families, and especially low-income women, had a lot to gain from the health care reform legislation. In early December 2009, during the fraught write-up of health care reform, Marcus detailed the conundrum women's groups and leaders faced: "There is no way to avoid an abortion fight in health care. The pro-choice side has no options, only less bad ones. The worst one of all would be to take a step that punished women in the name of protecting their rights" (2009: 50). Open and unabashed lobbying by the United States Conference of Catholic Bishops against federal financing of abortion in health care options was part of the controversy and strife (Goodnough 2009; L. Miller 2010; Toobin 2009). Emily's List made an exception to its no-lobbying policy to pressure women it helped elect to "Stop Stupak" and protect reproductive rights in health care reform (D. Kirkpatrick 2009b).

Passage of health care reform included "for the Democrats, a shameful and costly retreat on abortion" (Michelman and Kissling 2009: 31). Many women's rights leaders interpreted the House acceptance of the Stupak-Pitts amendment in November 2009 as, "The Democratic majority has abandoned its platform and subordinated women's health to short-term political success. In doing so, these so-called friends of women's rights have arguably done more to undermine reproductive rights than some of abortion's staunchest foes" (Michelman and Kissling 2009).

In the U.S. Senate, Democrat Ben Nelson of Nebraska demanded provisions to prohibit federal money to fund abortions and for any health exchange to not fund abortions as well. NOW asked members to call their Senators and tell them that three factors made the Senate bill unacceptable: the abortion coverage ban, the lack of a public plan and the possible no Medicare buy-in option for individual states. NOW's position was that members should ask their senators to vote against the entire bill if these amendments were adopted. NOW's email stated, "The Senate does not HAVE to pass this flawed bill before Christmas, but they MUST fix the bill to remove onerous abortion restrictions! And the senators should restore the public option and the Medicare buy-in as well" (NOW National Action Center 2009b; copy of email in author files).

Documents examined for this study, also, chillingly warned as early as 2009 that members of Congress wanted to defund Planned Parenthood specifically. After the 2016 elections, this played out more fully.

Under the Bus: Final Countdown Compromises

When President Obama signed the ACA in March 2010, he also signed a separate executive order on abortion funding. How he got to this point, signing an agreement on abortion restrictions along with his ACA, was an "unexpected victory" for antichoice groups in the 2010 ACA (Halva-Neubauer, Zeigler, and Zientek 2011). Antiabortion forces successfully cast the reproductive health choices in the ACA as an expansion of abortion rights that included public funding for abortion. Antiabortion adherents challenged the ACA as toppling the status quo of no public funding for abortion. Early in 2009 antiabortion groups "had shifted attention from the complexities of the service and funding options to the question of whether abortion services would be covered by publicly funded plans" within the ACA (Halva-Neubauer, Zeigler, and Zientek 2011: 9). Protecting the status quo is an advantageous political position in American politics. In the meantime, pro-choice and pro-ACA reproductive choice groups did not have as united a message and were castigated by opponents for pulling a fast one with inclusion of abortion funds in the ACA.

Pro-choice interests maintained that they were the defenders of the status quo by only agreeing to the limits in annual Hyde Amendment legislation. However, their claim for stability in abortion legislation did not resonate with congressional elites. Representative Lois Capps (D-CA) offered a compromise amendment setting up separate, segregated accounts within exchanges wherein beneficiaries could purchase with their own funds policies that covered legal abortions. The Capps amendment gave pro-choice members of the Congress a way to protect what they saw as the status quo on abortion.

To ensure passage of the ACA, President Obama went to Congress in early September 2009 and promised no public funding for abortion within health care reform. He also agreed to the executive order codifying this compromise. When President Obama did this, antichoice forces achieved more than acceptance of the status quo. A more restrictive status quo was created with a pro-choice Democratic president agreeing to their demands and adding to the basic outlines of the Hyde Amendment a promise that even future health exchanges would not indirectly allow beneficiaries to pay for a legal abortion with their own funds through ACA programs.

Congressional women and their staffs pressed for broad coverage of preventive health care in the ACA. They included the benefits women needed to choose from for their reproductive health in addition to mammogram and gynecological care. At one point in the process, Senate Majority Leader Harry Reid (D-NV) dropped a broad group of women's preventive health care services as a cost-cutting move. However, "Women [in the U.S. Senate] played key roles in behind-the-scenes negotiations seeking to restore the benefits" (Swers 2013: 235). The combination of congressional women's and women's rights groups' pressure also limited the scope of "conscience clauses" in the ACA "that would prioritize women's health" (Swers 2013: 235). The double teaming of the women both inside and outside of the Congress was also assisted by cogent policy analysis from women's rights groups like the National Women's Law Center, Planned Parenthood, the National Partnership of Women and Girls, the FMF, NOW, and IWPR, to name a few. These groups were also important members of the NCWO. Health care reform was also achieved through the efforts of other large coalitions such as Health Care for America Now (HCAN).

Regarding passage of health care reform, Swers's study of women in the U.S. Senate found "the debate over contraceptive coverage reaffirms the importance of women having a seat at the table when policies are negotiated. Moreover, the controversy highlights the significance of social identity and intensity of commitment to a policy. Democratic women were among the most aggressive advocates for wide contraceptive coverage as President Obama sought to find a compromise that would be acceptable to the disparate elements of the Democratic coalition" (2013: 236). In the end, however, women's groups had to cut their losses since there were not enough votes in the Congress to pass the ACA without the guaranteed abortion restrictions. In this contest, "taxpayer choice was pitted against a women's choice" (Halva-Neubauer, Zeigler, and Zientek 2011: 4).

Conclusion

Regarding health care reform politics between 2009 and 2010, my interviews and fieldwork showed

1. NCWO members deeply favored comprehensive health care reform realizing that it would result in progress for women and their families.
2. House passage of the Stupak Amendment surprised the choice and women's rights communities.
3. Their shock led to outrage and mobilization against further erosion of choice Stupak represented to them. Their mobilization moderated the Stupak restrictions in the Senate but did not defeat them.
4. President Obama's willingness to compromise on abortion was very disappointing to members of the NCWO. Many of them chalked it up to his desire to pass the ACA as a keystone of his presidential legacy.
5. The women's rights community in DC, in the final push for health care reform, did not push for expanded access to legal abortion or repeal of Hyde Amendment policies. For the sake of passing health care reform, in their words, they "stood down."

The ACA is not perfect, by any means. However, it moved forward several aspects of the women's movement agenda: coverage of preventive health screenings women need (mammograms, pap smears), inclusion of birth control as preventive health care, end of gender ratings in insurance premiums, and more. One of President Obama's oft-repeated admonitions seems apt here as well, "We should not let the perfect be the enemy of the good."

In spring of 2010 *Ms.* magazine categorized the ACA as "A Title IX for Health Care" (Smeal 2010: 12). Credit to women's groups was front and center:

> To achieve this recent legislative victory, which eliminates sex discrimination in pricing and many benefits, women's organizations

such as Planned Parenthood Foundation of America, NARAL Pro-Choice America, NOW, Feminist Majority, National Women's Law Center, National Partnership for Women and Families, National Council of Women's Organizations, YWCA USA, National Council of Jewish Women and National Older Women's League worked tirelessly together—attending countless meetings with administration officials and members of Congress, delivering millions of emails, sponsoring lobby days and more. (Smeal 2010: 14)

Since President Obama signed the ACA on March 24, 2010, it has continued to be a political lightening rod. The ACA is anathema to neoliberal, free market activists and theorists. It is a social program based on linked fate, shared cost, and mutual benefits policy making. Neoliberal reforms and ideology impacted the climate and agenda for the ACA. For instance, there was most likely a political effect on already existing private health care saving accounts. "Piling tax break upon tax break permitting wealthy and healthy Americans to opt out of our tattered institutions of social insurance does harm" (J. Hacker 2008: 180).

The House of Representatives has since voted at least sixty times to repeal "Obamacare." Provisions for birth control coverage have been eviscerated by court challenges and close U.S. Supreme Court decisions. Fascinating coalitions of Catholic bishops, Tea Party activists, and neoliberal conservatives have combined efforts to fight the ACA in the courts and state legislatures, and at the ballot box (Goodstein 2012). At the same time, another coalition of industry, health, consumers, labor unions, and NGOs worked to enroll the uninsured and facilitate implementation of the ACA (Alonso-Zaldivar 2011).

In the 2015–2016 Republican presidential nomination contest all seventeen candidates vowed to repeal "Obamacare" or ACA. The U.S. Supreme Court has on the one hand upheld the basic tenets of the ACA yet allowed exceptions (*Burwell v. Hobby Lobby Stores*, 2014). Pending in the court as this book is written are further cases regarding religious freedoms and the ACA, issues particularly central to women's bodily agency (again, birth control).

After the victory of President Donald J. Trump, groups continued to sign people up for the ACA. President Trump has promised to repeal and replace the ACA. The Trump administration, however, faced a situation on the ground of more than twenty million Americans relying on the ACA. Only time will tell if being a woman goes back to being a preexisting condition or not with regard to American health care reforms.

To many advocates' disappointment, the ACA health care reforms, from their perspective, were not enough. What was needed was a single-payer system, universal citizenship based rights to health care, rather than means tested or state-by-state criteria, options, buy-ins, or refusals. Many health care and social insurance gaps and incongruous coverage criteria still make life very difficult for many Americans. Politicians say they are helping and providing "a hand up," not a handout. Yet many of the situations people find themselves in are more like boots on their necks to keep them poor, beleaguered, and stigmatized (Campbell 2014).

The ACA, for example, should have included dental care and eye care. In South Carolina, for instance, periodic free medical care events are held at one of the University of South Carolina's huge athletic facilities. They are for poor and working poor people. People line up overnight, the line winds around the block, and people are turned away because of excess demand. Medical doctors, eye doctors, dentists, and nurse practitioners volunteer their time and work all day to treat as many people as possible. Thousands of people come to these events. They need a lot. I noticed how dental care (tooth extractions for the most part) and eye care are a big part of the procedures requested. These events occur even after passage of the ACA.

In South Carolina, then governor Republican Nikki Haley and the Republican-controlled legislature refused to expand Medicaid and accept the ACA money. It is fascinating politics that South Carolina leaders were not moved when essential medical care is doled out person-by-person in charity events such as the one just described. The people seeking health care at USC's basketball facility were supplicants who had to verify their worthiness and had to stand in line and accept an unsystematic and spotty philanthropic effort to fill in the gaps in their basic health care needs. These events are only periodically held and people are turned away because of excess demand. As discussed previously and in Chapter 8 and the Conclusion some people work to prevent problems such as people making do without needed dental or eye care. They "go up the river" to find the source of an issue and work to eliminate the origin of the problem in the hope of preventing future similar hardships.

Comprehensive health insurance could be a right of being a citizen. It could be systematic, automatic, and consistent. The NCWO and many women's groups, labor unions, public health advocates, civil rights groups, and disability and human rights groups worked hard for this vision of health care reform. They all had to compromise to a "new normal" regarding neoliberal theories and the "great risk shift." One big compromise was on women's bodily autonomy in regard to legal abortion. Although the majority in the U.S. Congress did not "trust women" to make their own decisions regarding the full panoply of their possible health care decisions, the U.S. Congress and policy makers moved forward toward criteria for healthy citizens that do not see being female as a preexisting condition.

Further steps by groups like the NCWO will advance critiques that corporations are not citizens, but women actually are. In Chapter 8 the analysis continues of the actions, theory, and effect (and affect) of the NCWO as they addressed global women's issues. Here, too, the take home point is to take women seriously, with gravitas, as a matter of course.

8

The NCWO and Global Feminism

> Only a transnational polity has the capacity to confront
> transnational capital.
>
> —WALBY, *Crisis*

An American Women's Coalition and Global Issues

Gender politics increasingly takes on international dimensions. Globalization is gendered since it "affects men and women differently, and it produces
new modes of gender power and disadvantage" (Hawkesworth 2006: 2). The
American women's movement has woven into its agenda several issues related
to globalization and inequality. Theoretically blending critiques of neoliberalism and free market ideology with aspects of multiculturalism and liberal
individualism, leaders of the American women's movement tried to balance
their Western-infused philosophy of women's individual rights with respect
and acknowledgment of culturally diverse ethics regarding family, community, tradition, and culture. This chapter explores these tensions in three
clusters: (1) funding and social change issues; (2) the NCWO and Women
in Afghanistan, and (3) the NCWO's support for the Convention on the
Elimination of all Forms of Discrimination against Women (CEDAW). An
overview of women's economic vulnerabilities as regards neoliberal globalization forces concludes the chapter.

As governments have retreated from their responsibilities for citizen welfare, women's domestic burdens and economic vulnerabilities have increased
(see Jaggar 2014a). Neoliberal market forces and modern communication
technologies have accelerated attention to global gender dynamics. Women
are active in many global and international movements in addition to actions
concerned with gender. It has been a truism, however, in politics worldwide

that "movements often gain more from women than women gain from movements" (Basu 2010: 15).

The NCWO "Women's Leadership Handbook" (1999) contained a section on international women. The section highlighted women's worldwide poverty and the prevalence of domestic violence for women. The 1999 Women's Equality Summit and Congressional Action Day (WESCAD) sponsored by the NCWO focused on six main issues. Five of these issues were domestic policy concerns: social security, pay equity, child care, access to family planning and reproductive health, and elimination of discrimination against women. The sixth and final issue was the plight of women in Afghanistan (NCWO meeting minutes, January 19, 1999).

Women's Issues and Globalization

Care work, reproductive labor, and service jobs dominate employment possibilities for women in the global economy. In addition, sex work and sex trafficking are part of the global picture for women and girls. Legal and illegal immigration, displacement, migration, and statelessness are part and parcel of local economic and social disruptions that girls and women experience. Terms such as "informal" work or "flexible" jobs might mask the hardships these positions pose for women: unsettled work schedules, lack of a contract, vagueness about wages, and no clarity on where someone works, or when, or for whom (K. Arnold 2008; Hawkesworth 2006). For many girls and women it amounts to a "peculiarly gendered form of serfdom" (Hawkesworth 2006: 15). The routine, unheralded work that women do around the world "underwrites the entire global economy by subsidizing the indispensable tasks of cleaning and care and especially by producing the next generation of the global labor force" (Jaggar 2014a: 29). These issues distilled down indicate that "financial crises are gendered around the world" (Walby 2015: 76).

Endemic gendered inequalities make women more vulnerable to violence and abuse. Jacqui True asserted, "It is not just poverty that heightens women's vulnerability to violence; it is women's impoverished situation relative to men that is at the root of violence." True concluded, "The gendered inequalities that fuel the violence against women are rooted in structures and processes of political economy that are increasingly globalized" (2012: 5). Foundational to these inequalities and injustices is the lack of representation of women and women's issues in most governments. These result in "procedural unfairness in the decision-making processes of global institutions" (Kang 2014: 43). These socioeconomic and hermeneutical injustices combine to establish that "many women experience epistemic constraints due to narrow and dominant conceptual frameworks which unduly limit their understanding of themselves (as women, persons, and agents), thereby thwarting their self-development and self-determination" (Gosselin 2014: 101; see also Brock 2014).

Global perspectives in the American women's movement added strength to activists' analysis of the interconnected nature of economic inequalities and opportunities for girls, women, and their families. At the same time, expanding the women's movement agenda to critiques of American foreign policy and neoliberal market forces had the potential to make coalitions in national and international politics more fragile. Important to remember are the insights of scholars like Kristin Goss (*The Paradox of Gender Equality*) and S. Laurel Weldon (*When Protest Makes Policy*) that general interest women's groups in the past were influential on issues such as the formation of the United Nations, international human rights treaties, and arms agreements. Groups today are less broad and more niche positioned.

Neoliberalism and Gender

Neoliberal market contexts are gendered. Public state expenditures are often the focus for budget cuts, privatization, or elimination. Employment disruptions and weakened social supports rattle women's economic securities (Walby 2015: 142–143). Since the 1980s the global economy has been dominated by institutions and structures aligned with neoliberalism. Neoliberalism's foundation "is an acceptance of the basic principles of market capitalism in a country's internal and external economic policies" (Everett and Charlton 2014: 3).

Neoliberalism, with free markets expanded, governments shrunk, and negligible worker protections, pushes onto women increased care work and social welfare burdens that add to their unwaged work and social and economic vulnerabilities. The Washington consensus on the blessings of unfettered free trade foresaw global general equilibrium and maximum prosperity (Madrick 2014: 165–166). The belief became a one-size-fits-all economic template, which during "post–World War II globalization was unleashed with an ideological intensity mostly blind to compromise, nuance, and history. It's unstated central assumption was that laissez-faire, spread everywhere, is almost all the governance the world needs" (Madrick 2014: 165).

Structural adjustment was how the neoliberal Washington consensus was implemented. Included were "fiscal discipline, tax reform, market-determined interest rates, competitive exchange rates, trade liberalization, openness to foreign direct investment (FDI), privatization of state enterprises, deregulation, and security for property rights" (Everett and Charlton 2014: 61–62). Woven tightly into all of these reforms were decentralization and shrinking of governments. In general, "without explicit feminist organizing efforts around economic, social, educational, health, and welfare policies, women's needs are often not recognized or addressed in the legislation" aimed at development, reform, and market-based neoliberalism (Everett and Charlton 2014: 181).

When human service programs are cut, women workers and clients are disproportionately affected. Neoliberalism, therefore, regenders the state by "shoring up male-dominant institutions (finance, commerce, defense/military), while delegitimizing and diminishing the social welfare agencies in which women have gained ground" (Hawkesworth 2006: 20). One observer reflected that social problems might be addressed with more nuance "but the ideological sweep of globalization overwhelmed thoughtfulness" (Madrick 2014: 168).

Comparatively, women's movements worldwide were more successful in addressing gendered violence than in challenging income inequalities (Basu 2010: 2; Weldon 2002b). Feminist organizations internationally were more successful regarding civil and political rights, such as antigendered violence efforts. Yet social and economic rights reforms remained less successful. One implication was "that Western feminist agendas reap benefits from the hegemonic force of liberalism and neoliberalism" (Hawkesworth 2006: 141).

Nationally based NGOs have received international and foundation funding to address the needs of women. However, foreign funding can be problematic for movement-based groups. Elaine Zuckerman (a past chair of the Global Task Force of the NCWO) recommended to me the work of AWID (Association for Women's Rights in Development). They published a series of research reports on women in development. The AWID series was entitled, *"Where Is the Money for Women's Rights?"* Zuckerman steered me in particular to the fourth in the series by AWID entitled, "Watering the Leaves, Starving the Roots: The Status of Financing for Women's Rights Organizing and Gender Equality" (Arutyunova and Clark 2013). In the study, "The 'leaves'—the individual women and girls—are receiving growing attention, without recognizing or supporting 'the roots'—the sustained, collective action by feminist and women's rights activists and organizations that has been at the core of women's rights advancements throughout history" (Arutyunova and Clark 2013: 17).

A 2011 AWID global survey of over one thousand women's organizations displayed moderate growth in group budgets and resources. The groups primarily relied on project support from external funders for direct service provision efforts rather than on long-term, capacity-building, flexible funding to empower women (Arutyunova and Clark 2013: 17).

Targeted strategic philanthropy by foundations, based on measurable outcomes and timelines, sometimes meant that NGOs funded thusly disengaged from the movements they were a part of. AWID's research found that grantees described foundation funding as based on a preset project portfolio rather than on listening to community needs and plans. NGOs were treated as contractors for the foundations. The NGO, as contractor, was hired to carry out the donor's vision of what is to be done (Arutyunova and Clark 2013: 81). Concerns about donor-driven agendas were rampant in domestic and international politics and the role of NGOs (Arutyunova and Clark 2013: 116; see also Kohl-Arenas 2016; MacFarquhar 2016; Poppendieck 1998). To push back against funder prepackaged projects and agendas, AWID emphasized the need to broadly document the impact of the women's rights and development movements. If the women's groups working globally could work together collectively in a movement coalition, they could reshape the context of individual groups competing for funding and large foundations shaping groups' approaches and agendas (Arutyunova and Clark 2013: 131–132, 136). The Global Women's Task Force of the NCWO consistently raised many of these issues at council meetings and events. In addition, activists working on seemingly domestic policy–oriented task forces in the NCWO were acutely aware that their projects were also infused with global dynamics.

Money, as the old saying goes, makes the world go round. AWID's analysis concurred and emphasized that flexible multiyear and core funding foster financial resilience and best support work to transform gender inequalities. As donors are increasingly concerned with measurable results, they tend to support narrowly focused and time-bound projects. Funders want returns on their investments, which paradoxically "makes it difficult to secure meaningful results in terms of women's empowerment and gender equality" (Arutyunova and Clark 2013: 125).

Nation-states that have strengthened market forces, bolstered by the safe flow of capital and assets, diminished labor unions, social programs, and communal obligations, have increased economic inequalities worldwide with harsh impacts on women and families (Banaszak, Beckwith, and Rucht 2003a; K. Arnold 2008; Basu 2010: 24–25; Ehrenreich and Hochschild 2002; Hawkesworth 2006; Smith and Johnston 2002). Many women, therefore, work triple shifts, doing subsistence-level paid labor, child and family care, and community-building labor (Hawkesworth 2006: 149).

Global aspects of gender and politics, NCWO activists and scholars point out, should also incorporate attention to the status of people who are sexually diverse. Many regimes are heteronormative and deny rights and dignity to sexually diverse people. Research on participation of diverse groups (such as women and ethnic and religious minorities) in a nation's politics and civil society often does not include questions about LGBTQ citizens. Future research and advocacy should include the heteronormative dimensions of global political institutions and public policies (see also Lind 2013: 189–213).

Individual and Systemic: Linked Fates

For gender justice adherents, action is shaped by particular issues that are both societal and individual. "Women's inferiority is produced, one might say, at once wholesale and retail: that is, both through their location in 'macro' social structures and through 'micro,' interpersonal, self-other encounters and idiosyncratic experiences" (Kruks 2012: 66). Thus, "When prejudice, bigotry, and injustice are entrenched, egregious, and sanctioned," explains Anna Quindlen, "we're looking at big-muscle-group remedies—the lawsuit, the amendment, the marches. But we're now more often in the small-muscle-group area, the business of personal behavior and attitudes" (2012: 127–128; see also West and Blumberg 1990). For feminist scholars and activists, "the question that faces us is not whether to engage in cultural recognition, economic struggle, or democratic activity. But to do all at the same time" (Squires 2013: 741).

Women's communities and organizations in the South African struggle for democracy engaged in many of these messy, overlapping, and contingent efforts. At neighborhood and community levels women often consistently found ways to provide for women's practical needs such as savings clubs, burial insurance, day care centers, health clinics, solidarity networks for women, religiously based women's forums, and social clubs (Hassim 2006). Hassim drew on Temma Kaplan's work to help explain the political significance of these routine and unheralded efforts: "Such grassroots support groups can be important sources for the emergence of social movements, and their 'unspectacular' concerns to 'accomplish necessary tasks, to provide services rather than to build power bases' can seem politically insignificant" (Hassim 2006: 27).

Attention must be paid, however, to group-based women's work (see Miller 1949). The American Southern Black Baptist women's movement for generations practiced an ethos of mutual aid with "the duty to help others [which] was serious, immediate, and practical" (Ransby 2003: 19). Women's everyday "unspectacular" interactions in these organizations need to be part of a more fluid understanding of gender and politics, since "in their everyday life within these nonpolitical structures women often develop a collective consciousness that can be mobilized when the survival of communities is at stake" (Hassim 2006: 27). In other words, "by treating political action as what one exclusively does in the public sphere and outside of the local community, these approaches effectively ignore how gender shapes activism and universalize men's experiences as 'normal'" (Kretschmer and Meyer 2013: 392).

My observations of the NCWO traced these insights. My work added that the issues are also taken up by organized, institutionalized NGOs with bylaws, which are staffed with women's movement adherents. These activists were communities of memory and hope made up of feminist and civil rights warhorses, labor union stalwarts, stewards of the earth, protectors of the least of these, religious communities, and people who "get it" that women should be full and equal citizens (see Bellah et al. 1985; Brown-Guinyard 2013; Chavez 2010; Collins 2013; hooks 2000; Jaggar and Rothenberg 1993; Katzenstein 1998; Freedman 2002; C. Payne 1990; U. Taylor 2010; B. Thompson 2010; Woliver 1993). Attention must be paid, also, to radical feminists who came directly to the women's movement on their own, not through awakenings while working in the U.S. civil rights movement or the antiwar movement of the New Left (Whittier 1995: 78).

In my fieldwork I observed many instances of linked fate solidarity. One example is the NCWO's efforts to include women's aid issues in foreign aid programs and education initiatives. The student lobbyists I shadowed at the 2008 Women's Equality Summit in DC, for instance, advocated for global women often overlooked by U.S. aid programs. While the 2008 student lobbyists also pressured for cheaper birth control for American college students, they wove into the analysis the plight of poor people not able to access birth control at all. Recognizing their relatively privileged standpoint as Western, educated women, they also admonished policy makers to make sure girls in underdeveloped countries have schools they can attend, and that foreign aid not discriminate against schoolgirls' mothers, grandmothers, and aunts. They continued the thread within the larger women's movement to break silences about poverty, discrimination, violence, and abuse even when the speaker or the group itself is not currently experiencing those depravations. Their advocacy deliberately included international women and global issues.

Strengths and Weaknesses of NGOs: Alleviating or Eliminating Injustices

As government social programs were cut while economic conditions declined, many NGOs filled in the gaps by providing ameliorative aid to the needy and beleaguered. NGOs provided needed services that governments exited from or left underfunded and hanging by threads. In addition, domestic and international NGOs "pick up problems that states in fiscal crisis or under the mandate of structural adjustment policies disdain. Working on soft money and without job security, NGO staff offer cheaper means to alleviate poverty or provide health care than state employees" (Hawkesworth 2006: 106). The NGOs also must raise money through charitable and philanthropic foundations, government grants, business sponsorship, and individual contributions. One longtime NGO worker reflected that these practices could mean "we might be tempted to follow the money rather than follow the work" (Guil-louci and Cordery 2007: 111). Critiques of private social service providers organized as nonprofit organizations and other NGOs and buttressed with 501(c)(3) status (contributions are tax exempt) to some observers conjure up the specter of group oligarchy.

In the United States and worldwide only a small percentage (about 6 percent) of charitable and foundation philanthropy goes to groups working on gender issues. The reason women's rights leaders might chase the same funding sources is partly based on the low percentage of funding available to women's groups. Joan Williams, director of the Center for Work Life Law at UC Hastings College of Law, observed "this is another way that bias against women feeds conflict among women" (Williams quoted in Rhode 2014: 21; see also Arutyunova and Clark 2013). A recent development reflects aware-ness of these inequities. One effort was that the Women's Funding Network had secured pledges from about 160 foundation members to channel three-quarters of their grants to women-led projects (Rhode 2014: 158; see also Elayne Clift 2005; Whittier 1995: 86). Time will tell if this has a positive impact on future funding issues for the women's rights community.

U.S. Department of Justice grants to help battered women and address domestic violence have reoriented many NGO efforts from decreasing vio-lence and empowering women to working with police, courts, jails, and pris-ons. The programs helped channel resources to jails and prisons as the answer to domestic violence (Durazo 2007: 115–124; Bumiller 2008; N. Matthews 1995: 291–305; Templeton 2004: 254–277). The NGOs ineluctably were often "tethered to the state" by tax status rules such as 501(c)(3)s and funding arrangements. In addition, "grassroots organizations that labor in the shadow of the state should consider this: that the purpose of the work is to gain libera-tion, not to guarantee the organization's longevity" (R. Gilmore 2007: 51).

International or domestic coalition work for entities like the NCWO was weakened by member's needs to secure funding, sometimes from the same sources. Domestically, one study of women's groups in the 1980s, for instance, found an omission of class analysis and interpreted the lack as "an effort to avoid tensions and divisiveness, to continue to use inclusive language in order to increase women's economic participation, mollify corporate funders, avoid additional backlash, and keep the focus on women's losses in abortion rights" (Spalter-Roth and Schreiber 1995: 124). Recent books such as *Dead Aid, The Revolution Will Not Be Funded,* and *Just Advocacy,* to name a few, explored these dynamics as well. One example out of many: "Rather than challenging state power, the non-profit model actually encourages activists to negotiate, even collaborate with the state—as those police permits for anti-police bru-tality marches illustrate" (P. Rojas 2007: 206). A scathing critique, edited by Incite! Women of Color against Violence, states that resource competition "promotes a social movement culture that is non-collaborative, narrowly focused, and competitive. To retain the support of benefactors, groups must compete with each other for funding by promoting only their own work, whether or not their organizing strategies are successful" (A. Smith 2007: 10).

There are many instances of women's groups who confronted the paradoxes of working for radical social change while accepting funds from and contracting with government agencies or private foundations who sought to shape their agenda and activism. Social movements powerful enough to force social change, however, need united fronts. In present circumstances, though, "likely allies have all become constricted by mission statements and hostile laws to think in silos rather than expansively, grassroots organizations can be the voices of history and the future to assemble the disparate and sometimes desperate non-profits who labor in the shadow of the shadow state" (R. Gilmore 2007: 5; see also Lang 2013).

The state can be used by change agents if laws, rules, and regulations by the government can be leveraged by activists. While the state exercises social control, Tarrow explained, "by these efforts, states not only penetrated society; they created a standard set of roles and identities that were the basis of modern citizenship. Within this matrix, citizens not only contested state expansion; they used the state as a fulcrum to advance their claims against others" (Tarrow 1998: 58; see also Jones 1986; Marilley 1996; Wheeler 1995). One fulcrum often used, to be discussed near the end of this chapter, was international treaties.

We should reflect on the insights of the Incite! Women of Color against Violence edited book regarding shadow states. Chasing foundation funding and nonprofit management paperwork and accountability, for instance, "not only exhausts us and potentially compromises our radical edge; it also has us persuaded that we cannot do our work without their money and without their systems" (Perez 2007: 98; see also King and Osayande 2007). Reformist solutions might mitigate but not prevent gendered inequalities.

One tactic to advance the larger goals of a movement would be a coordinated coalition of groups working on their niche specialties and convening periodically to assess and validate the bigger picture for the movement. The NCWO displays the potential for this, yet it also reveals the fragile nature of these coalitions given the funding situations they are embedded within to begin with.

The NCWO and Women in Afghanistan

The FMF (an important NCWO member) has been very active on behalf of Afghan women. They were some of the few voices before the 9/11 attacks documenting the gendered human rights abuses of the Taliban in Afghanistan (Maloney 2008: 210). The FMF spearheaded the "Campaign to Stop Gender

Apartheid in Afghanistan." They had 160 cosponsoring organizations. The FMF publicized the abuses and degradations Afghan girls and women experienced under the Taliban.

My observations at NCWO meetings from 1999 to 2014 were that usually at least two (sometimes four) women from the FMF attended the bimonthly NCWO meetings. Principals of the FMF regularly attended council meetings. Among other things, they briefed the group on the status of the girls and women under the Taliban, the situation in Congress regarding emergency aid for Afghan refugees, possible political asylum status for women who fled Afghanistan, and votes on sanctions against the ruling regime.

In the fall of 2000, The FMF held a "Back to School" campaign for Afghan girls. They highlighted the point that while the world's children were going back to school, girls in Afghanistan were not permitted to be educated any more. The NCWO embraced the Afghan women's issue on many levels. Several of the founding principles of the NCWO touch on the plight of women in Afghanistan, for example, the NCWO's commitment to equal education for girls and women. For years the NCWO has also highlighted the hostilities to girls' educations in Afghanistan and Pakistan.

Given that representatives from forty to fifty organizations were sitting in the NEA conference room during the bimonthly meetings (and that 120 groups received NCWO meeting minutes and updates), the FMF's actions helped keep the issue of the gendered apartheid by the Taliban an issue in the national women's (and civil) rights communities. One member of the NCWO even stated at the March 20, 2001, meeting that she thought without the constant pressure from the NCWO and the FMF, the Taliban would be recognized by the probusiness Bush administration. As another delegate member to a bimonthly NCWO meeting put it, "All the government [of the United States] wants to talk about is Osama Bin Laden. It is also an issue of these girls and women and we remind them of that constantly."

From my observations, the NCWO responded forcefully to the situation of girls and women in Afghanistan under the Taliban. The March 20, 2001, NCWO meeting had a wrenching effect on everyone in the NEA's conference room. Three women spoke toward the end of the meeting about their efforts in France to help Afghan women. One of the women, through an interpreter, told us she would don the required full body, meshed face mask burka the women must wear whenever they leave their houses in Afghanistan. When she put the burka on, the normally noisy group became eerily and poignantly quiet and somber. The woman wearing the blue covering was completely invisible behind the cloth and mesh. She looked like a blue ghost, vaguely shaped like a human. She said through the mesh and her interpreter told us regarding the clothing, "This is a one woman at a time concentration camp." To be clear, the speakers addressed issues of the Taliban in Afghanistan. They did not castigate all of Islam or Muslim societies.

When Western groups and activists position themselves as saviors of global women, aspects of Edward Said's *Orientalism* (1978) seem to echo. When feminism in the Middle East looks different than Western feminism, in orientalist thinking, the Middle East feminists look less correct. Many scholars and activists with in-country histories and legacies critique emphatic, universalizing positions about groups of global women. Cultural insensitivity and Western templates concerning human rights and gender justice are detrimental to international cooperation and understanding. Blanket statements about Islamic women by Western activists and NGOs are particularly problematic to many observers and community members.

In *Do Muslim Women Need Saving?* activists and scholars are advised to recall that local conditions of women's lives, which concern Western feminists, are often national and international in origin (Abu-Lughod 2013: 24). An entire culture or community should not be stigmatized by women's rights and human rights adherents. Otherwise, there are taints of a new sort of Western imperialism (Abu-Lughod 2013: 114). "Things can go wrong for people everywhere." One culture does not have "a monopoly on violence against women" (Abu-Lughod 2013: 126). We should be circumspect about generalizations regarding cultures, religions, and communities. If not, then, "gendered Orientalism has taken on a new life and new forms in our feminist twenty-first century" (Abu-Lughod 2013: 202). Less biased appraisals are possible if activists "look and listen carefully, think hard about the big picture, and take responsibility" (Abu-Lughod 2013: 224). The basis of careful analysis also includes "critical self-reflection, and constant recognition of our common humanity, a humanity subjected to different forces and expressed in different registers" (Abu-Lughod 2013: 227).

NCWO activists were aware of these pitfalls. At the WESCAD 2002 conference, sample letters participants could sign and send to their congressional representatives included domestic welfare reform and safety net issues as well as this paragraph: "Finally, I want to encourage you to continue to work for restoration of the rights of women in Afghanistan. International peacekeeping forces must be expanded and substantial funds must be immediately contributed by the Afghan interim administration, especially the Ministry of Women's Affairs. Without security and without adequate funds, the future of Afghanistan is at risk and the rights of Afghan women are in jeopardy" (WESCAD 2002; in author files). The concerns about girls and women in Afghanistan also included pressure for the United States to ratify CEDAW as well as admonitions about how the convention would enhance the rights of women in other countries such as Afghanistan.

CEDAW: Big Muscled Policy

Support for U.S. ratification of CEDAW was a consistent focus of both the COP and then the NCWO. Attention to global women's issues has been enhanced since 1985 by UN conferences and programs (Basu 2010: 8–13). Many principals in the NCWO have attended UN conferences where they gathered information and built international networks of individual and group support. Globally, international statutes, like CEDAW, and the Beijing Platform were tools for local feminists (Chappell 2013: 603–626; see also Everett and Charlton 2014: 35–43, 195; Baldez 2014). However, treaties and statutes like CEDAW, with their focus on formal individual rights (to include women's individual rights), left systemic inequalities and gender regimes largely uncontested (Everett and Charlton 2014: 183–184). Women's activism, however, from the grassroots level to international NGOs such as Peace Women across the Globe, have contested these enduring structures of inequality (Everett and Charlton 2014: 183, 187–190).

CEDAW was adopted by the United Nations General Assembly in 1979. The United States has not ratified CEDAW. Two aspects of American politics help explain the failure to ratify CEDAW. The first is structural; the U.S. Constitution requires a high threshold for international treaty approval: a two-thirds vote or a supermajority in favor of a treaty in the U.S. Senate plus presidential approval. The second reason is a medley of American domestic political issues—abortion politics, pride over sovereignty, suspicions of international, United Nations–appointed CEDAW experts, and the back and forth about women's formal equality and women's actual well-being in the U.S. regarding issues such as domestic violence—all of which illustrate some of these dynamics. CEDAW stipulates that nation-states are obligated to respond to violence against women, even by private actors like family members or intimate partners. Under CEDAW women in states that have ratified the treaty can "demand that state actors, namely police, respond to violations of protection orders in cases of intimate violence" (Baldez 2014: 197).

Ratifying nations must also submit reports to CEDAW experts at the UN on the status of women in their countries. CEDAW experts can advise ratifying countries on how to improve the status of women in nation-states. These dynamics engendered many concerns about big government (here big international government), American domestic sovereignty, and the power of appointed elite experts within the ratifying countries.

The NCWO was a stalwart advocate for ratification of CEDAW. As a member of the more than 186 organization strong U.S. CEDAW Task Force and also working separately, the NCWO tried to counter the concerns antiratification groups and U.S. Senators had about the treaty. In advocating for CEDAW ratification, many groups, including members of NCWO, emphasized the need for the treaty and the positive impact it would have on American women. One conundrum was, however, that the advocates' points stoked the fears of opponents. If CEDAW is a powerful treaty and mechanism to advance a globally based women's rights agenda, that built opposition to ratification. The argument assumed, also, that women in the United States were not equal and they needed CEDAW to protect and enhance their prospects. Opposition built around these issues and many conservative groups and leaders, to include conservative women's groups and women pundits and activists, rejected ratifying CEDAW (see also Baldez 2014; Deckman 2016; Jaggar 2014a).

Bridge Building at the NCWO

NCWO chairs regularly applied for grants from foundations to fund information, analysis, and conferences on globalization and women's issues. In addition, NCWO chairs met with groups of international women visiting Washington, DC, and regularly briefed them on the work of the NCWO and separate groups within the American women's movement. Finally, NCWO officials sometimes traveled abroad as gender ambassadors, so to speak, to emerging democracies and women residing in postconflict communities. Countries visited for on-site training, dialogue, and information exchange included the Balkans, the Baltics, Kuwait, Bosnia, Romania, and Russia, through U.S. Department of State sponsorship. The Open Society Institute funded activism and policy analysis in 2003 to help encourage the United States to ratify CEDAW (NCWO 2004a; in author files).

The NCWO also monitored efforts to prevent international trafficking in persons, especially women and children. Reports from United Nations–affiliated groups and task forces outside of the NCWO (for instance, the International Human Rights Network) received agenda status at the full council meetings and were added to the information disseminated to member organizations.

The spring 2003 issue of *Ms.* magazine included a two-page "Special Alert" statement from the NCWO on the war with Iraq (*Ms.*: 2003: 64–65). The NCWO spoke out several times regarding reversals of women's rights in Iraq and Afghanistan. Constantly monitored by member organizations, the issue of reproductive choices, including legal abortion, was highlighted by press releases, announcements to members, and invitations to briefings and conferences by and with the NCWO (in author files).

There are many vociferous critiques of different actions by Western, particularly American, feminists on global women's issues. Questions were raised if a project seemed like a "rescue" by more enlightened Western women, or if the incursion is publicized, formatted, and started without input from the women in the areas targeted (see, for example, Hesford and Kozel 2005).

The NCWO was fully aware of the global nature of gender inequalities and tried to address many international gender issues through task forces, the general council meetings, and their consistent support for the FMF efforts to highlight the Taliban's oppression of women, and pressured the U.S. Senate to ratify CEDAW.

Conclusion

Issues of economic inequality and people suffering dire poverty, while addressed and acknowledged by global feminist activists, have often not resulted in many changes, in part because "the emergence and growth of women's movements, and particularly their success in achieving increased political representation and securing measures to prevent violence against women, have rested on their attaining support from the state, civil society, and international forces. Women's movements have been much less successful in addressing poverty and class inequality because of a lack of domestic and international support" (Basu 2010: 18). Important to the context was that "most states are less responsive to women's movements—or any social movements—on matters of economic policy than around a range of social issues" (Basu 2010: 27). Scholars of the American women's movement agree that DC policy makers proved more amenable to passing measures in support of formal equality than to enacting social programs needed to ameliorate the situation of vulnerable women.

Feminist scholars have pointed out the economic subsidy that mostly women give to the world capitalist system through their unpaid and often undervalued domestic work (see Rai 2013: 263–288; L. Ferguson 2013: 337–361). Under neoliberal economic policies, for example, social reproduction mostly by women filled in the gaps between public welfare and private markets. Globalization reshapes the commons through privatization and individualizes human alternatives (Rai 2013: 275). "The neoliberal discourses on rational choice, competition instead of cooperation, and rights rather than freedoms have also worried feminist scholars" (Rai 2013: 276). These shortfalls are based on deep and wide resistance to programs and policies that begin to build equity for everyone. In sum, "The feminist agenda was inclusive; the nation's political agenda was not" (Harrison 2008: 43).

Women's work internationally was impressive given the underfunding of many gender equality efforts and the enormous amount of work and effort that has to be done. AWID summed this up: "We have to communicate in creative ways that make what we do and why we do it in specific ways almost self-evident! This is not often the case—and thus, the incredible history and achievements of vibrant and diverse women's organizations and movements across the world are scarcely visible outside our own world" (Arutyunova and Clark 2013: 130).

While the American women's movement was not insulated and focused on domestic U.S. politics exclusively, nevertheless, the agenda of coalitions like the NCWO concerning global issues and gender were different than previous activism by Western women on world affairs. Current women's activism is less general and more country and issue specific. An exception to this is the broad critique of globalization as epitomized by neoliberal, free market capitalism, which is also part of the modern women's movement in the United States. The NCWO, then, balanced two agendas in regard to global issues: country specific issues as with Afghanistan and critiques of neoliberalism and globalization.

The Conclusion underscores the foundational work many groups, like the NCWO, took on, which preserved social programs fundamental to whatever modicum of economic security women and their families have. While activists pushed back neoliberal forays against communal efforts and programs, they also tried to move forward with admonitions and proposals to strengthen and enlarge many programs and policies. The NCWO is currently no longer operating, as will also be discussed in the next chapter.

Conclusion

Pushing Back Neoliberal Agendas via Women's Coalitional Activism

> One Woman Can Change the World . . . But It's Easier When You Work in Groups
> —NCWO brochure

Conclusion: Speaking for Women

The NCWO's roots went deep, to progressive black women, suffragists, labor unions and workers on strike, civil rights groups, church ladies, and feminists. Part of their pushing back aimed to highlight the gender injustice of ideas that assumed an unencumbered, solely market-oriented, rational, and economic man. People who do care work or need care were not part of these logical, individualistic calculations. Many people, groups and coalitions, however, pushed back. The NCWO, as displayed, was a steadfast guardian for social justice and the public good. Corporations are not citizens, the NCWO asserted, but women are.

Eleanor Smeal, president of FMF, directed women's rights activists to not reify opponents and to stop debating feminism's popularity. "What I say (as Eleanor Smeal) is that I speak for all who believe in equality. Not for women. I don't know what all women . . . [pauses/shrugs shoulders/raises arms toward sky] . . . But equality? [pause] Yes! And, we should be proud of that. Proud of them, the people who believe in equality" (Smeal, interview, September 4, 2014). She emphasized that she and the FMF fight for the obvious: equal pay, respect, and dignity.

In their classic study of poor people's mobilization, Piven and Cloward asserted, "What was won must be judged by what was possible" (1977: xiii). Working around the edges is sometimes all reformers can hope for in an era of super capitalism and democratic weakness. The best solution for many of our collective issues is political and community-wide. Many public fig- ures admonish us to take our citizenship duties seriously and hold politicians accountable (Reich 2007: 225; Warren 2014; Gillibrand 2014). Reformers know that it is our political system that can make wrongs such as child labor illegal and possibly preventable. People can go up the river and address the sources of problems. In the meantime, current economic crises affect people's access to real choices. The roots of economic problems have contested mean- ings. Financial crises like in 2008, although based in failures to regulate capital, are often diverted to austerity solutions targeting social programs (Walby 2015: 18).

Within the progressive lobbying community, government was usually not the enemy. The attitude, instead, was "government, after all, is society; it is all of us getting together. The economy is not" (Madrick 2014: 80). The 2008 economic meltdown was ironically headed off by large government intrusion into the very same markets championed as reliably self-correcting (Madrick 2014: 163).

Embedded in neoliberal, free market policies and ideology was a paternal- ism about the irrationality of marginalized people and the need to channel their behavior and choices toward "proper conduct" (Denbow 2015: 106–107, 116). Health care politics and women's bodily agency in the ACA, then, showed that "neoliberalism and gendered power relations are intertwined and the way social and economic anxiety is often displaced onto issues of sexuality and reproduction challenges a common narrative regarding recent battles over women's health care" (Denbow 2015: 103). The story line was that restrictions on women's bodily agency were "merely political distractions" intended to "dis- tract the public from the *real* issues, like economic inequality, corporate power, and war" (Denbow 2015: 103–104, italics in original). Attacks on women and other "others," however, were not a distraction, but really the main show. Personal responsibility slogans especially vilified mothers on welfare. Demoni- zation of poor mothers was central to neoliberal slashing of public assistance (Denbow 2015: 104). Hence, "acting in one's self-interest is often perceived as good or natural in the context of the market. However, when an activity is *framed* as publicly subsidized, which is more likely the more disenfranchised the beneficiaries are, action in one's self-interest is likely to be maligned and understood as irresponsible" (Denbow 2015: 105, italics in original).

Fears of not being an autonomous, individualistic "real man" bring on political fights over whether we created a "nanny state," which was feminized, nurturing, and maternal instead of armored and unsentimentally rational (McDonagh 2009). The neoliberal narrative shifts the origins of economic crisis away "from the excessive deregulation of finance towards excessive state spending on welfare" (Walby 2015: 18). The NCWO was one of the entities trying to refocus rescues of faltering economies away from blaming social programs and the poor and steer the agenda back toward the sources of the collapse: the markets, super capitalism, and unfettered competition for short-term profits often conducted globally.

Broad Agendas and Critical Needs

One observation, from attending twenty-five NCWO bimonthly meetings and forty-seven related and sponsored events and conducting sixty-nine interviews with activists in the NCWO, is that it is almost impossible for a huge, diffuse coalition to say "no." Their interests and agenda are enormous. Additional items kept getting added to their domain. As long as work was delegated to task forces, the NCWO was not necessarily burdened by extra work. However, overseeing the integrity of the work and the use of the NCWO stamp of approval and cosponsorship became difficult as their agenda expanded. Given the size of the NCWO, many representatives of causes approached the NCWO for endorsements, cosponsorship, or a chance to address NCWO members at their every-other-month meetings. At the January 1999 NCWO meeting, to give one example, representatives from NASA came to publicize the first female commander of a NASA launch. The visitors urged the NWCO members to help recruit more girls into the study of science, math, and engineering.

Future iterations of this study of the NCWO, for example, could easily focus further on the area of women's health and representation issues the NCWO was involved in (The Women's Vote Project, The Names Project), the NCWO's work for the three-state strategy to ratify the ERA, or on child care, fair pay, paid sick leave, expansion of the Family and Medical Leave Act (FMLA), full implementation of Title IX, and enforcement of the Lilly Ledbetter Act, to name a few. One weakness of huge coalitions, therefore, could be the diffusion of energy, the possible burnout of leaders and members, and the sense that the coalition cares about everything but might not accomplish much about these issues.

For the NCWO, the use of task forces, which marshaled compelling information and framed it in a way that brought women into discussions, made a difference. The data the Social Security Task Force of the NCWO put together was widely discussed. Social Security reform now includes discussions of gender. Within the Social Security Task Force Report of the NCWO the authors alluded to the dynamic of the dual nature of being a powerful voice for women's policy, yet a coalition that must compromise:

> Because the NCWO is a coalition of organizations with different political strategies, consensus on a single set of reform proposals may not

be possible. The purpose of this report, therefore, is not to present a single comprehensive plan for Social Security reform, but rather to present a menu of options that reflect the different perspectives and strengths of the participating organizations. Speaking with a single voice can be powerful, but a well-orchestrated chorus can be effective as well. (Hartmann and Hill 2000: 2)

Within the chorale, however, a single, targeted message might get drowned out.

To achieve social change, people have to work together, not just individually. Myles Horton of Highlander Folk School reflected, "[I] had to turn my anger into a slow burning fire, instead of a consuming fire" (1990: 80). People have to organize in order to "relate what you believed to the real situation" (Horton 1990: 43). Instead of a hot and furious focus on the short term, relative calm is often needed so long-term change can be built step by step. Horton told himself, "Get ready for the long haul and try to determine how you can live out this thing and make your life useful" (1990: 81). Enduring social movements understand these measures of justice and long views.

Groups anathema to the NCWO were also wise to this perspective. Antilegal abortion activists, for instance, played a long game wherein many of their lengthy court cases, even when a majority of justices did not support their positions, left them "limited in victory, enabled in defeat" (Joshua Wilson 2013: 111).

Coalitions between feminists in different parts of the social hierarchy are difficult to sustain and need individuals and organizations to act as bridge builders across race/ethnicity, sexuality, and especially social class divides. "Continuing inequality between groups of feminists, then, makes coalition making both necessary and difficult; inclusive solidarity is only possible when partners at once take notice of inequality and strive not to reproduce dominance. That kind of process takes time and energy, and it is somewhat fragile, as it is hard to battle oppressions while fighting internal conflicts generated by those same injustices" (Roth 2004: 223). Power differentials within alliances and coalitions by group or individual members have to be addressed and recognized or intersectional work and cooperation will be impeded (Cole, 2008).

Memoirs by feminist activists echo my own fieldwork observations. Susan Brownmiller, for one, wrote, "Of course it is wildly unrealistic to speak in one voice for half the human race, yet that is what feminism always attempts to do, and that is what Women's Liberation did do, with astounding success, in our time" (1999: 330). Even though the American women's movement "was the largest and farthest-reaching social movement of the era, feminism and women's activism are often relegated to a sidebar of social movement histories of the 1960s and 1970s" (S. Gilmore 2008a: 1). Many feminist coalitions arose at the grassroots levels and included the intersecting hierarchies of women's lives. "They brought multiple consciousnesses to their coalition work, and in these coalitions, they incorporated, or at least sought and tried to incorporate, many perspectives and experiences into their activism on a number of issues. They faced common oppression and discrimination *as women*, even if this oppression was mediated by other social and cultural factors" (S. Gilmore 2008a: 2–4, italics in original).

The NCWO was not the only coalition or activist voice monitoring changes to Social Security, pressuring for health care reform, or expressing outrage over the treatment of girls and women in Afghanistan. The NCWO was an element within a large coalition of coalitions and groups working to ensure that concerns about human rights, the poor, social change, and societal health include women and children.

A Conscious Coalition

In addition to acknowledging that all activists will one day, if they are lucky, be older, with weaker voices and hearing, and perhaps representing groups and causes that have lost their luster and might, instances of linked fate solidarity were observed several times. One example was the NCWO's efforts to include women's aid issues into foreign aid and education initiatives.

In a study of contemporary feminism, the important work of noticing what was not discussed, not on the agenda, not visible in many young women's feminism found that discussions of economic inequalities and social class were missing (Reger 2012: 134, 153–156). Contemporary feminism had a more cultural focus. A cultural emphasis, however, was not a retreat from politics. The strategy stemmed from the experience of coming to feminism in a generation where institutional gains faced vociferous backlash. "It is this focus on culture that often makes contemporary feminism appear everywhere and nowhere" (Reger 2012: 186).

To their credit, these mostly professional, middle- to upper-middle-class women in the NCWO raised questions on behalf of poor, disabled, and working poor women who they believed would be hit the hardest by the reforms advocated by the Clinton administration in 1998, the new Bush administration in 2000–2002 and again in 2004, and then the Obama administration. Poor, elderly, and disabled women remain difficult to organize and exercise little collective (or individual) power in DC. The questions the NCWO raised on their behalf, then, indicate a feminist ethic of care manifested in national political coalition lobbying.

It is also clear that there were few bright line boundaries between Washington women's movement interest groups and fellow travelers in government agencies, congressional offices, law firms, political party apparatuses, and staffers in many other DC-, New York–, Chicago-, and Philadelphia-based interest groups and nonprofit organizations. Like many others have noticed (Costain 1992; Flammang 1997; Katzenstein 1998; McBride and Mazur 2008a; Banaszak, Beckwith, and Rucht 2003b), there were many people working to advance feminism inside, outside, and in between the formal state or formal institutional governing boards of organizations and the advocacy community.

While relatively better-resourced groups such as the FMF, the AAUW, the Business and Professional Women's Organization, and NOW were dominant players in the NCWO, the coalition as a whole made sure to speak for the poor, the unorganized, and the voiceless. In addition, the NCWO gave equal voting status and agenda access to small coalition member groups. However, realistically, at council and task force meetings, when leaders or delegates of the largest, most historically established groups spoke up, much more attention was paid. Strong, experienced, battle weary, and wise women seemed also to carry more power and engender more attention during meetings or even when not at meetings themselves, when their names were evoked. Two examples were "Ellie [Smeal, FMF] thinks that" or "We need to check with Heidi [Hartmann of IWPR] about this."

Like many coalitions and institutionalized social movements, NCWO group members belonged to several overlapping women's and progressive groups as well as the one's they officially worked for. In addition, the tight networks of women's rights attorneys, lobbyists, policy researchers, and politicos were woven with the complex job experiences of the activists. One woman, for example, might have interned as a college student at one NGO in DC, worked as a staffer on the Hill or in her state legislature, and over the course of time worked at four or five of the groups or labor unions in DC, New York, Chicago, or Los Angeles that were part of the larger women's movement.

Another dynamic observed over the years in the NCWO was a delicate, gentle, and patient respect fostered by several NCWO chairs toward "older and wiser" women in the coalition who regularly attended council meetings. At council meetings moving through the agenda was of manifold importance. The women were busy and needed to keep on schedule. They needed to catch trains, metros, carpools, etc., round up children from schools and day cares, and fulfill their numerous kin work obligations as well as attend some of the fund-raisers and receptions held most evenings in DC. The council meetings were made up of two groups of women: leaders and key activists in the NCWO and interns and young staffers from myriad organizations in the DC area belonging to the NCWO. Interns were sent to keep an eye on what was going on, and bring back to the office packets of materials passed around at the meeting.

Within the old guard there were a couple of much older women who might have come from small organizations, could not hear all the discussion unless everyone spoke up, and regularly had a lot to say at the council meetings. NCWO chairs consistently paid homage to these women by making sure they were called on, listened to, and given time to have their say, even if it slowed down the agenda. Sometimes the older women forgot what they were going to say in the middle of their comments, and everyone waited for them to collect their thoughts.

People at NCWO meetings seemed to realize that the older attendees had logged decades and lifetimes of work and effort in the civil rights movement, women's movement, and antiwar, environmental, and labor organizations, to name a few. Their legacies included still-standing organizations as well as organizations that had faded away or were absorbed by other entities or regrouped into other efforts. They spoke from hard-won wisdom and experience. They fought in campaigns for the long haul.

The young interns watched this carefully and a little impatiently. I wondered if they thought that issues raised like reintroduction of the ERA were over and done with. Yet, I believe the young interns (and some of the also-impatient attorneys mashing their Blackberry buttons during the 1990s meetings) were being schooled. After all, "Learning . . . lies at the heart of social movements" (Jasper 1997: 98).

In *Freedom Is an Endless Meeting*, Polletta (2002) described similar behaviors in her analysis of 1960s and 1970s women's groups. The women were often friends and they cared about each other and believed deeply in the equality of each group member. This had pluses and minuses, of course. The NCWO also had a sense of the larger women's community with a "complex equality" incorporating the norms of professional collegiality. Polletta warned activist communities about hierarchical structures and what she called a "simple equality" where differences of skill, interest, and opinion were unrecognized and not permitted. Simple equality's denials of inequalities risk group success. Healthy groups need rules and relationships. Organizational efficiency and accountability benefits from formal rules and protocols. "However, absent relationships of mutual trust, respect, and concern, not only are formal deliberative systems likely to become rigid, but the learning that is one of the most important products of joint decision making is also likely to suffer" (Polletta 2002: 174–175). Viable coalitions need formal rules plus personal relationships. In fact, "In many cases, they also emerge around shared *emotions*, which become a vital source of solidarity and a significant reason why diverse activists pool resources" (Kaminski 2008: 290, italics in original).

Throughout the years of my fieldwork I noted expressions of affection and appreciation within the people in the coalition. The NCWO community (group leaders, members, staff, interns, and veterans who retired from the field) would throw aside busy schedules and dozens of appointments to mourn a friend's death, to honor a legacy, and to celebrate accomplishments and milestones. My meeting minutes note health updates concerning their champions: U.S. Senator Ted Kennedy, activist Mal Johnson, Dr. Dorothy Height, Representative Patsy Mink. They stood tall around the U.S. Capitol grounds when the late Senator Ted Kennedy's funeral cortege circled the Hill. They attended Dr. Height's funeral and wore beautiful hats in her honor. All of this was of a piece with their politics, ethics, and solidarities.

One skill central to the NCWO was humor. Periodically, a tense discussion of policy and action would break out into laughter, joy, and comic relief. During the debates about including the full agenda of women's reproductive health into the ACA, for instance, NCWO chair Susan Scanlan quipped, "You know, they really do want us barefoot and pregnant, in the chicken yard." My fieldwork notes document that attendees "fell out laughing and nodding in agreement."

Throughout my fieldwork, I witnessed many instances of the interweaving of gender-based solidarity. My teenage daughter and I accompanied a busload of University of South Carolina undergraduates to the 2004 March for Women's Lives in Washington, DC. For many of the young women (and a few young men) this was their first giant demonstration and national march. When we emerged from the Smithsonian Metro Station escalators up to the castle-like buildings and the National Mall, we were overwhelmed at the size of the crowd and the extent of the advanced organization the march must have entailed. The young students looked around carefully, reading people's T-shirts, placards, and signs. We found our assigned spot on the mall and started listening to speakers and announcements. I overheard the following conversation between two young South Carolina college women. The first one said, "Look at all these older women here at this march. It is amazing. They won't get pregnant any more or need legal abortions." The second student responded, "Yes, but they care about us." The circle of young listeners all nodded.

Leadership

Social movement leadership takes many forms. Jane Addams believed that a person's actions were central to their work of helping communities. She called it the power and example of *being* great, without doing dramatic and striking actions. She formulated and lived "an acceptable and understated 'woman's' way of being" (Sicherman 2010: 161). Contemporary social theorists advise us to always struggle for justice, without the illusion of attaining it. Ta-Nehisi

Coates wrote that it is in the constant struggle for justice that we maintain our sanity and it is the only part of this world we can control (2015: 107). Addressing his young son, Coates continued, "I never wanted you to be twice as good as them, so much as I have always wanted you to attack every day of your brief bright life in struggle. The people who must believe they are white can never be your measuring stick. I would not have you descend into your own dream. I would have you be a conscious citizen of this terrible and beautiful world" (2015: 108). The participatory process helps build the strength and confidence of individuals who, when they work together, can endure for "the long haul" (Horton 1990). "If emotion is the glue of solidarity," however, "then movements depend on an emotional infrastructure" (Jasper 1997: 207).

Cynthia Enloe (2013) emphasized that democracies should make sure women count and are taken seriously, with gravitas. Tax codes, public/private events, political campaigns, a gender-inclusive ACA, global issues, the social safety net, and more, the NCWO helped move forward with gravitas. Included were movement stalwarts, interns, activists, church ladies, and inspirational poets and authors.

The young interns at NCWO meetings, then, might have learned about deliberative decision making, layered social movements, relationships, conflict, and respect as they watched NCWO chairs give the floor to those whose voices might not be the most politically powerful or vigorous, where instrumental and rational cost-benefit analysis rendered the interchanges unproductive. Yet in this social movement, institutionalized within the NCWO, they remained important based on distaff side of life calculations.

In the fifteen years between 1999 and 2014 four chairs led the NCWO: Susan Bianchi-Sand from the beginnings of COP to 2000; Dr. Martha Burk, 2000–2005; Susan Scanlan, 2005–2013; and Shireen Mitchell, from 2013 to the end (about 2015). As Susan Scanlan often put it, "this is like herding cats." Each woman had her own style of leadership and came to the office with different backgrounds, priorities, and resources. In many quantitative studies of social behavior, the impact individuals have on a group or a cause is sometimes elided or overlooked. In sum, "Individuals, with their idiosyncrasies, neuroses, and mistakes, are troublesome for social science" (Jasper 1997: 216). However, leadership is vital to organizations. "Not only the ability to innovate, but selecting the best move, making it at just the right time, and the symbolic resonance we label charisma: all these things come from very subtle aspects of individuals. Movements flourish when they have leaders with these traits, and flounder when they do not" (Jasper 1997: 330). When examining the life and activism of Dorothy Day of the Catholic Worker's movement, Robert Coles reflected, "She remembered many dilemmas of leadership—*the tension between high purposes and their daily, attempted realization*" (2000:

139, italics in original). In movements, causes, and group dynamics, leaders set a tone, inspire people, keep the faith during hard times, and articulate a vision for the future for a group operating with a sense of "linked fate." Of course, leaders can also do the opposite and weaken an organization.

The American women's movement, when seen as a fluid and diffuse cultural and political social movement, has had its share of critics from within. On issues of racial, sexual, and social class diversity in group memberships and policy agendas, many women's movement adherents have evolved and learned over time. "The fact that participants in the feminist movement could face critique and challenge while still remaining wholeheartedly committed to a vision of justice, of liberation, is a testament to the movement's strength and power," bell hooks recounted. "It shows us that no matter how misguided feminist thinkers have been in the past, the will to change, the will to create the context for struggle and liberation, remains stronger than the need to hold on to wrong beliefs and assumptions" (hooks 2000: 58).

In many group efforts, no matter how hard their work and struggles were, people often reflected that it was one of the best times of their lives. They belonged to a cause bigger than themselves. They felt the companionship and appreciation of fellow activists. "And the deepest satisfaction, perhaps, is the devotion of one's entire life to a career in pursuit of social change. This can be a source of profound meaning and personal identity" (Jasper 1997: 209).

As a social movement coalition, the NCWO did not hold back from criticism of Democratic administrations when warranted. In 2014–2015 a series of meetings, editorials, and debates ensued over President Barack Obama's "My Brother's Keeper" program for its gender exclusivity and seeming insensitivity to the plight of girls of color (see, for example, Crenshaw 2015; O'Neill 2014). The Obama administration's willingness to meet with leaders of the women's community in DC, including the chair of the NCWO, Shireen Mitchell, indicated the recognition of Obama officials that the women's groups were "enduring publics of accountability" (Stout 2010: 109–110). Yet many NCWO leaders saw the My Brother's Keeper project of the Obama administration as unhelpfully making a split between the needs of boys of color and girls of color (Shireen Mitchell, interview, September 4, 2014). Messages from the NCWO and member groups like NOW that a better policy would be to help all children of color were not appreciated, to say the least.

Nonlinear, Forward Movement

Little of this was linear. The works of multiracial feminist activists "help show that the struggle against racism is hardly linear, that the consolidation of white-biased feminism was clearly costly to early second wave feminism, and that we must dig deep to represent the feminist movement that does justice to an antiracist vision" (B. Thompson 2010: 55–56). Depending on the context, a failure to zigzag can harm individual and group efforts.

Deepening democracy by lifting up poor and struggling people, while seemingly hopeless, was also presented as leading to economic collapse. "The rich and the lucky benefit from making large-scale democratic reform appear hopeless" (Stout 2010: 278). While there was no doubt that social movements and interest groups for social change, including feminism, could be stronger and more coordinated in their efforts, even movements that twist and turn, reconstitute like kaleidoscopes, stumble and fall, often make big differences. They can reset the political game.

U.S. senator Kristen Gillibrand (D-NY) is a champion for many silenced and disregarded people, especially women in the U.S. military who are survivors of sexual assaults and harassment. In her biography, *Off the Sidelines*, she lamented the lack of a functional women's movement in American politics (Gillibrand 2014: xvii, 184–185). Her story revealed, however, that when she prepared for her first congressional race she attended three different women candidate trainings, joined the Women's Fund of New York, mentored other women, was herself in turn mentored by other women, and was endorsed and funded by Emily's List. These are aspects of an engaged women's movement.

If public policy and fiscal issues were analyzed as if women mattered it would require "keeping an eye not only on private employers and public economic officials but also on the purveyors of meanness and their often seductive rationales" (Enloe 2013: 87). One reason social spending gets targeted for reductions is because the state is not efficiently collecting taxes from businesses, corporations, and the wealthy. Since women are not the dominant gender in those categories, tax is a gender issue. In addition to falling revenues, in part because of tax inequalities and tax dodging, there are other parts of a government budget that take up enormous resources like military expenditures (Walby 2015; Thorpe 2014). War, defense, and military spending have opportunity costs for countries, as well. "Funds spent on military procurement could be spent on other purposes, including investments in infrastructure, health care, or education. The borrowing used to finance the military procurements will also constrain future U.S. taxpayers who might have chosen to spend the money in other ways" (Thorpe 2014: 91–92). Therefore, "The fiscal is a gendered and feminist issue" writ large (Walby 2015: 97, see also 93; Barker and Feiner 2004; Scholzman, Verba, and Brady 2012).

Misrepresentation in legislatures also impacts gender, race, social class, and sexuality justice efforts. For instance, "The shortage of people from the working class in our legislatures and the overrepresentation of white-collar Americans means that tax policies are more regressive, business regulations are more probusiness, and social safety net programs are thinner. Who wins and who loses in this country depends in large part on who governs" (Carnes 2013: 111). "However, there is more to the story than just participation and organization. Whether our political process listens to one voice or another depends not just on who's doing the talking or how loud they are: it also depends on who's doing the listening" (Carnes 2013: 147).

"But feminists already possess one thing necessary for making successful coalitions—an expansive vision of social change that links issues" (Roth 2004: 224). People might join in these coalitions who did not even define themselves as feminists but want to save their communities. There are legitimate fears of coalition work by people and groups with less power. Bernice Johnson Reagon in 1981 spoke honestly and eloquently about these concerns by women of color trying to work with white feminists. Reagon pointed out that coalitions should not be like a safe home. Political coalitions are necessarily "both uncomfortable and indispensable places for feminists if they [are] to make progress" (Roth 2004: 223). It is hard, messy work since women's "rights do not 'trickle-down' to those below from above (especially when they are only incompletely built above)" (Roth 2004: 224). Remember that feminists have worked together in multiracial coalitions in the past when it mattered (Roth 2004: 225). A coalition is, in sum, "a mess worth making" (Smooth 2006).

There is also pain and hardship in social movements. Political activists can have difficult personalities combined with their stalwart commitment to a cause that can manifest as the arrogance of certainty (Jasper 1997: 220–226). As many people who worked in NGOs and policy institutes know, low wages and benefits along with long hours and many responsibilities add to the burdens (see, for example, Susanne Beechey in Reger 2005: 117–136). In *The Art of Moral Protest*, Jasper sums up many of these dynamics:

> Virtually all the pleasures that humans derive from social life are found in protest movements: a sense of community and identity; ongoing companionship and bonds with others; the variety and challenge of conversation, cooperation, and competition. Some of the pleasures are not available in the routines of daily life: the euphoria of crowds, a sense of pushing history forward with one's projects, or simply of making the evening news, of working together with others, of sharing a sense of purpose. And, perhaps most of all, the declaration of moral principles. (1997: 220)

As earlier works on the American women's movement have noted, "Organizational change need not necessarily lead to any one outcome, but it surely should not be understood as the death knell of feminism" (Gelb 1995: 134).

"Is it worth it?" is the question many people who worked in a coalition confront (Matsuda 2013: 332). "Working in coalition forces us to look for both the obvious and non-obvious relationships of domination, helping us to realize that no form of subordination ever stands alone" (Matsuda 2013: 336). To form theory out of coalition takes time and patience. Matsuda named it "the long, slow, open-ended efficiencies of coalition." The processing of ideas, concepts, and tactics through writings, art, and discourse is important work for movement adherents (Ferree and Martin 1995a: 18). "As often happens in the slow-cooking school of theory-building, the organizers wondered whether all this talk was getting anywhere. Cutting off discussion and avoiding conflict would have saved hours early on, but a coalition at its best never works that way. The slow and difficult early work gives us efficiencies when we need them: when the real challenges come, when justice requires action, when there is not time to argue over how to proceed" (Matsuda 2013: 338–339).

Decades of biracial justice work by Church Women United (CWU) illustrates these culture changes, discourse work, and ultimately political readiness when the time is ripe (Neumann 2008). The bottom line is, "American feminism may be unique in its blending of disparate wings with different orientations, and organizational styles. This hybrid style is not without its tensions and costs, but it also offers the potential for significant influence on policy" (Gelb 1995: 132). In addition, "The women's movement is perpetuated not only by its movement organizations but also by its cultural achievements" (Staggenborg 1995: 353).

Intergenerational conflict and cooperation within social movements also shape how and if they endure (Whittier 1995: 258). A local women's community network might be in relative abeyance, a latent interest potentially mobilized when issues arise. Grassroots communities, or even larger networks of feminists, can be sustained during quiet times as "a 'submerged network' of feminist activities and institutions that periodically erupted into public protest" (Whittier 1995: 26; see also Woliver 1993). Therefore, "even when the national level of a movement looks nowhere, in the communities the movement can be everywhere—in classrooms, coffee shops, bookstores, restaurants, co-ops and bars" (Reger 2012: 24). For young Americans, it can be like a "Generation Fluoride" where feminism is in the water, taken for granted, so feminism is present but not readily identified as such (Reger 2012: 56).

Progressive social movements have achieved a lot; credit must be given where credit is due. In the United States, for instance: "It is no small matter to outlaw slavery, enfranchise women, or get blacks to the front of the bus. We ought to be able to celebrate such accomplishments and gather their wind in our sails without being tricked into thinking that the current financial system and the military industrial complex uphold liberty and justice for all" (Stout 2010: 250–251).

Weakened, Abeyance, Disintegration

The NCWO became a legitimate, visible political presence. Based on its research and the breadth and depth of membership, the NCWO lobbied effectively for inclusion of women's issues on the national political agenda. The impetus of the NCWO's broad agenda was "a social democratic project" advocating for the wider public interest (Walby 2015: 124–125).

Holding the line in politics counts as a victory during political retrenchments. The NCWO spent a lot of talent and energy pushing back against neoliberal agendas in national politics. *Push Back, Move Forward* theorized political representation during policy backlashes, framing shifts, and fractious partisan divisions. To illustrate these points previous chapters discussed the politics of two social programs (Social Security and reproductive politics within the ACA). Points about gender framing also drew from Chapter 4 on the Masters Golf Tournament and the NCWO in 2003. When questions about power and powerlessness are trivialized to spats between individuals (Hootie vs. Martha), justice issues drain out.

As foreshadowed throughout this study, coalitions have fissures: the whole cannot overshadow the parts, money is short and should not be hijacked from member groups, foundation funding has limitations, and cohesion can be tough. In large, fluid social movements, "scholars must be careful not to interpret the proliferation of diverse organizations as evidence of 'schism' or 'fracture' in itself . . . it is precisely when such organizations exist and advocate for their members within the movement that they will contribute most significantly to movement strength" (Weldon 2011: 126).

NCWO council meetings in the later years of my fieldwork, as many participants also noticed, were increasingly attended by interns and young staff instead of "the principals." The internet, smartphones, and tweets meant that for many overbusy people traveling through DC traffic to NCWO meetings became a lower priority. Some of the pieces of the NCWO coalition were, by mutual consent, transferred to other DC-area NGOs. One, the Younger Women's Task Force was moved to the AAUW. A second restructuring was when Susan Scanlan retired from her chairpersonship. The NGO she headed, WREI, was folded into the Women's Policy Inc. organization.

The NCWO's finances were modest. Grants and cosponsored events continued to dry up. Movement leaders reflected on how the women's movement has diffused across the country (and the world) yet "is characterized by a lack of common purpose, the failure to create or push a broad women's agenda, and the absence of strategic and unified collective action to achieve major goals" (Hartmann and Burk 2012: 17). Conservative activist gains and Republican Party victories are part of the reasons for these shortcomings. Other influences offered were: (1) the failed ERA movement's toll on women's organizations; (2) the strong but single issue women's groups that lack a grassroots base; (3) the challenging economic times that stressed progressive groups including women's groups; (4) the lack of response to the cultural consequences of the employment opportunities for women that the women's movement helped create; (5) the thriving right-wing movement that has put the women's movement on the defensive: "The perennial top concerns of the vast majority of women," therefore, "such as better jobs and wages and work-life balance, as measured by surveys, have fallen further down the agenda as women's groups struggle to maintain a fundamental principle of women's equality: control over fertility" (Hartmann and Burk 2012: 18), and (6) the funding issues that result in a "'flea-market feminism,' with each bit of issue turf staked out and guarded by an organization seeking to attract customers to its booth" (Hartmann and Burk 2012: 18). Groups tailoring activities for foundation funding (as discussed in Chapter 8) exacerbate the problem.

In July 2015, Heidi Hartmann and five other members of the twelve member NCWO Steering Committee resigned because of spending and financial issues, and the lack of clear direction under the new chair (emails in author files). As the coalition declined, my numerous attempts to talk to the chair, Shireen Mitchell, were unsuccessful. The NCWO was unable to resolve many of the problems that manifested during this period of time. The NCWO then rapidly went from inactivity and abeyance to disintegration. As discussed throughout this study, coalitions are fragile and uncomfortable, yet indispensable to large social movements. A confluence of factors led to the crumbling of the NCWO.

Nevertheless, the movement persists. As discussed in the precursors for modern women's coalitions, many groups, conferences, consolidated efforts, and united campaigns have come and gone. The movement, however, is "not dead yet." Future scholars will pick up the trail of the NCWO. Recall, also, when policies have made citizens, struggles will happen (Campbell 2003). The NCWO's decline is a natural process for a large coalition in the United States. Chapter 2's discussion of the context and foundation for the NCWO discussed several once strong, then weakened coalitions and federations. There are several avenues future coalitions of women's groups could take. Given several disappointing gender justice decisions by the U.S. Supreme Court among other factors, a revitalized Equal Rights Amendment coalition formed in 2014 named the ERA Coalition with leadership from many, including Roberta Francis (Neuwirth 2015: 103). The Clearinghouse on Women's Issues, for instance, has sought to facilitate increasing collaborations among feminist organizations (www.womensclearinghouse.org email sent June 27, 2017; in author files). In addition, women's groups in DC have had joint press conferences to defend the ACA and denounce attempts to repeal it (Davison 2017). Keep in mind that "separate organizing of marginalized constituencies, which looks divisive to some observers, may in fact provide an avenue for strengthening social movements and making democratic policy-making more inclusive" (Weldon 2011: 127; see also J. Kirkpatrick 2010; Naples 2005: 215–235).

The 2016 elections shocked many people, groups, and coalitions. When keeping the faith, and never giving up is part of your ethos, regrouping and carrying on is unquestioned. As President Barack Obama reflected shortly after the 2016 election, "You say, O.K., where are the places where I can push to keep moving it forward." (President Obama, quoted in Remnick 2016: 63). President Obama also pointed out, "This is not a period. This is a comma in the continuing story of building America" (K. Reilly 2017).

The bottom line for the NCWO is that women's lives were highlighted, their stories told, the golfing masters had their fun and heritage troubled, research about women's situations was deftly gathered and utilized in politics, people were encouraged to vote, Social Security was not privatized, the ACA passed, and international women were a point of concern. The NCWO is still part of the fluid, political rights and culturally based women's movement. Linked fates, conscious coalitions, intersectional, nonlinear, and zigzagging the NCWO through its groups and activists pushed back and moved forward one of American's largest social movements: the American women's movement. The NCWO had a good run.

Appendix A

Interviews Conducted as of December 12, 2016

1. May 17, 1999: Allison Herwitt, director of Government Relations, NARAL, Washington, DC.
2. May 18, 1999: Katherine Levy, AAUW, Washington, DC.
3. June 16, 1999: Roger Evans, Planned Parenthood Federation of America, Columbia, SC.
4. July 21, 2000: Jan Ericson, NOW.
5. July 21, 2000: Leslie Ramsey, NOW intern.
6. August 14, 2000: Pat Reuss, NOW-LDF.
7. September 1, 2000: Martha Burk, NCWO chair.
8. September 4, 2000: Susan Bianchi-Sand, past NCWO chair, telephone interview.
9. September 5, 2000: Gail Shaeffer, BPW (Business and Professional Women).
10. September 5, 2000: Nicole Irvin, NAF (National Abortion Federation).
11. November 29, 2000: Ruth Nadell, OWL (Older Women's League; Clearinghouse Women's Issues).
12. November 30, 2000: Ardie Hollifield and Beth Raboin, Feminist Majority Foundation, Campus Coordinators, joint interview, Washington, DC.
13. November 30, 2000: Alice Cohan, Feminist Majority Foundation, Arlington, VA.
14. December 1, 2000: Jill Miller, Women Work!
15. December 1, 2000: Jan Ericson, NOW.
16. March 9, 2001: Carol Rosenblatt, Coalition of Labor Union Women, Washington, DC.
17. March 19, 2001: Beth Kanter, National Women's Political Caucus, Washington, DC.
18. March 21, 2001: Patricia Gibson, National Council of Negro Women, Washington, DC.
19. March 21, 2001: Zina Pierre, National Council of Negro Women, Washington, DC.
20. March 21, 2001: Jan Ericson, NOW, Washington, DC.

21. April 2, 2001: Heidi Hartmann, Institute for Women's Policy Research, telephone interview.
22. November 15, 2007: Kimberly Otis, executive director, NCWO, and Nicole Nesbary, Administrative Aid.
23. July 18, 2008: Susan Scanlan, NCWO chair.
24. January 27, 2009: Kimberly Otis, executive director, NCWO.
25. June 16, 2009: Jan Ericson, NOW.
26. June 16, 2009: Susan Scanlan, WREI and NCWO.
27. June 17, 2009: Liz Anderson, NCWO.
28. June 17, 2009: Shannon Lynberg, NCWO and Younger Women's Task Force.
29. July 7, 2009: Susan Scanlan, NCWO and WREI.
30. July 8, 2009: Shannon Lynberg, NCWO and Younger Women's Task Force.
31. July 8, 2009: Liz Anderson, NCWO.
32. July 9, 2009: Kim Otis, progressive consultant.
33. July 15, 2009: Susan Scanlan, chair of NCWO.
34. July 20, 2009: Amy Allina, National Women's Health Network.
35. July 22, 2009: Laura Hessburg, National Partnership for Women and Families.
36. July 28, 2009: Judy Waxman, National Women's Law Center, telephone interview.
37. September 16, 2009: Shireen Mitchell, Digital Sisters.
38. September 16, 2009: Terry O'Neill, president of NOW.
39. July 8, 2010: Shannon Lynberg, YWTF, NCWO headquarters, Washington, DC.
40. July 8, 2010: Liz [Elizabeth] Anderson, NCWO headquarters, Washington, DC.
41. July 9, 2010: Susan Scanlan, chair NCWO, Washington, DC.
42. July 13, 2010: Alice Cohan, Feminist Majority Foundation, Arlington, VA.
43. July 19, 2010: Jan Ericson, NOW, Washington, DC.
44. July 19, 2010: Rene Redwood, consultant and Church Ladies Project. Interview by Annie Boiter-Jolley (I sat in), Washington, DC.
45. July 21, 2010: Karen Mulhauser. Interview by Annie Boiter-Jolley, Washington, DC.
46. July 23, 2010: Alice Cohan, Feminist Majority Foundation. Interview by Annie Boiter-Jolley, Arlington, VA.
47. July 23, 2010: Emily Kadar, National Campus Organizer, Feminist Majority Foundation. Interview by Annie Boiter-Jolley, Arlington, VA.
48. July 28, 2010: Eleanor Hinton Hoyt, Black Women's Health Imperative, Washington, DC.
49. August 2, 2010: Susan Scanlan, NCWO chair, lunch meeting, Washington, DC.
50. August 11, 2010: Jeanette Senecal, League of Women Voters. Telephone interview by Annie Boiter-Jolley.
51. September 22, 2010: Heidi Hartmann, IWPR.
52. January 18, 2011: Susan Scanlan, NCWO chair, telephone interview.
53. June 24, 2011: Susan Scanlan, NCWO chair, lunch interview.
54. July 20, 2011: Joan Kuriansky, ex-director, WOW, Washington, DC.
55. July 26, 2011: Eleanor Smeal, president, Feminist Majority Foundation, Arlington, VA.
56. January 15, 2013: Dawn Aldrich, director of Programs and Policy, NCWO, Washington, DC.
57. August 12, 2013: Susan Scanlan, NCWO chair.
58. August 4, 2014: Susan Scanlan, NCWO ex-chair, lunch interview, Washington, DC.

59. August 18, 2014: Jan Ericson, lunch interview, NOW, Washington, DC.
60. September 4, 2014: Kim Otis, consultant, Washington, DC.
61. September 4, 2014: Shireen Mitchell, president NCWO, Washington, DC.
62. September 11, 2014: Karen Mulhauser, political consultant, Washington, DC.
63. September 17, 2014: Rev. Nancy Neal, associate for Denominational Women's Organizations Relations, Bread for the World, Washington, DC.
64. September 18, 2014: Elaine Zuckerman, GenderAction, Washington, DC.
65. September 19, 2014: Heidi Hartmann, president, Institute for Women's Policy Research, Washington, DC.
66. September 19, 2014: Rene Redwood, political consultant, Washington, DC.
67. October 3, 2014: Lisa Maatz, American Association of University Women, telephone interview, Washington, DC.

Appendix B

NCWO Meetings Attended

1. May 1999
2. July 2000
3. November 28, 2000
4. March 20, 2001
5. July 17, 2001
6. March 10–11, 2008, two-day Women's Equality Summit
7. May 20, 2008
8. July 15, 2008
9. September 16, 2008
10. November 18, 2008
11. July 21, 2009
12. September 15, 2009
13. November 17, 2009
14. January 19, 2010
15. March 16, 2010
16. May 18, 2010
17. July 20, 2010
18. September 21, 2010
19. November 16, 2010
20. March 8, 2011 (combination January/March meeting, because of January snow-storm)
21. May 17, 2011
22. July 19, 2011
23. November 18, 2014, via conference call
24. January 27, 2015, via conference call
25. March 31, 2015, via conference call

Appendix C

NCWO-Related Events Attended and Observed

1. May 17, 1999: Small Lobbying Task Force meeting, NARAL, Washington, DC.
2. July 20, 2000: House Judiciary Committee Subcommittee on the Constitution hearings on "The Born Alive Protection Act."
3. July 21, 2000: Congressional Staff briefing by NCWO, Women in 2000 Elections.
4. December 1–2, 2000: NOW Quarterly Board of Directors meeting, Washington, DC.
5. April 12, 2003: NCWO protest at Masters Golf Tournament, Augusta, GA.
6. April 25, 2004: "March for Women's Lives," Washington, DC.
7. May 13–14, 2005: NNAF Southern Region Organizing Summit, Atlanta, GA.
8. March 11, 2008: shadowed NCWO college student lobbyists for "Women's Equality Summit," Washington, DC.
9. July 17, 2008: Fair Pay Act Rally (i.e., Lilly Ledbetter Bill) Capitol Hill, Senate side, Washington, DC.
10. June 18, 2009: New Faces, More Voices, interns training, Session #2, Washington, DC.
11. July 10, 2009: NCWO Domestic Priorities Task Force, Health briefing, Russell Senate Office Building, U.S. Senate, Washington, DC.
12. July 14, 2009: Prevent Cervical Cancer briefing, NCWO Women's Health Task Force, Washington, DC.
13. July 14, 2009: IWPR interns reception, Heidi Hartmann, Washington, DC.
14. July 16, 2009: New Faces, More Voices, interns training, Session #3 or 4, Washington, DC.
15. July 21, 2009: Press Conference on Reintroduction of the ERA, Washington, DC.
16. July 21, 2009: NCWO, ERA. Task Force meeting, Washington, DC.
17. July 23, 2009: New Voices, intern training, NCWO, Washington, DC.
18. July 27, 2009: Society for Women's Health Research briefing; cervical cancer prevention. U.S. House of Representatives Office building, Washington, DC.

19. July 28, 2009: NCWO Domestic Priorities Task Force meeting, Washington, DC.
20. September 15, 2009: Younger Women's Task Force, DC Metro Area Chapter, "Dialogue between feminist generations," Washington, DC.
21. November 18, 2009: U.S. Senate lobbying day to "Stop Stupak" organized by Planned Parenthood. Shadowed lobbyists; attended meetings with key Senators and House leadership, Washington, DC.
22. July 8, 2010: Intern training session. Younger Women's Task Force, New Faces, More Voices Program. Topic: racial and sexual diversity. At the Alliance for Justice Conference room, 3:00–5:00 p.m., Washington, DC.
23. July 16, 2010: Congressional briefing. Women, Unemployment, and the Recession. Rayburn House Office Building. 11:00 a.m.–12:15 p.m., Washington, DC.
24. July 21, 2010: Interns Training and Congressional Visits. Feminist Majority Foundation organized. Russell Senate Office Building, Caucus room, Washington, DC.
25. July 22, 2010: Younger Women Task Force, intern training, New Faces, More Voices program. Topic: international women's issues, 3:00–5:00 p.m. Annie Boiter-Jolley attended, Washington, DC.
26. July 24, 2010: Advocacy Panel. National Association of Commissions on Women, Rockville, MD.
27. July 28, 2010: OWES (Older Women and Economic Security) Task Force, NCWO meeting, Washington, DC.
28. July 29, 2010: Strengthen Social Security campaign launch. National Press Club, Washington, DC.
29. July 29, 2010: Alyse Nelson, Vital Voices Global Partnership. Talk at Women's National Democratic Club, Washington, DC.
30. July 30, 2010: Panel discussion. "Lessons Learned from Health Care and What It Means for Progressive Organizations," at the Alliance for Justice, Washington, DC.
31. May 16, 2011: WREI (Women's Research and Education Institute) fellows lunch/briefing on CEDAW, Washington, DC.
32. June 21, 2011: Paycheck Fairness demonstration at U.S. Supreme Court (day after *Wal-Mart v. Dukes* decision), Washington, DC.
33. June 22, 2011: ERA Reintroduction press event/demonstration, House Triangle, Washington, DC.
34. June 22, 2011: WIN/Women Opening Doors Reception at NEA headquarters, Washington, DC.
35. June 24, 2011: Congressional briefing on Strengthen Social Security; Russell Senate Office Building, Washington, DC.
36. June 28, 2011: Clearinghouse on Women's Issues meeting, Washington, DC.
37. June 29, 2011: Economic Policy Institute. Work-life lunch. Economic security/paid sick days, Washington, DC.
38. June 30, 2011: "Budget Battles: Threats to Medicaid Webinar," Wider Opportunities for Women and Family USA. 3:00–4:00 p.m., Washington, DC.
39. July 6, 2011: OWES Task Force meeting; at NOW offices, Washington, DC.
40. July 8, 2011: Congressional Hearings, Subcommittee on Social Security, House Ways and Means Committee, Washington, DC.
41. July 14, 2011: "Women's History in Three Acts," panel at Sewell-Belmont House, Washington, DC.
42. July 21, 2011: Feminist Majority Foundation, summer intern briefing, Washington, DC.

43. July 27, 2011: NCWO Training "Ins and Outs of Lobbying for Nonprofits," Washington, DC.
44. July 28, 2011: "Save the American Dream" rally [Cosponsors: MoveOn.org and Common Cause], U.S. Capitol lawn, Washington, DC.
45. August 26, 2014: Panel Discussion. "Women's History on the Horizon: The Centennial of Women's Suffrage in 2020," cosponsored by the National Archives and the Sewall-Belmont House and Museum, Washington, DC.
46. September 11, 2014: Open mike discussion. NCWO event: open mike with author at Bus Boys and Poets restaurant. Martha Burk and new edition of book *Your Voice, Your Vote: 2014–2015 Edition.* Wednesday, 6:30–8:00 p.m., Washington, DC.
47. February 18, 2015: Webinar. National Women's Law Center. A State Roadmap to Economic Justice. Online.

Appendix D

Interviews, Meetings, and Observations by Year

1999

May 17, 1999: Allison Herwitt, director of Government Relations, NARAL, interview, Washington, DC.

May 17, 1999: Small Lobbying Task Force meeting, Washington, DC.

May 18, 1999: Katherine Levy, AAUW, Washington, DC.

May 18, 1999: NCWO meeting, Washington, DC.

June 16, 1999: Roger Evans, Planned Parenthood Federation of America, interview, Columbia, SC.

2000

July 18, 2000: NCWO meeting, Washington, DC.

July 20, 2000: Attended and observed: House Judiciary Committee Subcommittee on the Constitution hearings on "The Born Alive Protection Act," Washington, DC.

July 21, 2000: Attended and observed: Congressional Staff briefing by NCWO "Women in 2000 Elections," Washington, DC.

July 21, 2000: Jan Ericson, NOW, interview, Washington, DC.

July 21, 2000: Leslie Ramsey, NOW intern, interview, Washington, DC.

August 14, 2000: Pat Reuss, NOW-LDF, interview, Washington, DC.

September 1, 2000: Martha Burk, NCWO chair, interview, Washington, DC.

September 4, 2000: Susan Bianchi-Sand, past NCWO chair, telephone interview.

September 5, 2000: Gail Shaeffer, BPW (Business and Professional Women), interview, Washington, DC.

September 5, 2000: Nicole Irvin, NAF (National Abortion Federation) interview, Washington, DC.

November 28, 2000: NCWO meeting, Washington, DC.

November 29, 2000: Ruth Nadell (Older Women's League; Clearinghouse Women's Issues), interview, Washington, DC.

November 30, 2000: Ardie Hollifield and Beth Raboin, Feminist Majority Foundation, Campus Coordinators, joint interview, Washington, DC.

November 30, 2000: Alice Cohan, Feminist Majority Foundation, interview, Arlington, VA.

December 1, 2000: Jill Miller, Women Work! Interview, Washington, DC.

December 1, 2000: Jan Ericson, NOW, interview, Washington, DC.

December 1–2, 2000: Attended and observed: NOW Quarterly Board of Directors meeting, Washington, DC.

2001

March 9, 2001: Carol Rosenblatt, Coalition of Labor Union Women, interview, Washington, DC.

March 20, 2001: NCWO meeting, Washington, DC.

March 19, 2001: Beth Kanter, National Women's Political Caucus, interview, Washington, DC.

March 21, 2001: Patricia Gibson, National Council of Negro Women, interview, Washington, DC.

March 21, 2001: Zina Pierre, National Council of Negro Women, interview, Washington, DC.

March 21, 2001: Jan Ericson, NOW, interview, Washington, DC.

April 2, 2001: Heidi Hartmann, Institute for Women's Policy Research, telephone interview.

July 17, 2001: NCWO meeting, Washington, DC.

2003

April 12, 2003: Attended and observed: NCWO protest at "Masters" Golf Tournament, Augusta, GA.

2004

April 25, 2004: Attended and observed: "March for Women's Lives," Washington, DC.

2005

May 13–14, 2005: NNAF Southern Region Organizing Summit, Atlanta, GA.

2007

November 15, 2007: Kimberly Otis, executive director, NCWO and Nicole Nesbary, Administrative Aid, interview, Washington, DC.

2008

March 10–11, 2008: NCWO meeting, two-day Women's Equality Summit, Washington, DC.

March 11, 2008: Attended and observed: shadowed NCWO college student lobbyists for "Women's Equality Summit, Washington, DC.

May 20, 2008: NCWO meeting, Washington, DC.

July 15, 2008: NCWO meeting, Washington, DC.

July 17, 2008: Attended and observed: Fair Pay Act Rally (i.e., Lilly Ledbetter Bill) Capitol Hill, Senate side, Washington, DC.

July 18, 2008: Susan Scanlan, NCWO chair interview, Washington, DC.

September 16, 2008: NCWO meeting, Washington, DC.

November 18, 2008: NCWO meeting, Washington, DC.

2009

January 27, 2009: Kimberly Otis, executive director, NCWO interview, Washington, DC.

June 16, 2009: Jan Ericson, NOW interview, Washington, DC.

June 16, 2009: Susan Scanlan, WREI and NCWO interview, Washington, DC.

June 17, 2009: Liz Anderson, NCWO interview, Washington, DC.

June 17, 2009: Shannon Lynberg, NCWO and Younger Women's Task Force, interview, Washington, DC.

June 18, 2009: Attended and observed: New Faces, More Voices, intern training, Session #2, Washington, DC.

July 7, 2009: Susan Scanlan, NCWO and WREI, interview, Washington, DC.

July 8, 2009: Shannon Lynberg, NCWO and Younger Women's Task Force, interview.

July 8, 2009: Liz Anderson, NCWO interview, Washington, DC.

July 9, 2009: Kim Otis, progressive consultant, interview, Washington, DC.

July 10, 2009: Attended and observed: NCWO Domestic Priorities Task Force; Health briefing, Russell Senate Office Building, U.S. Senate, Washington, DC.

July 14, 2009: Attended and observed: Prevent Cervical Cancer briefing, NCWO Women's Health Task Force, Washington, DC.

July 14, 2009: Attended and observed: IWPR Interns reception, Heidi Hartmann, Washington, DC.

July 15, 2009: Susan Scanlan, chair of NCWO interview, Washington, DC.

July 16, 2009: Attended and observed: New Faces, More Voices, intern training, Session #3 or 4, Washington, DC.

July 20, 2009: Amy Allina, National Women's Health Network interview, Washington, DC.

July 21, 2009: Attended and observed: Press Conference on reintroduction of the ERA., Washington, DC.

July 21, 2009: Attended and observed: NCWO, ERA. Task Force meeting, Washington, DC.

July 21, 2009: NCWO meeting, Washington, DC.

July 22, 2009: Laura Hessburg, National Partnership for Women and Families, interview, Washington, DC.

July 23, 2009: Attended and observed: New Faces, More Voices, intern training, NCWO, Washington, DC.

July 27, 2009: Attended and observed: Society for Women's Health Research briefing; cervical cancer prevention. U.S. House of Representatives Office building, Washington, DC.

July 28, 2009: Attended and observed: NCWO Domestic Priorities Task Force meeting, Washington, DC.

July 28, 2009: Judy Waxman, National Women's Law Center, telephone interview.

September 15, 2009: NCWO meeting, Washington, DC.

September 15, 2009: Attended and observed: Younger Women's Task Force, DC Metro Area Chapter, dialogue between feminist generations, Washington, DC.

September 16, 2009: Shireen Mitchell, Digital Sisters interview, Washington, DC.

September 16, 2009: Terry O'Neill, president, NOW, interview, Washington, DC.

November 17, 2009: NCWO meeting, Washington, DC.

November 18, 2009: Attended and observed: U.S. Senate lobbying day to "Stop Stupak" organized by Planned Parenthood. Shadowed lobbyists; attended meetings with key Senators and House leadership, Washington, DC.

2010

January 19, 2010: NCWO meeting, Washington, DC.

March 16, 2010: NCWO meeting, Washington, DC.

May 18, 2010: NCWO meeting, Washington, DC.

July 8, 2010. Shannon Lynberg, YWTF, NCWO, interview, Washington, DC.

July 8, 2010. Liz [Elizabeth] Anderson, NCWO, interview, Washington, DC.

July 8, 2010: Attended and observed: intern training session. Younger Women's Task Force, New Faces, More Voices Program. Topic: racial and sexual diversity. At Alliance for Justice Conference room, 3:00–5:00 p.m., Washington, DC.

July 9, 2010: Susan Scanlan, chair NCWO, interview, Washington, DC.

July 13, 2010: Alice Cohan, Feminist Majority Foundation, interview, Arlington, VA.

July 16, 2010: Attended and observed: Congressional briefing. Women, Unemployment, and the Recession. Rayburn House Office Building, 11:00 a.m.–12:15. p.m., Washington, DC.

July 19, 2010: Jan Ericson, NOW, interview, Washington, DC.

July 19, 2010: Rene Redwood, consultant and Church Ladies Project. Interview by Annie Boiter-Jolley (I sat in), Washington, DC.

July 20, 2010: NCWO meeting, Washington, DC.

July 21, 2010: Karen Mulhauser. Interview by Annie Boiter-Jolley, Washington, DC.

July 21, 2010: Attended and observed: interns training and congressional visits. Feminist Majority Foundation organized. Russell Senate Office Building, Caucus room, Washington, DC.

July 22, 2010: Attended and observed: Younger Women task force, intern training, New Faces, More Voices Program. Topic: international women's issues. 3:00–5:00 p.m., Annie Boiter-Jolley attended, Washington, DC.

July 23, 2010: Alice Cohan, Feminist Majority Foundation. Interview by Annie Boiter-Jolley, Arlington, VA.

July 23, 2010: Emily Kadar, National Campus Organizer, Feminist Majority Foundation. Interview by Annie Boiter-Jolley, Arlington, VA.

July 24, 2010: Attended and observed: Advocacy Panel. National Association of Commissions on Women, Rockville, MD.

July 28, 2010: Eleanor Hinton Hoyt. Black Women's Health Imperative, interview, Washington, DC.

July 28, 2010: Attended and observed: OWES (Older Women and Economic Security) Task Force, NCWO meeting, Washington, DC.

July 29, 2010: Attended and observed: Strengthen Social Security campaign launch. National Press Club, Washington, DC.

July 29, 2010: Attended and observed: Alyse Nelson. Vital Voices Global Partnership. Talk at Women's National Democratic Club, Washington, DC.

July 30, 2010: Attended and observed: Panel discussion. "Lessons Learned from Health Care and What It Means for Progressive Organizations," at Alliance for Justice, Washington, DC.

August 2, 2010: Susan Scanlan, NCWO chair, lunch meeting, interview, Washington, DC.

August 11, 2010: Jeanette Senecal, League of Women Voters. Telephone interview done by Annie Boiter-Jolley.

September 21, 2010: NCWO meeting, Washington, DC.

September 22, 2010: Heidi Hartmann, IWPR, interview, Washington, DC.

November 16, 2010: NCWO meeting, Washington, DC.

2011

January 18, 2011: Susan Scanlan, NCWO chair, telephone interview, Washington, DC.

March 8, 2011: NCWO meeting, (combination January/March meeting, because of January snowstorm), Washington, DC.

May 16, 2011: Attended and observed: WREI (Women's Research and Education Institute) fellows lunch/briefing on CEDAW, Washington, DC.

May 17, 2011: NCWO meeting, Washington, DC.

June 21, 2011: Attended and observed: Paycheck Fairness demonstration at U.S. Supreme Court (day after *Wal-Mart v. Dukes* decision), Washington, DC.

June 22, 2011: Attended and observed: ERA Reintroduction press event/demonstration, House Triangle, Washington, DC.

June 22, 2011: Attended and observed: WIN/Women Opening Doors Reception at NEA, Washington, DC.

June 24, 2011: Attended and observed: Congressional briefing on Strengthen Social Security; Russell Senate Office Building, Washington, DC.

June 24, 2011: Susan Scanlan, NCWO chair, lunch interview.

June 28, 2011: Attended and observed: Clearinghouse on Women's Issues meeting, Washington, DC.

June 29, 2011: Attended and observed: Economic Policy Institute. Work-life lunch. Economic security/paid sick days, Washington, DC.

June 30, 2011: Attended and observed: "Budget Battles: Threats to Medicaid Webinar," Wider Opportunities for Women and Family USA. 3:00–4:00 p.m., Washington, DC.

July 6, 2011: Attended and observed: OWES Task Force meeting; at NOW offices, Washington, DC.

July 8, 2011: Attended and observed: Congressional Hearings, Subcommittee on Social Security, House Ways and Means Committee, Washington, DC.

July 14, 2011: Attended and observed: "Women's History in Three Acts," panel at Sewell-Belmont House, Washington, DC.

July 19, 2011: NCWO meeting, Washington, DC.

July 20, 2011: Joan Kuriansky, ex-director, WOW, Washington, DC.

July 21, 2011: Attended and observed: Feminist Majority Foundation, summer intern briefing, Washington, DC.

July 26, 2011: Eleanor Smeal, president, Feminist Majority Foundation, Arlington, VA.
July 27, 2011: Attended and observed: NCWO Training on "Ins and Outs of Lobbying for Nonprofits," Washington, DC.
July 28, 2011: Attended and observed: "Save the American Dream" rally [Cosponsors: MoveOn.org and Common Cause], U.S. Capitol lawn, Washington, DC.

2013

January 15, 2013: Dawn Aldrich, director of Programs and Policy, NCWO, interview, Washington, DC.
August 12, 2013: Susan Scanlan, NCWO chair, Washington, DC.

2014

August 4, 2014: Susan Scanlan, NCWO ex-chair, lunch interview, Washington, DC.
August 18, 2014: Lunch interview with Jan Ericson, NOW, Washington, DC.
August 26, 2014: Attended and observed: Panel Discussion. "Women's History on the Horizon: The Centennial of Women's Suffrage in 2020," cosponsored by the National Archives and the Sewall-Belmont House and Museum, Washington, DC.
September 4, 2014: Kim Otis, Consultant, Washington, DC.
September 4, 2014: Shireen Mitchell, chair NCWO, Washington, DC.
September 11, 2014: Karen Mulhauser, political consultant, Washington, DC.
September 11, 2014: Attended and observed: Open mike discussion. NCWO event: open mike with author at Bus Boys and Poets restaurant, Martha Burk and new edition of book Your Voice, *Your Vote: 2014–15 Edition*. Wednesday, 6:30–8:00 p.m., Washington, DC.
September 17, 2014: Rev. Nancy Neal, Associate for Denominational Women's Organizations Relations, Bread for the World, interview, Washington, DC.
September 18, 2014: Elaine Zuckerman, GenderAction, Washington, DC.
September 19, 2014: Heidi Hartmann, president, Institute for Women's Policy Research, Washington, DC.
September 19, 2014: Rene Redwood, political consultant, Washington, DC.
October 3, 2014: Lisa Maatz, American Association of University Women, telephone interview. Washington, DC.
November 18, 2014: NCWO meeting, via conference call.

2015

January 27, 2015: NCWO meeting, via conference call.
February 18, 2015: National Women's Law Center Webinar. A State Roadmap to Economic Justice.
March 31, 2015: NCWO meeting, via conference call.

Notes

CHAPTER 1

1. In late April 2017, tennis champion Serena Williams responded to inappropriate comments regarding her pregnancy with direct quotes from "Still I Rise" by Maya Angelou (Hendricks 2017).

CHAPTER 2

1. Please note that most black women in America did not secure access to ballots until after passage of the 1965 Voting Rights Act (see, for example, Brown and Gershon 2016; Smooth 2006).

2. At the same time, thirteen of the eighteen congresswomen responded to a questionnaire requesting their women's issues priorities for the Ninety-Fifth Congress. Job creation, and more responsible jobs for women in the federal government, were respondents' highest priority. A less gender discriminatory Social Security system was their second priority. They also advocated for support for day care, displaced homemakers, and health care for women (Gertzog 1984: 184).

3. As a nonpolitical group, WREI was able to attract funding from the Ford Foundation and the Rockefeller Family Fund. The biggest funder was the Charles H. Revson Foundation, which financed ten WREI congressional internships (Gertzog 1984: 191–192). Eventually, additional internships were underwritten by R. J. Reynolds Industries (two internships), the Phillip Morris Company (one internship), and the Helena Rubenstein Foundation (one internship) (Gertzog 1984: 192–193).

CHAPTER 3

1. A sign-in sheet from the September 9, 1982, meeting showed representatives of the following groups attended (in alphabetical order):

AFL-CIO: American Federation of Labor and Congress of Industrial Organizations
ANA: American Nurses Association
CLUW: Coalition of Labor Union Women
LWVUS: League of Women Voters of the United States
NARAL: National Abortion Rights Action League
NASW: National Association of Social Workers
NEA: National Education Association
NCJW: National Council of Jewish Women
NOW: National Organization for Women
NWPC: National Women's Political Caucus
WEAL: Women's Equity Action League

Author Note: The following entities were signed in by individuals at the meeting. They are listed here as questions because I cannot determine what groups these might be or I cannot read the cursive writing of some of the signatories. Future scholars can perhaps figure out these unknowns: NCNW (might be National Council of Negro Women), NCWW (might be National Council of Working Women), NNEdF, WCF (probably Women's Campaign Fund), WLD8.

2. The full text of the 1994/1995 COP pledge is as follows:

Our Pledge to the Women of America

In 1995, our organizations will work to raise the visibility of the following five-point agenda in the public arena and to promote legislative action and social advocacy on as many of the components of the plan as possible:

W ORKPLACE FAIRNESS
Pay equity for women; livable minimum wage; protections for workplace organizing; benefits for part-time and temporary workers; freedom from harassment; and effective antidiscrimination remedies and enforcement.

O NGOING SUPPORT FOR FAMILIES
Affordable, quality child care; effective enforcement of child support; financial assistance for low-income families through expanded tax credits, feeding and nutrition programs, and Head Start; and comprehensive welfare reform that truly gets women and children out of poverty and does not exclude children because of the age or behavior of their parents.

M EDICAL CARE FOR ALL
Access to health care and coverage to all; including long-term care; increased funding for family planning and HIV prevention; access to reproductive health care for women of all ages and incomes; and equitable allocation of medical research funds for women's health needs.

E DUCATIONAL AND ECONOMIC EQUITY
Equal access to educational and economic opportunities; vocational education and job training that meet women's needs; encouragement of business

enterprise for women, including improved access to federal and state contracts and sources of capital; and tax equity for working women and homemakers.

N EW GUARANTEES OF RIGHTS
Safety from violence and all forms of abuse; full reproductive rights including safe access to women's health clinics; human and civil rights for all; enforcement of current civil rights protections; implementation of women's rights internationally, including ratification of CEDAW; and ratification of the Equal Rights Amendment to the U.S. Constitution.

In order to achieve this positive agenda for women, we pledge to make women's voices heard through education, outreach, and mobilization. We will work to heighten women's political power through:

V OTER EDUCATION AND REGISTRATION
Our organizations will work to register and educate women voters—through community groups, religious congregations, workplaces, and public and private agencies.

O RGANIZATION OF OUR COMMUNITIES
Our organizations will work through our constituencies and networks, locally and/or globally, to help women become effective advocates in support of this five-point pledge.

T URN OUT
Our organizations will work to bring women to the polls to increase our clout through the ballot box.

E QUAL REPRESENTATION
Our goal is equal representation of women in *all* elective and appointive offices. We will work to ensure women real choices at the polls by encouraging women who support our agenda to run for all offices.

WOMEN VOTE!

Adopted by the Council of Presidents, December 1994

3. The NCWO "POLICY AGENDA" adopted in November 1998 listed the following ten items:

1. Protecting Social Security and ending disadvantages to women in Social Security
    a. Opposition to privatization
    b. End policies and practices that disproportionately disadvantage women in Social Security
    c. Ensure that any proposed reform of social security does not disproportionately disadvantage women
2. Securing affordable, quality child care as a national priority for all who need it
3. Supporting the principles of the National Women's Equity Act for the 21st Century
4. Winning economic security for all women raising the minimum wage and establishing pay equity regulations for government contractors either through federal legislation or executive orders

5. Improving access to health care by increasing funding for family planning, requiring contraception insurance coverage, enacting patient bills of rights, removing gender bias from Medicare and Medicaid, stopping restrictions to abortion access, and funding for enforcement and measures to counter antiabortion clinic terrorism

6. Enacting Violence Against Women Act II and enacting Hate Crimes Legislation to include gender, sexual orientation, and disability

7. Supporting affirmative action in public education, employment, and contracting

8. Opposing the weakening of Title IX and increasing opportunities for higher education for poor women

9. Supporting the ratification of the Equal Rights Amendment and

10. Supporting the ratification of the United Nations Convention for the Elimination of All Forms of Discrimination Against Women (CEDAW) by the Senate and measures to oppose gender apartheid in Afghanistan ("National Council of Women's Organizations: Policy Agenda." Adopted November 1998. One page Xerox in author files.)

4. Detailed list of COP, then NCWO growth:

As of January 20, 1998:	15 groups (COP)
As of February 12, 1998:	29 groups (COP)
As of April 16, 1998:	54 groups (NCWO)
As of April 30, 1998:	64 groups (NCWO)
As of May 15, 1998:	77 groups (NCWO)
As of June 2, 1998:	78 groups (NCWO)
As of August 4, 1998:	82 groups (NCWO)
As of October 29, 1998:	94 groups (NCWO)

5. Funders: Lists are incomplete. A funder might have only funded one part of one conference, the printing costs, a reception, or a research report. Funders listed below might not have funded an entire event or activity.

Conference Funders/Sponsors (alphabetically):

AARP
AFL-CIO
AFSCME—Women's Rights Department
Feminist Majority Foundation
Barbara Lee Family Fund
Ms. Foundation for Women
National Abortion Federation
NOW and NOW LDEF
Women Leaders Online

Other Funders (alphabetically):

Acra Foundation (Reynolds's tobacco interest)
Atrea (tobacco interest)

Brookings Institution
Ford Foundation
General Motors Corporation
Bill & Melinda Gates Foundation
Hadassah
Heinz Family Foundation
Lifetime Television
MacArthur Foundation
Ms. Foundation
Pew Charitable Trust
Planned Parenthood Federation of America
Rockefeller Foundation
Russell Sage Foundation

Other Funders—Pharma or Health Companies (alphabetically):

GYNAGEN
Hologic
Eli Lilly
Merck
Qiagen
Sanofi-Aventis

CHAPTER 5

1. Although more women still voted for John Kerry than for George W. Bush, the gap was smaller than average and the Republican Party captured more "undecided" women (S. MacManus 2006: 378).

CHAPTER 6

1. Peter G. Peterson is a hedge fund billionaire. Among many entities he supports the Committee for a Responsible Federal Government. The Peterson Foundation, which he funds, was quoted as a neutral think tank by some media outlets.

2. Timeline of reform proposals to Social Security.
Social Security Reform Proposals (a.k.a. Forays against Social Security):

- 1998: Clinton Administration Deficit Reduction Study/commission.
- December 4, 1998, White House Conference on Social Security.
- July 19–23, 1999, NCWO sponsored retreat; Airlie House, Virginia. "Working Conference on Women and Social Security."
- 2000–2001: President George W. Bush during presidential campaign and newly in office. Private account plans.
- Women's Equality Summit, Congressional Action Day (WESCAD) was funded, organized, and led by NCWO people in the spring of 2002 and 2008.
- 2005: Deficit reduction plan.
- Early 2010: Obama administration. National Commission on Fiscal Responsibility and Reform.

3. Women and Social Security Task Force member organizations were:

- AAUW, BFW USA, Center for Advancement of Public Policy, FMF, IWPR, MANA, A National Latina Organization, MA'AMAT USA, National Committee on Pay Equity, National Council of Negro Women, NOW, National Partnership for Women and Families, National Women's Law Center, OWL, WOW, WAND, Women's Institute for a Secure Retirement. (Task Force, NCWO September 21, 1999; in author files).

4. The four short-term policy initiatives were:

1. Eliminate an earnings test for workers between age sixty-two and the normal retirement age since it would encourage workers to retire early, resulting in diminished benefits over time.
2. Any amendments to SSI should help the poorest recipients instead of making them worse off. A raise to SSI income disregards from $20 a month to $80 a month, to bring the disregard up to the 1972 level after accounting for inflation. [author note: A disregard concerns income a recipient is allowed to earn without losing SSI benefits.] Protections for Medicaid eligibility even if Social Security benefits increase.
3. Opposition to using the budget surplus to give tax cuts to the wealthy. Emphasis that the key to a strong economy is a strong workforce.
4. Budget surpluses should be invested in education, training, health care, housing, child care, and other programs for today's and tomorrow's workforce.

The five reforms to strengthen Social Security for women were:

1. Raise benefits payable to survivors to 75 percent of a married couple's combined benefits.
2. Raise benefits for divorced spouses to 75 percent of the former spouse's benefits (while he is alive). Upon death of the former spouse, widow's benefits of 100 percent should continue. In addition, consider changing the eligibility requirement for divorce benefits to a seven-year marriage minimum and a total of ten years in marriage and work history combined.
3. Raise Social Security benefits for the lowest earners.
4. Remove the early retirement reduction for disabled widows and surviving divorced spouses; also, remove the seven-year limit on benefit eligibility and age fifty provision on widows; and make disabled divorced spouses eligible on the same basis as widows.
5. Value unpaid child care and/or elder care with: a "Family Service Credit"; make changes to the special minimum benefit requirement; allow the lower-earning spouse (or a single parent) a certain number of family care years.

The three solvency recommendations derive from their premise that women must play a significant role in any reforms to Social Security. A bottom line position is "we oppose any attempt to privatize the heart of our nation's social insurance program." To enhance revenue they recommend

- Increasing the maximum wage base subject to the payroll tax for Social Security
- Investing some of the Trust Funds in equities
- If needed, a possible future payroll tax increase

(Task Force, NCWO, September 21, 1999a; in author files).

5. The AFL-CIO remained steady in the fight, for example, sharing with the NCWO a focus group study conducted by Peter D. Hart Research Associates on Social Security privatization (Peter D. Hart Research Associates 2002; in author files) and in 2005 results of their polling on Social Security (NCWO 2005a; in author files). The NCWO and the BPW/USA along with the YWCA had Turner Strategies advise them on talking points and strategies for protecting Social Security (Howard 2005).

6. The symbol links the eye to women because it looks like the pink ribbons for breast cancer fund-raising and awareness. The red ribbon for AIDS Awareness is also echoed in the green dollar ribbon. The task force literature (and the OWL literature, which also used the symbol) explained that anyone can fold a dollar up in this manner and wear it as a statement about protecting Social Security for women.

CHAPTER 7

1. For example, in 2005, twenty-six organizations supporting women's health and access to reproductive services wrote to the U.S. House of Representatives with concerns about the Small Business Fairness Act of 2005 (National Partnership for Women and Girls 2005).

References

Aaron, Henry J., Alan S. Blinder, Alicia H. Munnell, and Peter R. Orszag. 2000. "A New Analysis of Governor Bush's Individual Account Proposal: Implications for Retirement Benefits" (October 16). Institute for America's Future. In author files.

Abelson, Reed. 2010. "In Health Care Reform, Boons for Hospitals and Drug Makers," *New York Times* (March 22): 1–2B.

"Abortion Foes Capitalize on Health Law They Fought." 2010. *State Newspaper* (May 17): 5.

"Abortion Still Threatens Health Care Vote." 2010. *State Newspaper* (March 7).

Abu-Lughod, Lila. 2013. *Do Muslim Women Need Saving?* Cambridge, MA: Harvard University Press.

Acker, Joan. 1995. "Feminist Goals and Organizing Processes." In *Feminist Organizations: Harvest of the New Women's Movement*, Myra Marx Ferree and Patricia Yancey Martin, eds., 137–144. Philadelphia: Temple University Press.

Ackerly, Brooke, and Jacqui True. 2013. "Methods and Methodologies." In *The Oxford Handbook of Gender and Politics*, Georgina Waylen, Karen Celis, Johanna Kantola, and S. Laurel Weldon, eds., 135–159. New York: Oxford University Press.

Adcox, Seanna. 2007. "Bill: Must See an Ultrasound before Abortion," *The Charlotte Observer* (March 17): 6B.

Adichie, Chimamanda Ngozi. 2012. *We Should All Be Feminists*. New York: Random House.

AFL-CIO. n.d. "Fact Sheet: Equal Pay and Retirement," forwarded by Alison Stein, NCWO on December 21, 2004, to third party. In author files.

AFL-CIO Public Policy Department. 2001. "Breaking the Covenant with America's Working Families: Bush Plan to Privatize Social Security Imperils Future Retirement Security for Millions" (February). In author files.

————. 2001. "Social Security Fact Sheet" (February). In author files.

Ainsworth, Scott H., and Thad E. Hall. 2011. *Abortion Politics in Congress: Strategic Incrementalism and Policy Change*. New York: Cambridge University Press.

Alonso-Zaldivar, Ricardo. 2011. "Unusual Coalition Boosts Health Care Overhaul," *State Newspaper* (September 15): 4–5B.

————. 2009. "For Public, Plan Will Hurt before It Helps," *State Newspaper* (December 23): 4.

————. 2009. "Health Bill Has Loopholes: Senate Plan Caps Coverage for Those with Costly Ailments," *State Newspaper* (December 12): 7.

————. 2009. "House Health Care Bill 'Dead on Arrival': S.C.'s Graham Says Bill Won't Get Past Senate," *State Newspaper* (November 9): 4.

Alptraum, Lux. 2017. "bell hooks on the State of Feminism and How to Move Forward under Trump: BUST Interview," *Bust*, Vol. 103 (February/March): 56–59.

Alter, Jonathan. 2009. "Health Care as a Civil Right: Obama Needs to Reframe the Debate," *Newsweek* (August 24 and 31): 33.

Alvarado, Donna. 1992. "Book about Women's Health Still Raising Eyebrows," *State Newspaper* (September 29): 3D.

American Association of University Women (AAUW). 2001a. "Social Security: AAUW Principles for Reform" (January). Washington, DC. In author files.

————. 2001b. "AAUW FAX Sheets: Get the Facts: Privatizing Social Security Will Hurt Women." (May 18).

American Political Science Association. 2004. *American Democracy in an Age of Rising Inequality*. Task Force on Inequality and American Democracy. Washington, DC: APSA.

Ames, Katrine. 1990. "Our Bodies, Their Selves: A Bias against Women in Health Research," *Newsweek* (December 17): 60.

Amnesty International. 2000. "The International Criminal Court: Fact Sheet 7: Ensuring Justice for Women." London, England.

Andersen, Kristi. 1996. *After Suffrage: Women in Partisan and Electoral Politics before the New Deal*. Chicago: University of Chicago Press.

Arnold, Gretchen. 1995. "Dilemmas of Feminist Coalitions: Collective Identity and Strategic Effectiveness in the Battered Women's Movement." In *Feminist Organizations: Harvest of the New Women's Movement*, Myra Marx Ferree and Patricia Yancey Martin, eds., 276–290. Philadelphia: Temple University Press.

Arnold, Kathleen R. 2008. *America's New Working Class: Race, Gender, and Ethnicity in a Biopolitical Age*. University Park: Pennsylvania State University Press.

Arutyunova, Angelika, and Cindy Clark. 2013. "Watering the Leaves, Starving the Roots: The Status of Financing for Women's Rights Organizing and Gender Equality." The Association for Women's Rights in Development (AWID).Toronto, Ontario. www.creativecommons.org.

"Augusta, Ga., to Pay $120,000 to End Suit." 2004. Associated Press (July 30). From NCWO archive.

"Augusta National Golf Club Has Admitted Its First Female Members." 2012. *CNN Breaking News* (August 20).

"Augusta National Golf Club Members List," USATODAY.com. From NCWO archives.

"Background on the Women's Agenda and Council of Presidents," March 21, 1989. NCWO archives. AAUW, Washington, DC. In author files.

Baer, Denise L., and Heidi I. Hartmann. 2014. *Building Women's Political Careers: Strengthening the Pipeline to Higher Office* (May). Washington, DC: Institute for Women's Policy Research.

Baer, Judith. 1999. *Our Lives before the Law: Constructing a Feminist Jurisprudence.* Princeton, NJ: Princeton University Press.

Baker, Dean. 2002. "The Cost of the War on Terrorism and the Cost of Social Security" (February 1). Washington, DC: Center for Economic and Policy Research. In author files.

Baker, Dean, and David Rosnick. 2004. "Briefing Paper: Basic Facts on Social Security and Proposed Benefit Cuts/Privatization" (November 16). Center for Economic and Policy Research. In author files.

Baldez, Lisa. 2014. *Defying Convention: U.S. Resistance to the U.N. Treaty on Women's Rights.* New York: Cambridge University Press.

Bamberger, Michael. 2002. "She Means Business, and So Does He," *Sports Illustrated* (July 29): G35–36, 38.

Banaszak, Lee Ann. 2010. *The Women's Movement Inside and Outside the State.* Cambridge, Cambridge University Press.

———. 1996. *Why Movements Succeed or Fail: Opportunity, Culture and the Struggle for Women's Suffrage.* Princeton, NJ: Princeton University Press.

Banaszak, Lee Ann, Karen Beckwith, and Dieter Rucht, eds. 2003a. *Women's Movements Facing the Reconfigured State.* Cambridge: Cambridge University Press.

———, eds. 2003b. "When Power Relocates: Interactive Changes in Women's Movements and States." In *Women's Movements Facing a Reconfigured State,* Lee Ann Banaszak, Karen Beckwith, and Dieter Rucht, eds., 1–29. Cambridge: Cambridge University Press.

Barakso, Maryann. 2004. *Governing NOW: Grassroots Activism in the National Organization for Women.* Ithaca, NY: Cornell University Press.

Barker, Drucilla K., and Susan F. Feiner. 2004. *Liberating Economics: Feminist Perspectives on Families, Work, and Globalization.* Ann Arbor: University of Michigan Press.

Barnes, Robert. 2007. "Justices Affirm Ban on Partial-Birth Abortions," *State Newspaper* (April 19): 1, 8.

Barnett, Bernice McNair. 1995. "Black Women's Collectivist Movement Organizations: Their Struggles During the 'Doldrums.'" In *Feminist Organizations: Harvest of the New Women's Movement,* Myra Marx Ferree and Patricia Yancey Martin, eds., 199–219. Philadelphia: Temple University Press.

Bassett, Laura. 2012. "The Gender Gap in 2012 Election Aided Obama Win," *Huffington Post,* (November 7). www.huffingtonpost.com/2012/11/07/gender-gap-2012election -Obama.

Basu, Amrita, ed. 2010. *Women's Movements in the Global Era: The Power of Local Feminisms.* Boulder, CO: Westview Press.

Baucus, Max, U. S. Senator; Chairman Committee on Finance. 2002. "News Release," Re: Treasury Secretary O'Neill and Social Security (August 1). In author files.

Baumgartner, Frank R., Jeffrey M. Berry, Marie Hojnacki, David C. Kimball, and Beth L. Leech. 2009. *Lobbying and Policy Change: Who Wins, Who Loses, and Why.* Chicago: University of Chicago Press.

Becker, Jo. 2014. *Forcing the Spring: Inside the Fight for Marriage Equality.* New York: Penguin Press.

Beckwith, Karen. 1986. *American Women and Political Participation: The Impacts of Work, Gender, and Feminism.* Westport, CT: Praeger.

Beechey, Susanne. 2005. "When Feminism is Your Job: Age and Power in Women's Policy Organizations." In *Different Wavelengths*, J. Reger, ed., 117–136. New York: Routledge.

Begley, Sharon. 2009. "Attack! The Truth about Obamacare," *Newsweek* (August 24 and 31): 40–43.

———. 2009. "The Five Biggest Lies in the Health Care Debate," *Newsweek* (September 7): 42–43.

———. 1999. "From Both Sides Now: Women Do Research the Same Way Men Do, but the Questions They Ask Nature May Be Different. Has Feminism Changed Science?" *Newsweek* (June 14): 52–53.

Bejarano, Christina E. 2016. "New Expectations for Latina State Legislative Representation." In *Distinct Identities: Minority Women in U.S. Politics*, Nadia E. Brown and Sarah Allen Gershon, eds., 187–200. New York: Routledge.

———. 2014. *The Latino Gender Gap in U.S. Politics.* New York: Routledge.

———. 2013. *The Latina Advantage: Gender, Race, and Political Success.* Austin: University of Texas Press.

Bejarano, Christina E., Sylvia Manzano, and Celeste Montoya. 2011. "Tracking the Latino Gender Gap: Gender Attitudes across Sex, Borders and Generations," *Politics and Gender*, Vol. 7, No. 4: 521–549.

Bellah, Robert N., Richard Madsen, William M. Sullivan, Ann Swidler, and Steven M. Tipton. 1985. *Habits of the Heart: Individualism and Commitment in American Life.* Berkeley: University of California Press.

Bergan, Daniel E., Alan S. Gerber, Donald P. Green, and Costas Panagopoulas. 2006. "Grassroots Mobilization and Voter Turnout in 2004," *Public Opinion Quarterly*, Vol. 69, No. 5: 760–777.

Bernard, Tara Siegel. 2010. "What the New Legislation Will Mean to Consumers' Wallets," *New York Times* (March 22): 1, 18.

Berry, Jeffrey M. 1999. *The New Liberalism: The Rising Power of Citizen Groups.* Washington, DC: Brookings Institution Press.

Bianchi-Sand, Susan. 1999. "Memo to: Myrna Blyth, Editor in Chief," *Ladies Home Journal.* Re: Social Security (April 13). In author files.

———. 1998. Cover letter for grant request from NCWO (December 7). NCWO archives. Xerox in author files.

———. 1998. "Memorandum Re: National Women's Equality Act" (July 8). From NCWO archives. In author files.

———. 1997. "Draft Letter to C. O. P. Members" (March 11). In author files.

———. 1996. "Memo to: COP Steering Committee; Re: TWO ITEMS" (November 14). In author files.

Billingsley, Andrew. 1999. *Mighty Like a River: The Black Church and Social Reform.* New York: Oxford University Press.

Bland-Watson, Thelma. 1999. (National Committee to Preserve Social Security and Medicare). Letter to Ms. Susan Bianchi-Sand, President, National Committee on Pay Equity and NCWO chair [regarding budget cuts and Medicare] (September 7). In author files.

Blasius, Mark. 1994. *Gay and Lesbian Politics: Sexuality and the Emergence of a New Ethic.* Philadelphia: Temple University Press.

Boiter-Jolley, Annie, and Laura R. Woliver. 2010. "Gender, Labor and Progressive Co-alitions Working the Vote: Grass Roots Mobilization for Registration and Early Voting in the 2008 Election." Paper presented at the American Political Science Convention, Washington, DC.

Boles, Janet K. 1979. *The Politics of the Equal Rights Amendment: Conflict and the Decision Process.* New York: Longman.

Bonk, Kathy. 1996. "Memo to Dixie Horning, Gray Panthers and Susan Bianchi-Sand; Re: Media Strategy for Council of Presidents Policy Activities" (December 2). In author files.

———. 1988. "The Selling of the Gender Gap." In *Politics of the Gender Gap: The Social Construction of Political Influence,* Carol Mueller, ed., 82–101. Newbury Park, CA: Sage.

Bonk, Thomas. 2002. "Her Master Plan: Martha Burk Takes on Augusta, CBS and Hootie as She Seeks to End Discrimination," *Los Angeles Times* (September 5).

Bor, Jonathan. 1991. "Women Slighted by Cardiologists," *State Newspaper* (July 25): 1, 11.

Boston Women's Health Book Collective. 2011. *Our Bodies, Ourselves.* New York: Simon and Schuster.

Boswell, Thomas. 2002. "A Boys' Club Full of Little Rascals," *Washington Post* (September 7): D01.

Boyer, Peter J. 2003. "Club Rules: The Antagonists in the Augusta Controversy Are More Complicated Than You'd Think," *New Yorker* (February 17 and 24).

Bread for the World. 2014. "1,000 Days: The Issue and the Tools," pamphlet. In author files.

Brennan, Christine. 2012. "Will Augusta National Have Its First Female Member?" *USA Today* (March 29).

Briceland-Betts, Deborah, and Lisa M. Maatz, eds. 2000. *Women, Work and Pension: 2000.* OWL: The Voice of Midlife and Older Women (June). Washington, DC: OWL.

Bridge, J. 1997. "Presentation Notes for Council of Presidents" (February). In author files.

Brinson, Claudia Smith. 1992. "Retreat from Legalized Abortion Called Attack on Women's Health," *State Newspaper* (March 27): 6.

Brock, Gillian. 2014. "Reforming Our Taxation Arrangements to Promote Global Gender Justice." In *Gender and Global Justice,* Alison M. Jaggar, ed., 147–167. Malden, MA: Polity Press.

Broder, David. 2009. "Something Good, Something Rotten," *State Newspaper* (December 29): 9.

Brooks, David. 2010. "Democrats Rejoice over General Liberal Project," *State Newspaper* (March 24): 7.

———. 2010. "The Mire of Health Care Reform," *New York Times,* (February 23): 27A.

Brooks, Deborah Jordan. 2013. *He Runs, She Runs: Why Gender Stereotypes Do Not Harm Women Candidates.* Princeton, NJ: Princeton University Press.

Brown, Nadia E. 2014a. "Political Participation of Women of Color: An Intersectional Analysis," *Journal of Women, Politics and Policy,* Vol. 35, No. 4 (October-December): 315–348.

———. 2014b. *Sisters in the Statehouse: Black Women and Legislative Decisionmaking.* New York: Oxford University Press.

Brown, Nadia E., and Sarah Allen Gershon, eds. 2016. *Distinct Identities: Minority Women in U.S. Politics.* New York: Routledge.

Brown, Thomas J. 1998. *Dorothea Dix: New England Reformer.* Cambridge, MA: Harvard University Press.

Brown-Guinyard, Sherral. 2013. "Race, Class, Gender and Linked Fate: A Cross-Sectional Analysis of African American Political Partisanship, 1996 and 2004." Ph.D. dissertation, Department of Political Science. Columbia: University of South Carolina.

Brownmiller, Susan. 1999. *In Our Time: Memoir of a Revolution.* New York: Dell Publishing.

Brubach, Holly. 2003. "Rewriting the Rules," *Golf Digest* (April): 192, 194.

Bruck, Connie. 2017. "A Hollywood Story: Did the Movies Really Make Steve Bannon?" *New Yorker* (May 1): 34–45.

"Budget," from Engaging Women file, NCWO Archives. n.d. In author files.

Bumiller, Kristin. 2008. *In an Abusive State: How Neoliberalism Appropriated the Feminist Movement against Sexual Violence.* Durham, NC: Duke University Press.

Burbank, Matthew, and Melissa Goldsmith. 2010. "Targeting Voters: Citizens and Partisan Get-Out-the-Vote Efforts." Paper presented at the Annual Meeting of the Western Political Science Association, April 1–3, San Francisco, CA.

Burk, Martha. 2016. "The Vanishing Money Trick," *Ms.* (Summer): 411.

———. 2012. "Augusta National, Welcome to the 20th Century," CNN.Com (August 22).

———. 2005a. *Cult of Power: Sex Discrimination in Corporate America and What Can Be Done about It.* New York: Scribner.

———. 2005b. "Green Jacket Cronies," *Wall Street Journal* (April 7). From NCWO archives.

———. 2004. "Memo to: Steering Committee, RE: Follow-Up to Meeting Discussion on Corporate Accountability Project" (September 20). From NCWO archives.

———. 2002. "NCWO Memo to: Gerald A. Reynolds, RE: Single-Sex Notice of Intent Comments" (July 8). From NCWO archives.

———. 2000. "Father Figures," *Ms.* (October/November): 29.

———. 2000. "Lip Service Isn't Enough to Woo Women Voters," *Washington Post* (August 7).

———. 1998. "NOW Invokes Title IX to Fight an All-Girls School," *Ms.* (July/August): 24–25.

———. 1997. "A Family Law Center Closes," *Ms.* (January/February): 24.

———. 1997. "The Sperm Stops Here," *Ms.* (November/December): 18.

———. 1995. "Are You Too Young for a Mammogram?" *Ms.* (September/October): 29–30.

———. 1995. "Why Football Coaches Are Trying to Sack Title IX," *Ms.* (July/August): 93.

Burk, Martha, Heidi Hartmann, Lisa M. Maatz, Terry O'Neill, Joan Kuriansky, and NCWO signatories. 2002. "Letter to: Gerald A. Reynolds, Assistant Secretary for Civil Rights, U.S. Department of Education. Re: Single-Sex Notice of Intent Comments" (July 8). In author files.

Burrell, Barbara. 2010. "Political Parties and Women's Organizations: Bringing Women into the Electoral Arena." In *Gender and Elections: Shaping the Future of American Politics.* Susan J. Carroll and Richard L. Fox, eds., 210–238. New York: Cambridge University Press.

Burris, Roddie. 2009. "Outcry from GOP in S.C.: Lawmakers Assail Senate Health Care Plan," *State Newspaper* (December 22): 1, 5.

Burry, Matt (NUWS). 2004. "Understanding the Funding [Social Security]" (December 17).

Burstein, Paul. 2014. *American Public Opinion, Advocacy, and Policy in Congress.* New York: Cambridge University Press.

Burwell v. Hobby Lobby Stores. U.S. Supreme Court, June 30, 2014.

Byrd, Rudolph P., Johnnetta Betsch Cole, and Beverly Guy-Sheftall, eds. 2009. *I Am Your Sister: Collected and Unpublished Writings of Audre Lorde.* New York: Oxford University Press.

Bystrom, Dianne. 2010. "Advertising, Web Sites, and Media Coverage: Gender and Communication along the Campaign Trail." In *Gender and Elections: Shaping the Future of American Politics,* 2nd ed., Susan J. Carroll and Richard L. Fox, eds., 239–262. New York: Cambridge University Press.

———. 2008. "Confronting Stereotypes and Double Standards in Campaign Communication." In *Legislative Women: Getting Elected, Getting Ahead,* Beth Reingold, ed., 59–83. Boulder, CO: Lynne Rienner.

Camp, Zoe. 2016. "Pollsters and Reporters on the Gender Gap," *Ms.* (Summer): 25.

Campbell, Andrea Louise. 2014. *Trapped in America's Safety Net: One Family's Struggle.* Chicago: University of Chicago Press.

———. 2003. *How Policies Make Citizens: Senior Political Activism and the American Welfare State.* Princeton, NJ: Princeton University Press.

Canaday, Margot. 2009. *The Straight State: Sexuality and Citizenship in Twentieth Century America.* Princeton, NJ: Princeton University Press.

Capers, K. Juree, and Candis Watts Smith. 2016. "Linked Fate at the Intersection of Race, Gender, and Ethnicity." In *Distinct Identities: Minority Women in U.S. Politics,* Nadia E. Brown and Sarah Allen Gershon, eds., 29–48. New York: Routledge.

Carmon, Irin, and Shana Knizhnik. 2015. *Notorious RBG: The Life and Times of Ruth Bader Ginsburg.* New York: Dey St. Imprint of William Morrow.

Carnes, Nicholas. 2013. *White-Collar Government: The Hidden Role of Class in Economic Policy Making.* Chicago: University of Chicago Press.

Carpenter, Daniel, and Colin D. Moore. 2014. "When Canvassers Became Activists: Antislavery Petitioning and the Political Mobilization of American Women," *American Political Science Review,* Vol. 108, No. 3 (August): 479–498.

Carroll, Susan J. 2010. "Voting Choices: The Politics of the Gender Gap." In *Gender and Elections: Shaping the Future of American Politics,* Susan J. Carroll and Richard L. Fox, eds., 117–143. New York: Cambridge University Press.

Carroll, Susan J., and Kelly Dittmar. 2010. "The 2008 Candidacies of Hillary Clinton and Sarah Palin: Cracking the 'Highest, Hardest Glass Ceiling.'" In *Gender and Elections: Shaping the Future of American Politics,* 2nd ed., Susan J. Carroll and Richard L. Fox, eds., 44–77. New York: Cambridge University Press.

Caruso, David B. 2015. "Raise the Minimum Wage? Enforcement's a Problem," *State Newspaper* (August 10): 5.

Castells, Manuel. 2012. *Networks of Outrage and Hope: Social Movements in the Internet Age.* Cambridge, U.K.: Polity.

Cathcart, Thomas, and Daniel Klein. 2007. *Aristotle and an Aardvark Go to Washington: Understanding Political Doublespeak through Philosophy and Jokes.* New York: Harry N. Abrams.

Center for American Women and Politics (CAWP). 2012. "The Gender Gap: Voting Choices in Presidential Elections." Center for American Women and Politics (CAWP), Eagleton Institute of Politics. New Brunswick, NJ: Rutgers University. Accessed April 14, 2016. Available at www.cawp.rutgers.edu/sites/default/files/resources/ggpresvote.pdf.

Chapman Jr., Leroy. 2009. "McMaster, 7 Others to Probe Bill: Health Care: Nebraska's Medicaid Deal," *State Newspaper* (December 23): 1, 6.

Chappell, Louise. 2013. "The State and Governance." In *The Oxford Handbook of Gender and Politics.* Georgina Waylen, Karen Celis, Johanna Kantola, and S. Laurel Weldon, eds., 603–626. New York: Oxford University Press.

Chappell, Marisa. 2008. "Demanding a New Family Wage: Feminist Consensus in the 1970s Full Employment Campaign." In *Feminist Coalitions: Historical Perspectives on Second-Wave Feminism in the United States,* Stephanie Gilmore, ed., 252–284. Urbana: University of Illinois Press.

Chavez, Marisela R. 2010. "We Have a Long, Beautiful History: Chicana Feminist Trajectories and Legacies." In *No Permanent Waves: Recasting Histories of U.S. Feminism,* Nancy A. Hewitt, ed., 77–97. New Brunswick, NJ: Rutgers University Press.

"Church Ladies Project 2008." 2008. In author files.

"Church Ladies Project 2008 Voter Guide." 2008. In author files.

"The Church Ladies Project—Leadership by Women of Faith," n.d. NCWO archives. Xerox in author files.

Clark, Jeanne C. K. 2016. "This Is What a Revolution Looks Like," *Ms.* (Summer): 34–38.

Clark, Septima Poinsette, and Cynthia Stokes Brown. 1986. *Ready from Within: Septima Clark and the Civil Rights Movement.* Navarro, CA: Wild Trees Press.

Clarke, Adele E. 1998. *Disciplining Reproduction: Modernity, American Life Sciences, and the Problems of Sex.* Berkeley: University of California Press.

Clemens, Elizabeth S. 1997. *The People's Lobby: Organizational Innovation and the Rise of Interest Group Politics in the United States, 1890–1925.* Chicago: University of Chicago Press.

Clift, Elayne, ed. 2005. *Women, Philanthropy, and Social Change: Visions for a Just Society.* Medford, MA: Tufts University Press.

Clift, Eleanor. 1993. "The Gender Wars: Inside the White House, It Was the Women against the Men over Mental Health Benefits," *Newsweek* (October 4): 50.

Coates, Ta-Nehisi. 2015. *Between the World and Me.* New York: Spiegel and Grau.

Cohn, Victor. 1992. "How Can We Fix a Broken System? Paying for Health Care Reform Is Only the First Hurdle," *Washington Post National Weekly Edition* (February 3–9): 6–7.

Cole, Elizabeth R. 2008. "Coalitions as a Model for Intersectionality: From Practice to Theory," *Sex Roles,* Vol. 59 (September): 443–453.

Cole, Johnnetta Betsch, and Beverly Guy-Sheftall. 2003. *Gender Talk: The Struggle for Women's Equality in African American Communities.* New York: Ballantine Books.

Coles, Robert. 2000. *Lives of Moral Leadership: Men and Women Who Have Made a Difference.* New York: Random House.

Collins, Patricia Hill. 2013. *On Intellectual Activism*. Philadelphia: Temple University Press.

———. 2000. *Black Feminist Thought: Knowledge, Consciousness, and the Politics of Empowerment*. New York: Routledge.

"Concessions: Who Got What?" 2009. *State Newspaper* (December 22): 4.

Congressional Caucus for Women's Issues. 1991. "The Women's Health Equity Act of 1991" (February). In author files.

Conway, M. Margaret. 2008. "The Gender Gap: A Comparison across Racial and Ethnic Groups." In *Voting the Gender Gap*, Lois Duke Whitaker, ed., 170–184. Urbana: University of Illinois Press.

Conway, M. Margaret, David Ahern, and Gertrude Steuernagel. 1999. *Women and Public Policy: A Revolution in Progress*. Washington, DC: CQ Press.

Conway, M. Margaret, Gertrude A. Steuernagel, and David W. Ahern. 2005. *Women and Political Participation: Cultural Change in the Political Arena*, 2nd ed. Washington, DC: CQ Press.

Correspondents of *The New York Times*. 2005. *Class Matters*. New York: Henry Holt.

Corrigan, Rose. 2014. "Why Feminist Theory Matters for Feminist Practice: The Case of Rape Response," *Politics and Gender*, Vol. 10, No. 2: 280–284.

———. 2013. *Up against a Wall: Rape Reform and the Failure of Success*. New York: New York University Press.

Costain, Anne N. 1998. "Women Lobby Congress." In *Social Movements and American Political Institutions,* Anne Costain and Andrew McFarland, eds., 185–198. Lanham, MD: Rowman and Littlefield.

———. 1992. *Inviting Women's Rebellion: A Political Process Interpretation of the American Women's Movement*. Baltimore, MD: Johns Hopkins University Press.

———. 1982. "Representing Women: The Transition from Social Movement to Interest Group." In *Women, Power, and Policy*, Ellen Boneparth, ed., 19–37. New York: Pergamon Press.

———. 1980. "The Struggle for a National Women's Lobby: Organizing a Diffuse Interest," *Western Political Quarterly*, Vol. 33 (December): 476–491.

Cott, Nancy F. 1987. *The Grounding of Modern Feminism*. New Haven, CT: Yale University Press.

Cowley, Geoffrey. 1993. "What High Tech Can't Accomplish: Beyond the Clinton Plan," *Newsweek* (October 4): 60–63.

"Cracker Barrel Old County [*sic*] Store." 2004. *Washington Post* (August 12). From NCWO archives.

Crary, David. 2006. "Vote on Ban of Virtually All Abortions Confronts South Dakotans," *State Newspaper* (October 22): 1, 4D.

Crenshaw, Kimberle. 2015. "Black Girls Matter: When National Initiatives to Help Youth of Color Focus Only on Boys, the Needs of Our Most Vulnerable Young Women Become Invisible," *Ms.* (Spring): 26–29.

———. 1991. "Mapping the Margins: Intersectionality, Identity Politics, and Violence Against Women of Color," *Stanford Law Review* 43 (6): 1241–1279.

———. 1989. "Demarginalizing the Intersection of Race and Sex: A Black Feminist Critique of Antidiscrimination Doctrine, Feminist Theory and Antiracist Politics," *University of Chicago Legal Forum* 1989: 139–167.

Critchlow, Donald T. 2011. *The Conservative Ascendancy: How the Republican Right Rose to Power in Modern America*, 2nd ed. Lawrence: University of Kansas Press.

———. 2005. *Phyllis Schlafly and Grassroots Conservatism: A Woman's Crusade.* Princeton, NJ: Princeton University Press.

Crum, Elisabeth, and Ashley English. 2010. "IWPR Launches Roundtable Series on Women and the Economy," *Institute for Women's Policy Research Quarterly Newsletter* (Winter/Spring): 1, 4.

"Dan River Announced." 2004. *Washington Post* (August 12). From NCWO archives.

Dart, Bob. 2002. "Women's Leader Shakes Things Up," *State Newspaper* (September 14): 3, 5C.

Davenport, Jim. 2009. "'Sleazy Politics' Driving Senate's Health Care Votes, Graham Charges," *State Newspaper* (December 22): 4.

Davison, Ciarra. 2017. "Feminist Leaders Come Together to #StopTrumpcare." *Ms. Blog. Ms.*, June 23. http://msmagazine.com/blog/2017/06/23/feminist-leaders-come-together-stoptrumpcare/.

Dawson, Michael C. 2001. *Black Visions: The Roots of Contemporary African-American Political Ideologies.* Chicago: University of Chicago Press.

———. 1994. *Behind the Mule: Race and Class in African-American Politics.* Princeton, NJ: Princeton University Press.

Deckman, Melissa. 2016. *Tea Party Women: Mama Grizzlies, Grassroots Leaders, and the Changing Face of the American Right.* New York: New York University Press.

Deibel, Mary. 2002. "How Career Change Can Imperil Social Security," *Seattle Post-Intelligencer* (July 5).

———. 2002. "Why Women Still Rely So Much on Federal Safety Net," *Seattle Post-Intelligencer* (July 5).

Democratic Staff. 2001a. "Diverting 'Just 2 Percent' of Payroll Tax Cuts Revenue by 16 Percent." Prepared by the Office of Congressman Robert T. Matsui and Democratic Staff of the House Committee on Ways and Means (August 2). In author files.

———. 2001b. "Five Problems with Privatizing Social Security." House Ways and Means Committee (June). In author files.

"Democrats Dropping Medicare Expansion?" 2009. *State Newspaper* (December 15).

"Dems Stop Courting Abortion Foes for Health Care Votes." 2010. *State Newspaper* (March 12): 6.

"Dems Sweeten Bill; Showdown on Sunday." 2010. *State Newspaper* (March 19): 1.

Denbow, Jennifer M. 2015. *Governed through Choice: Autonomy, Technology, and the Politics of Representation.* New York: New York University Press.

DeRobles, Gloria. 1994. "Letter to Susan Bianchi-Sand" (May 4). National Committee for Responsive Philanthropy.

Dhamoon, Rita Kaur. 2013. "Feminisms." In *The Oxford Handbook of Gender and Politics*, Georgina Waylen, Karen Cellis, Johanna Kantola, and S. Laurel Weldon, eds., 88–110. New York: Oxford University Press.

Diaz, Jaime. 2003. "Welcome to the Bizarro Masters," *Golf Digest* (April): 127–130, 132, 134–135.

Dicker, Rory, and Alison Piepmeir. 2003. *Catching a Wave: Reclaiming Feminism for the 21st Century.* Boston: North Eastern University Press.

Dittmar, Kelly. 2015. *Navigating Gendered Terrain: Stereotypes and Strategy in Political Campaigns.* Philadelphia: Temple University Press.

Dodson, Debra L. 2006. *The Impact of Women in Congress*. New York: Oxford University Press.

———. 2001. "Acting for Women: Is What Legislators Say, What They Do?" In *The Impact of Women in Public Office*, Susan J. Carroll, ed., 225–242. Bloomington: Indiana University Press.

———. 1998. "Elections and the Politics of Reproduction: Implications for 1998: Highlights." Center for the American Woman and Politics, Upper Saddle River, NJ: Rutgers State University of New Jersey. Brochure in author files.

Dolan, Julie, Melissa Deckman, and Michele L. Swers. 2007. *Women and Politics: Paths to Power and Political Influence*. NJ: Prentice Hall.

Dolan, Chris J., Angela Ledford, and Laura R. Woliver. 2001. "The South Carolina Confederate Flag: The Politics of Race and Citizenship," *Politics and Policy*, Vol. 29, No. 4 (December): 708–730.

Dolan, Kathleen. 2008. "Women as Candidates in American Politics: The Continuing Impact of Sex and Gender." In *Political Women and American Democracy*, Christina Wolbrecht, Karen Beckwith, and Lisa Baldez, eds., 110–127. New York: Cambridge University Press.

Dolgon, Corey. 2017. *Kill It to Save It: An Autopsy of Capitalism's Triumph over Democracy*. Bristol, U.K.: Policy Press.

Donegan, Lawrence. 2004. "G2: Women: Club Culture: Today Laura Davies Will Make History as She Becomes the First Woman to Play on the European Men's Tour," *The Guardian* (London, U.K.; February 12). From NCWO Archives.

Dowd, Maureen. 2009. "Oval Man Cave," *New York Times* (October 28): 29.

Dowe, Pearl K. Ford. 2016. "African American Women: Leading Ladies of Liberal Politics." In *Distinct Identities: Minority Women in U.S. Politics*, Nadia E. Brown and Sarah Allen Gershon, eds., 49–62. New York: Routledge.

Drash, Wayne, and Jessica Ravitz. 2012. "Vagina Enters Stage Left—Or Is It Right?" CNN.com (March 28).

Duerst-Lahti, Georgia. 2010. "Presidential Elections: Gendered Space and the Case of 2008." In *Gender and Elections: Shaping the Future of American Politics*, 2nd ed., Susan J. Carroll and Richard L. Fox, eds., 13–43. New York: Cambridge University Press.

Dunham, Richard S. 2010. "What Follows Health Care Bill? Political Effects Uncertain," *State Newspaper* (March 23): 1, 6.

Durazo, Ana Clarissa Rojas. 2007. "We Were Never Meant to Survive: Fighting Violence against Women and the Fourth World War." In *The Revolution Will Not Be Funded: Beyond the Non-Profit Industrial Complex*, Incite! Women of Color against Violence, eds., 113–128. Cambridge, MA: South End Press.

Edelman, Murray. 1977. *Political Language: Words That Succeed and Policies That Fail*. New York: Academic Press.

Editorial. 2010. "Health Care Reform, at Last," *New York Times* (March 22): 24.

———. 2009. "The Ban on Abortion Coverage," *New York Times* (November 9): 34.

Ehrenreich, Barbara. 2014. "Time to Wake Up: Stop Blaming Poverty on the Poor." In *The Shriver Report: A Woman's Nation Pushes Back from the Brink; A Study by Maria Shriver and the Center for American Progress*, Olivia Morgan and Karen Skelton, eds., 36–39. New York: Palgrave MacMillan.

———. 2001. *Nickel and Dimed: On (Not) Getting by in America*. New York: Metropolitan Books.

Ehrenreich, Barbara, and Arlie Russell Hochschild, eds. 2002. *Global Woman: Nannies, Maids, and Sex Workers in the New Economy.* New York: Henry Holt.

Eisler, Riane, and Kimberly Otis. 2014. "Unpaid and Undervalued Care Work Keeps Women on the Brink." In *The Shriver Report: A Woman's Nation Pushes Back from the Brink; A Study by Maria Shriver and the Center for American Progress.* Olivia Morgan and Karen Skelton, eds., 67–68. New York: Palgrave MacMillan.

Eliasoph, Nina. 1998. *Avoiding Politics: How Americans Produce Apathy in Everyday Life.* New York: Cambridge University Press.

Emails received by AugustaDiscriminates.org. From NCWO archives. In author files.

English, Ashley, and Sunhwa Lee. 2010. "Who Are Social Security Beneficiaries?" IWPR. Fact Sheet (March).

————. 2010. "Women and Social Security: Benefit Types and Eligibility," IWPR. Briefing Paper (March).

Enloe, Cynthia. 2013. *Seriously! Investigating Crashes and Crises as if Women Mattered.* Berkeley: University of California Press.

————. 2007. *Globalization and Militarism: Feminists Make the Link,* 2nd ed. Lanham, MA: Rowman and Littlefield.

Entmacher, Joan. 2005. "Not Just Your Mom's Retirement: Why Privatizing Social Security Threatens Women and Their Families at All Stages of Their Lives: Presentation to Coalition on Human Needs" (January 7). In author files.

————. 2005. "Pitfalls of Privatization," Statement of Joan Entmacher, vice president and director, National Women's Law Center, for the National Committee to Preserve Social Security and Medicare (January 14). In author files.

————. 2005. "Proposals to Achieve Sustainable Solvency, with and without Personal Accounts." Testimony of Joan Entmacher, vice president for Family Economic Security, National Women's Law Center. To U.S. Senate Committee on Finance (April 26). In author files.

Entmacher, Joan, and Nancy Duff Campbell (National Women's Law Center), Heidi Hartmann (Institute for Women's Policy Research and Task Force on Social Security, National Council of Women's Organizations). 1999. Memo to: Gene Sperling, assistant to the president for Economic Policy and director, National Economic Council. Re: USA Accounts: Issues for Women (February 11). In author files.

The ERA Campaigner. 2001. Issue #5 (July).

Erdreich, Sarah. 2013. *Generation Roe: Inside the Future of the Pro-Choice Movement.* New York: Seven Stories Press.

Erickson, Jan. 2009. "Health Care Reform—Will the System Still Be Sick?" *National NOW Times,* Vol. 41, No. 1 (Spring): 7.

————. 2005. "Summary of the NCWO Social Security TF [Task Force] Meeting" (January 10). In author files.

Espo, David. 2009. "Compromise Raises Dems' Hopes on Health Care Overhaul," *State Newspaper* (December 10): 4.

————. 2009. "Dean's Prescription: Kill Health Bill and Start Over," *State Newspaper* (December 18): 4.

————. 2009. "Health Bill Survives Key Test on Medicare Cuts," *State Newspaper* (December 4): 14.

————. 2009. "Senate Sinks Public Option," *State Newspaper* (December 17): 4.

Espo, David, and Sam Hananel. 2010. "Tax Deal Seen as Breakthrough on Health Bill," *State Newspaper* (January 15): 10.

Estes, Carroll, Terry O'Neill, and Heidi Hartmann. 2012. *Breaking the Social Security Glass Ceiling: A Proposal to Modernize Women's Benefits* (May 11). Washington, DC: Institute for Women's Policy Research .

Evans, Sara. 1979. *Personal Politics: The Roots of Women's Liberation in Civil Rights and the New Left*. New York: Alfred A. Knopf.

Everett, Jana, and Sue Ellen M. Charlton. 2014. *Women Navigating Globalization: Feminist Approaches to Development*. Lanham, MA: Rowman and Littlefield.

Ewig, Christina, and Myra Marx Ferree. 2013. "Feminist Organizing: What's Old, What's New? History, Trends, and Issues." In *The Oxford Handbook of Gender and Politics*, Georgina Waylen, Karen Celis, Johanna Kantola, and S. Laurel Weldon, eds., 437–461. New York: Oxford University Press.

"Executive Summary," n.d. (on social security and women). In author files.

"Factors Help Avoid Hysterectomy," 1994. *State Newspaper* (October 24): 3.

Facts about Women and Social Security. n.d. Flyer at May 1999 National Council of Women's Organizations meeting.

Faludi, Susan. 2001. "Don't Get the Wrong Message," *Newsweek* (January 8): 56.

"Federal Reserve Fines Citigroup $70M." 2004. *USA Today* (May 28). From NCWO archives.

"'Feet on the Ground. Not Backing Down!': On Trump's First Day in Office, Women Delivered a Huge Message—Too Massive to Ignore" 2017. *Ms.*, Vol. 27, No. 1 (Spring):6–27.

"Female Executives Don't Get Equal Pay." 2013. *State Newspaper* (August 14).

"The Female Face of Foreclosure: [speaker] Bios." 2008. (July 25). In author files.

Feminist Daily News Wire. 2005. "Opposition to Alito Nomination Continues to Grow," from NCWO website (November 7). In author files.

Feminist Majority Foundation. 2001. "Afghan Women and Children Freedom Act of 2001: Fact Sheet."

———. 2000. "Emergency Assistance for Afghan Women and Girls" (November 28). Letter.

Ferguson, Doug. 2012. "Augusta National Adds Two Female Members," *State Newspaper* (August 21): 1, 2B.

———. 2012. "Augusta National Announces Inclusion of Women," Golf Channel (August 20).

———. 2002. "Augusta National Won't Yield: Johnson Says Club Won't Admit Women by 2003 Masters," *State Newspaper* (November 12): 1A.

———. 2002. "Johnson: 'We're Right': Augusta Chairman Says Club Has No Timetable to Admit Woman Member," *State Newspaper* (November 12): 1, 6C.

———. 2002. "'There Will Always Be a Masters,' Chairman Says," *State Newspaper* (November 12): 6C.

Ferguson, Lucy. 2013. "Gender, Work, and the Sexual Division of Labor." In *The Oxford Handbook of Gender and Politics*, Georgina Waylen, Karen Celis, Johanna Kantola, and S. Laurel Weldon, eds., 337–361. New York: Oxford University Press.

Ferguson, Michaele L. 2017. "Trump Is a Feminist, and Other Cautionary Tales for Our Neoliberal Age," *Theory and Event*, Vol. 20, No. 1 (January): 53–67.

Ferree, Myra Marx, and Patricia Yancey Martin. 1995a. "Doing the Work of the Movement: Feminist Organizations." In *Feminist Organizations: Harvest of the New Women's Movement,* Myra Marx Ferree and Patricia Yancey Martin, eds., 3–23. Philadelphia: Temple University Press.

———, eds. 1995b. *Feminist Organizations: Harvest of the New Women's Movement.* Philadelphia: Temple University Press.

Fierst, Edith U. 1999a. "Minutes of Meeting of the Technical Subcommittee of the Task Force on Social Security of the National Council of Women's Organizations" (June 30). In author files.

———. 1999b. "Minutes of Meeting of Technical Committee of Social Security Task Force of National Council of Women's Organizations" (June 14). In author files.

———. 1999c. "Minutes of the Technical Subcommittee of the Task Force on Social Security of the National Council of Women's Organizations" (June 1). In author files.

Fineman, Howard. 2001. "Move Over, Gray Panthers: Suddenly, Social Security Matters to Baby Boomers," *Newsweek* (September 10): 29.

Finney, Nikky. 2011. *Head Off and Split: Poems.* Evanston, IL: Triquarterly Books/ Northwestern University Press.

Flammang, Janet A. 1997. *Women's Political Voice: How Women Are Transforming the Practice and Study of Politics.* Philadelphia: Temple University Press.

Flexner, Eleanor. 1974. *Century of Struggle: The Woman's Rights Movement in the United States.* New York: Atheneum.

Ford, Lynn E. 2010. *Women and Politics: The Pursuit of Equality.* Boston: Houghton Mifflin.

Fosl, Catherine. 2002. *Subversive Southerner: Anne Braden and the Struggle for Racial Justice in the Cold War South.* Lexington: University Press of Kentucky.

Fox, Richard L. 2010. "Congressional Elections: Women's Candidacies and the Road to Gender Parity." In *Gender and Elections: Shaping the Future of American Politics,* 2nd ed., Susan J. Carroll and Richard L. Fox, eds., 187–209. New York: Cambridge University Press.

Fox, Richard L., and Jennifer L. Lawless. 2014. "Uncovering the Origins of the Gender Gap in Political Ambition," *American Political Science Review,* Vol. 108, No. 3 (August): 499–519.

Foxworth, Laura. 2014. "The Sacred Is Political." Ph.D. dissertation. March. Department of History. Columbia: University of South Carolina.

"A Fragile Deal on Abortion," 2009. *State Newspaper* (December 22): 4.

Franklin, John Hope, and Alfred A. Moss Jr. 1994. *From Slavery to Freedom: A History of African Americans,* 7th ed. New York: Alfred A. Knopf.

Fredrickson, Caroline. 2015. *Under the Bus: How Working Women Are Being Run Over.* New York: New Press.

Freedman, Estelle. 2002. *No Turning Back: The History of Feminism and the Future of Women.* New York: Ballantine Books.

Freeman, Jo. 2000. *A Room at a Time: How Women Entered Party Politics.* Lanham, MD: Rowman and Littlefield.

———. 1995. "From Seed to Harvest: Transformations of Feminist Organizations and Scholarship." In *Feminist Organizations: Harvest of the New Women's Movement,* Myra Marx Ferree and Patricia Yancey Martin, eds., 397–408. Philadelphia: Temple University Press.

Fridkin, Kim L., and Patrick J. Kenney. 2014. "How the Gender of U.S. Senators Influences People's Understanding and Engagement in Politics," *Journal of Politics*, Vol. 76, No. 4 (October): 1017–1031.

Fried, Marlene Gerber. 2003. "Introduction: Abortion in the U.S. Today, Legal but Inaccessible." In *Legal but Out of Reach: Stories from the National Network of Abortion Funds.*, 4th ed. Boston, MA: National Network of Abortion Funds.

Friedman, Thomas L. 2003. "Give It Up, Hootie," *Golf Digest* (April): 190, 192.

Fulcher, Juley. 2000. "Legislative Update: A Summary of the Violence against Women Act, 2000": National Coalition against Domestic Violence, and the National Task Force to End Sexual and Domestic Violence against Women. In author files.

Galinsky, Ellen, James T. Bond, and Eve Tahmincioglu, Families and Work Institute. 2014. In *The Shriver Report: A Woman's Nation Pushes Back from the Brink; A Study by Maria Shriver and the Center for American Progress*, Olivia Morgan and Karen Skelton, eds., 287–315. New York: Palgrave MacMillan.

Gallo, William. 2003. "A Masters Like No Other," *Sports Illustrated* (April 8).

Gandy, Kim (president, NOW). 2002. "Executive Summary of NOW's Comments on Notice of Proposed Rulemaking Regarding Single-Sex Classes and Schools" (July). From NCWO archives.

Gandy, Kim, and Jan Erickson. 2000. Government Relations Report: for NOW Board of Directors Meeting (November 20).

Garcia Bedolla, Lisa, and Melissa R. Michelson. 2012. *Mobilizing Inclusion: Transforming the Electorate through Get-Out-the-Vote Campaigns*. New Haven, CT: Yale University Press.

Garland, Susan B. 2000. "Making Social Security More Women-Friendly," *Business Week* (May 22): 103–104.

Gawande, Atul. 2006. "The Score: How Childbirth Went Industrial," *New Yorker* (October 9): 58–67.

Gelb, Joyce. 1995. "Feminist Organizations Success and the Politics of Engagement." In *Feminist Organizations: Harvest of the New Women's Movement*, Myra Marx Ferree and Patricia Yancey Martin, eds., 128–134. Philadelphia: Temple University Press.

"The Gender Gap, Then and Now: A *Ms.* Conversation with Eleanor Smeal," 2016. *Ms.* (Summer): 24–25.

"The Gender Gap: Voting Choices in Presidential Elections." 2008. *Center for American Women and Politics (CAWP)*. Eagleton Institute of Politics, New Brunswick, NJ: Rutgers University. Accessed November 2010. Available at http://www.cawp .rutgers.edu/fast_facts/voters/documents/GGPresVote.pdf.

"General Electric Violated." 2004. *Washington Post* (September 24): E2. From NCWO Archives.

Gerontological Society of America. 1999. "Press Briefing Announcement and Agenda: Older Women Are Being Ignored in Social Security Reform Packages" (July 1). In author files.

Gertz, M. 2010. "Breitbart Brings ACORN Videos Lie to MSNBC," (January 28). Available at http://mediamatters.org/research/2010/01/28/breitbart-brings-acorn-videos -lie-to-msnbc/159744.

Gertzog, Irwin N. 2004. *Women and Power on Capitol Hill*. Boulder, CO: Lynne Reinner.

———. 1984. *Congressional Women: Their Recruitment, Treatment, and Behavior.* New York: Praeger.

Giddings, Paula. 2002. *In Search of Sisterhood: Delta Sigma Theta and the Challenge of the Black Sorority Movement.* New York: Amistad, HarperCollins (first published in 1988 by Harper/Collins, New York).

———. 1984. *When and Where I Enter: The Impact of Black Women on Race and Sex in America.* New York: Harper and Row.

Gifford, Carolyn De Swarte, ed. 1995. *Writing Out My Heart: Selections from the Journals of Frances E. Willard, 1855–96.* Urbana: University of Illinois Press.

Gilens, Martin, and Benjamin I. Page. 2014. "Testing Theories of American Politics: Elites, Interest Groups, and Average Citizens," *Perspectives on Politics*, Vol. 12, No. 3 (September): 564–581.

Gilkes, Cheryl Townsend. 2001. *If It Wasn't for the Women . . . : Black Women's Experience and Womanist Culture in Church and Community.* Maryknoll, NY: Orbis Books.

Gillespie, Bob. 2012. "The Man Who Saved Augusta National: Former Masters Chairman Hootie Johnson," *State Newspaper* (May 6): 1, 7C.

———. 2012. "Women in the Club? Hootie Is Smiling," *State Newspaper* (August 21): 1, 4A.

———. 2009. "Even the Scalpers Are Taking a Hit: Economy Drives Down Ticket, Rental, Tee Time Prices, Demand," *State Newspaper* (April 8): 1, 10A.

———. 2006. "Payne Braces for Sudden Impact: Issues That Confronted Johnson and That Often Cast Him as a Lightning Rod Fall to a New Leader," *State Newspaper* (May 9): 1, 5C.

———. 2002. "Johnson Has Heart Surgery," *State Newspaper* (September 14): 5C.

Gillibrand, Kirsten. 2014. *Off the Sidelines: Raise Your Voice, Change the World.* New York: Ballantine Books.

Gilligan, Carol. 2014. "When We Were 9, We Were Honest." In *The Shriver Report: A Woman's Nation Pushes Back from the Brink; A Study by Maria Shriver and the Center for American Progress*, Olivia Morgan, and Karen Skelton, eds., 28–31. New York: Palgrave MacMillan.

———. 2011. *Joining the Resistance.* Cambridge, U.K.: Polity Press.

Gilligan, Carol, and David A. J. Richards. 2009. *The Deepening Darkness: Patriarchy, Resistance, and Democracy's Future.* New York: Cambridge University Press.

Gilmore, Glenda Elizabeth. 2008. *Defying Dixie: The Radical Roots of Civil Rights, 1919–1950.* New York: W. W. Norton.

———. 1996. *Gender and Jim Crow: Women and the Politics of White Supremacy in North Carolina, 1896–1920.* Chapel Hill: University of North Carolina Press.

Gilmore, Ruth Wilson. 2007. "In the Shadow of the Shadow State." In *The Revolution Will Not Be Funded: Beyond the Non-Profit Industrial Complex*, Incite! Women of Color against Violence, eds., 41–52. Cambridge, MA: South End Press.

Gilmore, Stephanie. 2008a. "Thinking about Feminist Coalitions." In *Feminist Coalitions: Historical Perspectives on Second-Wave Feminism in the United States*, Stephanie Gilmore, ed., 1–18. Urbana: University of Illinois Press.

———, ed. 2008b. *Feminist Coalitions: Historical Perspectives on Second-Wave Feminism in the United States.* Urbana: University of Illinois Press.

Goertz, Gary, and Amy G. Mazur, eds. 2008. *Politics, Gender, and Concepts: Theory and Methodology.* Cambridge: Cambridge University Press.

Gogoi, Pallavi, and Nedra Pickler. 2011. "BofA [Bank of America] to Pay $335 Million Settlement: Countrywide Fair-Lending Probe," *State Newspaper* (December 22): B4.

"Going to a Female Doc." 1993. *Newsweek* (August 23): 45.

Goodnough, Abby. 2009. "Rep. Kennedy and Bishop in Bitter Rift on Abortion," *New York Times* (November 12): 14.

Goodstein, Laurie. 2012. "Church Battle over Coverage Well Planned: Ruling on Birth Control Galvanized Bishops," *New York Times* (February 10): 1, 16.

"GOP Candidates Push for Privatizing Social Security," 2011. *State Newspaper* (September 18): A5.

Gordon, Linda. 1994. *Pitied but Not Entitled: Single Mothers and the History of Welfare 1890–1935.* New York: Free Press.

Gorney, Cynthia. 1998. "Punishment: The Struggle to Rewrite the Nation's Abortion Laws," *San Francisco Examiner Magazine* (February 10): 13, 22–25.

Goss, Kristin A. 2013. *The Paradox of Gender Equality: How American Women's Groups Gained and Lost Their Public Voice.* Ann Arbor: University of Michigan Press.

Goss, Kristin A., and Michael T. Heaney. 2010. "Organizing Women as *Women*: Hybridity and Grassroots Collective Action in the 21st Century," *Perspectives on Politics*, Vol. 8, No. 1 (March): 27–52.

Goss, Kristin A., and Theda Skocpol. 2006. "The Impact of Feminism on American Politics." In *Gender and Social Capital*, Brenda O'Neill and Elisabeth Gidengil, eds., 323–356. New York: Routledge.

Gosselin, Abigail. 2014. "Global Gender Justice and Mental Disorders." In *Gender and Global Justice*, Alison M. Jaggar, ed., 100–118. Malden, MA: Polity Press.

Grape, Nancy. 2002. "Golf Club's Ban on Women an Outrage," *Maine Sunday Telegram* (September 8): 3C.

Gravel, Tara. 2003. "U.S. Open: Then and Now," *Golf Magazine* (June): 191–192.

"The Great Debate: The Masters 2003." 2003. *Golf Digest* (April): 187.

Green, Donald P., and Alan S. Gerber. 2008. *Get Out the Vote: How to Increase Voter Turnout,* 2nd ed. Washington, DC: Brookings Institution Press.

Greenblatt, Alan. 2006. "Challengers to Abortion: States Are the Main Forum for Debate on Reproductive Issues, and the Trend Is for Greater Restriction," *Governing* (February): 16.

Gregory, Janice M., Thomas N. Bethell, Virginia P. Reno, and Benjamin W. Veghte. 2011. "Strengthening Social Security for the Long Run," *Social Security Brief.* National Academy of Social Insurance. No. 35 (November).

Grossman, Matt. 2012. *The Not-So-Special Interests: Interest Groups, Public Representation and American Governance.* Palo Alto, CA: Stanford University Press.

Grossman, Matt, and David A. Hopkins. 2016. *Asymmetric Politics: Ideological Republicans and Group Interest Democrats.* New York: Oxford University Press.

Guillouci, Stephanie, and William Cordery. 2007. "Fundraising Is Not a Dirty Word: Community-Based Economic Strategies for the Long Haul." In *The Revolution Will Not Be Funded: Beyond the Non-Profit Industrial Complex*, Incite! Women of Color against Violence, eds., 107–111. Cambridge, MA: South End Press.

Gutner, Toddi, with Mark Hyman. 2002. "More Heat on the Masters," *BusinessWeek* (August 12): 75.

Hacker, Andrew. 1992. *Two Nations: Black and White, Separate, Hostile, Unequal.* New York: Ballantine Books.

Hacker, Jacob S. 2008. *The Great Risk Shift: The New Economic Insecurity and the Decline of the American Dream*, revised and expanded ed. New York: Oxford University Press.

"Hall of Hypocrisy: An NCWO Project," from NCWO website. Xerox in author files.

Hall, Jacqueline Dowd. 2005. "The Long Civil Rights Movement and the Political Uses of the Past," *Journal of American History*, Vol. 91 (March): 1233–1263.

———. 1979. *Revolt against Chivalry: Jessie Daniel Ames and the Women's Campaign against Lynching.* New York: Columbia University Press.

Hall, Kevin G., and David Lightman. 2010. "With Social Security Proposal, Deficit Panel Touches Third Rail," *State Newspaper* (November 11): A10.

Halva-Neubauer, Glen A., Sara L. Zeigler, and Mark Zientek. 2011. "Unexpected Victories: Explaining Pro-Life Successes in the 2010 Health Care Bill," A paper presented at the 2011 Southern Political Science Convention.

Hamilton, Melinda. 2016. "LWV Gun Safety Coalition," *SC Voter* [LWV South Carolina newsletter] (Fall): 7.

Hancock, Ange-Mari. 2016. *Intersectionality: An Intellectual History.* New York: Oxford University Press.

———. 2011. *Solidarity Politics for Millennials: A Guide to Ending the Oppression Olympics.* New York: Palgrave McMillan.

———. 2004. *Politics of Disgust: The Public Identity of the Welfare Queen.* New York: NYU Press.

Hansen, Mark. 2007. "Following the Beat of the Ban: After a Loss in South Dakota, Many in the Anti-Abortion Movement Reassess Their Legal Strategy," *ABA Journal* (February): 32–37, 52.

Hanson, Jessica, and Anna Stanley. 2001. "Slavery, Violence against Women Continue Worldwide," *National NOW Times*, Vol. 33, No. 1 (Spring): 6.

Harder, Sarah. 1991. "The Council of Presidents of U.S. Women's Organizations" (April 10). In author files.

Harkness, Peter A. 2012. "Washington's Other 1-Percent Problem," *Governing* (September): 16–17.

Harris, Fredrick C. 1999. *Something Within: Religion in African-American Political Activism.* New York: Oxford University Press.

Harris, Gardiner. 2009. "Maine Finds a Health Care Fix Elusive," *New York Times* (November 11): 16, 20.

Harrison, Cynthia. 2008. "Creating a National Feminist Agenda: Coalition Building in the 1970s." In *Feminist Coalitions: Historical Perspectives on Second-Wave Feminism in the United States.* Stephanie Gilmore, ed., 19–47. Urbana: University of Illinois Press.

———. 1998. *On Account of Sex: The Politics of Women's Issues 1945–1968.* Berkeley: University of California Press.

Hartmann, Heidi. 2014. "Enhancing Social Security for Women and Other Vulnerable Americans: What the Experts Say" (June). Washington, DC: Institute for Women's Policy Research.

———. 2001. "Public Investment, Public Trust: Letter to the Editor," *Washington Post* (July 2).

————. 2000. "Vice President's Social Security Proposal Follows Recent Report by IWPR and NCWO," *Institute for Women's Policy Research Quarterly Newsletter* (Spring): 1, 4–5.

————. 1999a. (NCWO Women and Social Security Task Force chair). "Memo to Participants of the NCWO Airlie House Working Conference on Women and Social Security," Re: Conference Follow–Up and Group Photo (September 24). In author files.

————. 1999b. (NCWO Women and Social Security Task Force Chair). "Letter to Mr. Gene Sperling, Special Assistant to the President. Re: Asking for Meeting with Task Force on Social Security for the NCWO (August 25)." In author files.

————. 1999c. (NCWO Women and Social Security Task Force Chair). "Letter to: Caren Grown, Program Officer, John D. and Catherine T. MacArthur Foundation. Re: Invitation to Women and Social Security Reform Conference, July 19–22, 1999, in Warrenton, VA (July 7)." In author files.

————. 1997. "Women's Agenda for COP," to Susan Bianchi-Sand, March 3. In author files.

Hartmann, Heidi, and Martha Burk. 2012. *The Shape of Equality: An Overview of the U.S. Women's Movement.* New York: Rosa Luxemburg Foundation.

Hartmann, Heidi, and Ashley English. 2010. "Paid Sick Days Can Help Contain Health Care Costs," IWPR Fact Sheet (April). Washington, DC: Institute for Women's Policy Research.

Hartmann, Heidi, and Edith Fierst, [and twenty-six signatories]. 1999. "Letter to Mr. Gene Sperling, Chair, National Economic Council, Special Assistant to the President" [regarding Social Security] NCWO Task Force on Women and Social Security (June 24). In author files.

Hartmann, Heidi, Jeff Hayes, and Robert Drago. 2011. "Social Security: Especially Vital to Women and People of Color, Men Increasingly Reliant," Institute for Women's Policy Research (January). In author files.

Hartmann, Heidi, Ariane Hegewisch, Hannah Liepmann, and Claudia Williams. 2010. "The Gender Wage Gap: 2009," IWPR Fact Sheet (March). Washington, DC: Institute for Women's Policy Research.

Hartmann, Heidi, and Catherine Hill with Lisa Witter. 2000. *Strengthening Social Security for Women: A Report from the Working Conference on Women and Social Security.* Institute for Women's Policy Research (IWPR) and the NCWO Task Force on Women and Social Security (March).

Hartmann, Heidi, and Christopher Turman. 2002a. "Memorandum to NCWO Members; Re: Social Security Updates" (November 19). In author files.

————. 2002b. "Memorandum to NCWO Members; Re: Social Security Updates" (September 17). In author files.

————. 2002c. "Memorandum to NCWO Members; Re: Social Security Updates" (July 16). In author files.

————. 2001. "Project Highlights," Women and Social Security Project, NCWO (July 17).

Hartmann, Heidi, and Julie Whittaker. 1998. "Stall in Women's Real Wage Growth Slows Progress in Closing the Wage Gap," *Research-in-Brief,* (February). Washington, DC: Institute for Women's Policy Research.

Hartmann, Susan M. 1998. *The Other Feminists: Activists in the Liberal Establishment.* New Haven, CT: Yale University Press.

Hassim, Shireen. 2006. *Women's Organizations and Democracy in South Africa: Contesting Authority*. Madison: University of Wisconsin Press.

Hasson, Judi. 1994. "Women Say Alternative Health Plan Falls Short," *USA Today* (February 15): 4.

Hawkesworth, Mary. 2012. *Political Worlds of Women: Activism, Advocacy, and Governance in the Twenty-First Century*. Boulder, CO: Westview Press.

———. 2006. *Globalization and Feminist Activism*. Lanham, MA: Rowman and Littlefield.

Hayes, Jeff, Heidi Hartmann, and Sunhwa Lee. 2010. "Social Security: Vital to Retirement Security for 35 Million Women and Men." Briefing paper (March). Washington, DC: Institute for Women's Policy Research.

Hayes, Jeffrey, Youngmin Yi, and Heather Berg. 2011. "Fact Sheet: Latinas and Social Security," (April). Washington, DC: Institute for Women's Policy Research.

"Health Care Bill Logjam Broken." 2009. *State Newspaper* (December 20): 1, 15.

"Health Care Over Haul: Senate versus House," 2009. *The State Newspaper*, (December 21): 4.

"Health Care Over Haul: Employers Balk at Costs." 2010. *State Newspaper* (March 26): 6, 7B.

"Health Vote Highlights Medicare Cuts." 2009. *State Newspaper* (December 6): 6.

Hegewisch, Ariane, and Helen Luyri. 2010. "The Workforce Investment Act and Women's Progress: Does WIA Funded Training Reinforce Sex Segregation in the Labor Market and the Gender Wage Gap?" IWPR briefing paper (January). Washington, DC: Institute for Women's Policy Research.

Hegewisch, Ariane, and Iris Zhang. 2013–2014. "IWPR Cost Analysis Informs State and Federal Paid Leave Laws," *IWPR Quarterly Newsletter* (Fall-Winter): 1.

Heller, Joe. 2008. "Have You Noticed? No One Is Talking about Privatizing Social Security Any More" Political cartoon. *USA Today* (April 4): 9A.

Hendricks, Maggie. 2017. "Serena Williams Uses the Words of Maya Angelou to Respond to Racist Comment," *USA Today* (April 24).

Herbert, Bob. 2009. "A Less Than Honest Policy," *State Newspaper* (December 30): 9.

———. 1998a. "Hidden Agendas: Fetal Protection Isn't the Real Issue," *New York Times* (June 14).

———. 1998b. "Pregnancy and Addiction: South Carolina's Misguided Law," *New York Times* (June 11).

Hershey, Marjorie Randon. 2013. *Party Politics in America*, 15th ed. Boston: Pearson.

Herszenhorn, David M. 2009. "Abortion and Costs at Top of Senate Agenda," *New York Times* (December 8).

———. 2009. "Louisiana Republican Breaks Ranks on Health Bill," *New York Times* (November 9): 14.

———. 2009. "Reid Says Health Bill Will Be Done by Christmas," *New York Times* (November 11): 18.

———. 2009. "Spotlight Shifts to Senate Democrats," *New York Times* (November 9): 14.

Hertel-Fernandez, Alexander. 2014. "Who Passes Business's 'Model Bills'? Policy Capacity and Corporate Influence in U.S. State Politics," *Perspectives on Politics*, Vol. 12, No. 3 (September): 582–602.

Hesford, Wendy S., and Wendy Kozol, eds. 2005. *Just Advocacy? Women's Human Rights, Transnational Feminism, and the Politics of Representation.* New Brunswick, NJ: Rutgers University Press.

Hesse-Biber, Sharlene Nagy, and Patricia Leavy, eds. 2004. *Approaches to Qualitative Research: A Reader on Theory and Practice.* New York: Oxford University Press.

Hewitt, Nancy A. 2010a. "Introduction." In *No Permanent Waves: Recasting Histories of U.S. Feminism.* Nancy A. Hewitt, ed., 1–12. New Brunswick, NJ: Rutgers University Press.

———, ed. 2010b. *No Permanent Waves: Recasting Histories of U.S. Feminism.* New Brunswick, NJ: Rutgers University Press.

Hickey, Roger. 2001. "Commission's Mandate Clear from Whom It Excludes," *San Diego Union-Tribune* (September 6): B11.

Hill, Anita. 2011. *Reimagining Equality: Stories of Gender, Race, and Finding Home.* Boston: Beacon Press.

Hill, Catherine. 2000a. "News Release: Calculating the True Costs of Social Security Privatization." Institute for Women's Policy Research and Women and Social Security Project (November 2). Washington, DC: NCWO.

———. 2000b. "Why Privatizing Social Security Would Hurt Women: A Response to the Cato Institute's Proposal for Individual Accounts." NCWO Task Force on Women and Social Security. Washington, DC: Institute for Women's Policy Research.

Hill, Catherine, Christianne Corbett, and Andresse St. Rose. 2010. *Why so Few? Women in Science, Technology, Engineering, and Mathematics.* Washington, DC: American Association of University Women.

Himmelstein, Jerome L. 1990. *To the Right: The Transformation of American Conservatism.* Berkeley: University of California Press.

Hine, Darlene Clark, and Kathleen Thompson. 1998. *A Shining Thread of Hope: The History of Black Women in America.* New York: Broadway Books.

Hirshman, Linda. 2015. *Sisters in Law: How Sandra Day O'Connor and Ruth Bader Ginsburg Went to the Supreme Court and Changed the World.* New York: HarperCollins.

Hitch. 2011. "Social Security? That's A . . ." Political Cartoon. *State Newspaper* (September 18): D3.

Hitchens, Christopher. 2003. "Golf Is a Man's Game," *Golf Digest* (April): 188, 190.

hooks, bell. 2000. *Feminism Is for Everybody: Passionate Politics.* Cambridge, MA: South End Press.

Horton, Myles. 1990. *The Long Haul: An Autobiography.* With Judith Kohl and Herbert Kohl. New York: Doubleday.

Hounsell, Cindy. 2008. (President, Women's Institute for a Secure Retirement [WISER]). "Minority Women and Retirement Income: Your Future Paycheck: Pay, Social Security, Pensions, Savings and Investments" (May). In author files.

———. 1996. "Women and Pensions: A Policy Agenda." In *The American Woman 1996–97: Women and Work*, Cynthia Costello and Barbara Kivimae Krimgold, eds., 166–173. New York: W. W. Norton.

Howard, Greg (Turner Strategies). 2005. "Social Security Talking Points and Strategy Memo," To: NCWO, Business and Professional Women USA, YWCA (January 27). In author files.

Huddy, Leonie, Erin Cassese, and Mary-Kate Lizotte. 2008. "Sources of Political Unity and Disunity among Women: Placing the Gender Gap in Perspective." In *Voting the Gender Gap*, Lois Duke Whitaker, ed., 141–169. Urbana: University of Illinois Press.

Huffington, Arianna. 2009. "The Senate Health Care Bill: Leave No Special Interest Behind," Huffington Post online. December 21.

Hula, Kevin W. 1999. *Lobbying Together: Interest Group Coalitions in Legislative Politics.* Washington, DC: Georgetown University Press.

———. 1995. "Rounding Up the Usual Suspects: Forging Interest Group Coalitions in Washington." In *Interest Group Politics*, 4th ed., Allan J. Cigler and Burdett A. Loomis, eds., 239–258. Washington, DC: Congressional Quarterly Press.

Hull, Gloria T., Patricia Bell Scott, and Barbara Smith, eds. 1982. *All the Women Are White, All the Blacks Are Men, but Some of Us Are Brave.* Old Westbury, NY: Feminist Press.

Hulse, Carl. 2010. "Past Strife and Jeers, Another Long March in the Name of Change," *New York Times* (March 22): 17.

Hulse, Carl, and Robert Pear. 2009. "Schedule for Health Vote in House Could Slip," *New York Times* (November 6).

Hyde, Cheryl. 1995. "Feminist Social Movement Organizations Survive the New Right." In *Feminist Organizations: Harvest of the New Women's Movement*, Myra Marx Ferree and Patricia Yancey Martin, eds., 306–322. Philadelphia: Temple University Press.

Incite! Women of Color against Violence, eds. 2007. *The Revolution Will Not Be Funded: Beyond the Non-Profit Industrial Complex.* Cambridge, MA: South End Press.

Institute for Women's Policy Research (IWPR). 2010. "Separate and Not Equal? Gender Segregation in the Labor Market and the Gender Wage Gap." Briefing paper (September).

———. 2000. "Press Release: The Institute for Women's Policy Research Refutes the Cato Institute's Proposal to Privatize Social Security" (February 25). In author files.

Ireland, Patricia. 2005. "Insist on Equal Rights for Lesbians." In *50 Ways to Improve Women's Lives: The Essential Guide to Achieving Equality, Health, and Success*, NCWO, ed., 125–127. Maui, HI: Inner Ocean.

Iversen, Torben, and Frances Rosenbluth. 2010. *Women, Work, and Politics: The Political Economy of Gender Inequality.* New Haven, CT: Yale University Press.

"IWPR Refutes Cato Institute on Social Security." 2000. *Institute for Women's Policy Research Quarterly Newsletter* (Winter): 4.

Iyengar, Shanto. 1994. *Is Anyone Responsible? How Television Frames Political Issues.* Chicago: University of Chicago Press.

Jackson, Derrick Z. 2009. "Women Compromise on Health Care," *State Newspaper* (December 24).

Jacobs, Lawrence R. 2014. "Health Reform and the Future of American Politics," *Perspectives on Politics*, Vol. 12, No. 3 (September): 631–642.

Jaggar, Alison M., ed. 2014a. *Gender and Global Justice.* Malden, MA: Polity Press.

———. 2014b. "Transnational Cycles of Gendered Vulnerability: A Prologue to a Theory of Global Gender Justice." In *Gender and Global Justice*, Alison M. Jaggar, ed., 18–29. Malden, MA: Polity Press.

————, ed. 2014c. *Just Methods: An Interdisciplinary Feminist Reader*. Boulder, CO: Paradigm Publishers.

Jaggar, Alison M., and Paula S. Rothenberg. 1993. *Feminist Frameworks: Alternative Theoretical Accounts of the Relations between Women and Men*, 3rd ed. New York: McGraw Hill.

Janeway, Elizabeth. 1981. *Powers of the Weak*. New York: Morrow Quill Paperbacks.

Jasper, James M. 1997. *The Art of Moral Protest: Culture, Biography, and Creativity in Social Movements*. Chicago: University of Chicago Press.

Johnson, Lynn. 1993. "Survival Tactics, Photo Journal: A Pennsylvania Family Copes with Serious Illness and No Health Insurance," *Newsweek* (October 4): 56–59.

Jones, Jacqueline. 1986. *Labor of Love, Labor of Sorrow: Black Women, Work, and the Family from Slavery to the Present*. New York: Vintage Books.

Jones, Mary Lynn. 2000. "Think Tanks: Mindful of Gender," *Chicago Tribune* (May 31).

Junn, Jane, and Nadia Brown. 2008. "What Revolution? Incorporating Intersectionality in Women and Politics." In *Political Women and American Democracy*, Christina Wolbrecht, Karen Beckwith, and Lisa Baldez, eds., 64–67. New York: Cambridge University Press.

Kaminski, Elizabeth. 2008. "Learning from Coalitions: Intersections and New Directions in Activism and Scholarship." In *Feminist Coalitions: Historical Perspectives on Second-Wave Feminism in the United States*. Stephanie Gilmore, ed., 287–293. Urbana: University of Illinois Press.

Kang, Hye-Ryoung. 2014. "Transnational Women's Collectivities and Global Justice." In *Gender and Global Justice*, Alison M. Jaggar, ed., 40–61. Malden, MA: Polity Press.

Karpowitz, Christopher F., and Tali Mendelberg. 2014. *The Silent Sex: Gender, Deliberation and Institutions*. Princeton, NJ: Princeton University Press.

Kathlene, Lyn. 2001. "Words That Matter: Women's Voice and Institutional Bias in Public Policy Formation." In *The Impact of Women in Public Office*, Susan J. Carroll, ed., 22–48. Bloomington: Indiana University Press.

Katzenstein, Mary Fainsod. 1998. *Faithful and Fearless: Moving Feminist Protest inside the Church and Military*. Princeton, NJ: Princeton University Press.

Kelley, Robin D. G. 1990. *Hammer and Hoe: Alabama Communists during the Great Depression*. Chapel Hill: University of North Carolina Press.

Kellman, Laurie, and Jim Abrams. 2010. "Troubling Details, Scope of Threats Emerge," *State Newspaper* (March 26): 11.

"Kennedy, Bishop Clash over Communion," 2009. *State Newspaper* (November 23).

Kenski, Kate, Bruce W. Hardy, and Kathleen Hall Jamieson. 2010. *The Obama Victory: How Media, Money, and Message Shaped the 2008 Election*. New York: Oxford University Press.

Kessler, Glenn. 2001. "Paving the Way for Privatizing Social Security," *Washington Post* (June 26): 1, 2.

Kessler-Harris, Alice. 2001. *In Pursuit of Equity: Women, Men, and the Quest for Economic Citizenship in 20th-Century America*. New York: Oxford University Press.

King, Tiffany Lethabo, and Ewuare Osayande. 2007. "The Filth on Philanthropy: Progressive Philanthropy's Agenda to Misdirect Social Justice Movements." In *The Revolution Will Not Be Funded: Beyond the Non-Profit Industrial Complex*, Incite! Women of Color against Violence, eds., 79–89. Cambridge, MA: South End Press.

Kinnard, Meg. 2009. "S.C. Among 13 States Threatening Health Bill Suit," *State Newspaper* (December 31): 4.

Kirchhoff, Sue. 1998. "Proposed Fixes Could Widen Social Security Gender Gap," *Congressional Quarterly Weekly* (April 25): 1038–1044.

Kirkpatrick, David D. 2009a. "Catholic Hospitals Split with Bishops," *State Newspaper* (December 27).

———. 2009b. "Health Care Debate Revives Abortion Campaigners," *New York Times* (November 23).

Kirkpatrick, David D., and Robert Pear. 2009. "A Victory in Health Care Vote for Opponents of Abortion," *New York Times* (November 9): 1, 14.

Kirkpatrick, Jennet. 2010. "Introduction: Selling Out? Solidarity and Choice in the American Feminist Movement," *Perspectives on Politics*, Vol. 8: 241–245.

Klapper, Melissa R. 2013. *Ballots, Babies, and Banners of Peace: American Jewish Women's Activism, 1890–1940*. New York: New York University Press.

Klein, Ezra. 2013. "Let's Talk: The Move to Reform the Filibuster," *New Yorker* (January 28): 24–29.

———. 2012. "Unpopular Mandate: Why Do Politicians Reverse Their Positions?" *New Yorker* (June 25): 30–33.

Klein, Joe. 2003. "I'm for Duffers' Rights," *Golf Digest* (April): 192.

———. 1993. "Scenes from a Marriage: The Health Care Fight Will Tell Us a Lot about Hillary's Politics—And the Clinton Partnership," *Newsweek* (October 4): 52.

Klein, Naomi. 2008. *The Shock Doctrine: The Rise of Disaster Capitalism*. New York: Picador, A Metropolitan Book, Henry Holt and Co.

Kliff, Sarah. 2009. "The Abortion Evangelist: LeRoy Carhart Is Determined to Train as Many Late-Term-Abortion Providers as Possible—Or the Practice Just Might Die with Him," *Newsweek* (August 24 and 31): 44–49.

Klutchen, Rebecca M. 2009. *Fit to Be Tied: Sterilization and Reproductive Rights in America, 1950–1980*. New Brunswick, NJ: Rutgers University Press.

Knight, Louise W. 2005. *Citizen: Jane Addams and the Struggle for Democracy*. Chicago: University of Chicago Press.

Kohl-Arenas, Erica. 2016. *The Self-Help Myth: How Philanthropy Fails to Alleviate Poverty*. Berkeley: University of California Press.

Kornblut, Anne E. 2010. *Notes from the Cracked Ceiling: Hillary Clinton, Sarah Palin and What It Will Take for a Woman to Win*. New York: Crown Publishers.

Krauthammer, Charles. 2011. "The Great Ponzi Debate," *State Newspaper* (September 18): D3.

———. 2011. "Obama's Social Security Hoax," *State Newspaper* (March 13).

Kretschmer, Kelsy, and David S. Meyer. 2013. "Organizing around Gender Identities." In *The Oxford Handbook of Gender and Politics*, Georgina Waylen, Karen Celis, Johanna Kantola and S. Laurel Weldon, eds., 390–410. New York: Oxford University Press.

Kristof, Nicholas D. 2010. "Health Care: Is the Status Quo What We Want?" *State Newspaper* (February 19): 9.

———. 2010. "It's All about Access," *State Newspaper* (March 19): 13.

———. 2009. "Are We Going to Let John Die?" *State Newspaper* (December 4): 13.

———. 2009. "Unhealthy America," *New York Times* (November 4).

———. 2009. "Until Medical Bills Do Us Part," *New York Times* (August 29).

———. 2009. "The Wrong Side of History," *New York Times* (November 24).

Krugman, Paul. 2010. "The Attack on Social Security," *State Newspaper* (August 17): A5.

———. 2009. "Be Afraid if Health Care Reforms Fails," *New York Times* (December 6).

———. 2009. "A Dangerous Dysfunction," *State Newspaper* (December 22): 9.

Kruks, Sonia. 2012. *Simone de Beauvoir and the Politics of Ambiguity.* New York: Oxford University Press.

Kutner, Max. 2017. "Inauguration and Women's March, By the Numbers," *Newsweek* (January 21).

Labaton, Vivien, and Dawn Lundy Martin, eds. 2004. *The Fire This Time: Young Activists and the New Feminism.* New York: Anchor Books.

Lagemann, Ellen Condliffe. 1979. *A Generation of Women: Education in the Lives of Progressive Reformers.* Cambridge, MA: Harvard University Press.

Lang, Sabine. 2013. *NGOs, Civil Society, and the Public Sphere.* New York: Cambridge University Press.

———. 1997. "The NGOization of Feminism." In *Transitions, Environments, Translations: Feminisms in International Politics*, Joan W Scott, Cora Kaplan, Deborah Keates, eds., 101–120. London, U.K.: Routledge.

Lapham, Lewis. 2003. "The Augusta Eight," *Golf Digest* (April): 194.

LaReaux, Sherri. 2000. "Think Tank Thinks Pink: Institute for Women's Policy Research," *Washington Woman* (November): 49.

Lawless, Jennifer L., and Richard L. Fox. 2010. *It Still Takes a Candidate: Why Women Don't Run for Office*, rev. ed. New York: Cambridge University Press.

"A Lawsuit against Citigroup." 2004. *Washington Post* (August 12). From NCWO archives.

Leadership Council of Aging Organizations. 2004. Letter to the Honorable Jo Anne B. Barnhart, Commissioner, Social Security Administration (March 12). In author files.

League of Women Voters Education Fund. 2000. *Join the Debate: Your Guide to Health Issues in the 2000 Election.* League of Women Voters Education Fund and the Henry J. Kaiser Family Foundation.

Leibovich, Mark. 2009. "Senate Naysayer Spoiling for Health Care Fight," *New York Times* (October 30): 1, 17.

"Letter to Interested Parties" [Regarding Church Ladies Project]. 2008. NCWO Archives (April 3). Xerox in author files.

Leonhardt, David. 2010. "Health Care Overhaul Becomes Law of the Land: In the Process, Pushing Back at Inequality," *New York Times* (March 24): 1, 19.

———. 2009. "Real Choice? It's Off Limits in Health Bills," *New York Times* (August 26): 1, 15.

Lepore, Jill. 2015. "To Have and to Hold: Reproduction, Marriage, and the Constitution," *New Yorker* (May 25): 34–39.

———. 2013. "Long Division: Measuring the Polarization of American Politics," *New Yorker* (December 2): 75–79.

———. 2009. "The Politics of Death: From Abortion to Health Care—How the Hysterical Style Overtook the National Debate," *New Yorker* (November 30): 60–67.

Levenson, Michael. 2008. "The Anguish of Foreclosure: Fearing Sale of House, Woman Kills Herself before the Auction," *Boston Globe* (July 24). Available at www.boston.com/news/local/articlesw/2008/07/24/the_anguish_of_foreclosure?mode.

Levine, Susan. 1995. *Degrees of Equality: The American Association of University Women and the Challenge of Twentieth-Century Feminism.* Philadelphia: Temple University Press.

Levs, Josh. 2012. "Augusta National Admits One of 'Toughest' Women in Business," *CNN.US* (August 21).

Liepmann, Hannah. 2010. "IWPR Co-sponsors 'Making WIA Work for Women' Briefing," *IWPR Quarterly Newsletter* (Summer): 1, 3.

Lightman, David. 2011. "Social Security Support Slips: Amid Deficit Worries, Congress Looks for Ways to Save Money," *State Newspaper* (January 28): 1, 10A.

———. 2010. "Congress OKs Last of Health Care Measures," *State Newspaper* (March 26): 1, 11.

———. 2010. "Health Care Over Haul: On to the Senate, for the Next Challenge," *State Newspaper* (March 23): 1, 3.

———. 2010. "Historic Bill Passes: House Democrats Find Votes Despite Push to Detail Legislation," *State Newspaper* (March 22): 1, 6.

———. 2009. "The Battle over Health Care: The Real War Is for Public Opinion," *State Newspaper* (December 22): 4.

———. 2009. "Dems Get a Look at Senate Bill: Reid's Health Reform Proposal Sets Stage for Intense Debate," *State Newspaper* (November 19): 4.

———. 2009. "Expanding Medicare: Does It Make Sense?" *State Newspaper* (December 11): 7.

———. 2009. "Health Care Bill: Impact of Plan Confusing to Many," *State Newspaper* (December 24): 1, 4.

———. 2009. "Health Care Plans: Pay More Now, See Changes Later?" *State Newspaper* (November 26): 13.

———. 2009. "House Passes Health Care Bill," *State Newspaper* (November 8): 6.

———. 2009. "Senate Health Debate to Begin: Some Democrats May Block Bill's Way," *Myrtle Beach Sun Times* (November 22): 1, 14.

———. 2009. "Senate Stepping into a Health Care Minefield," *State Newspaper* (November 23): 4.

———. 2009. "Today's Vote Could Kick Off Senate Health Debate," *State Newspaper* (November 21): 4.

Lightman, David, and William Douglas. 2009. "Senate's Health Plan: When the Doors Close, the Negotiations Open," *State Newspaper* (December 23): 4.

Lightman, David, William Douglas, and Margaret Talev. 2009. "Senate Overhaul Plan Passes: Sunrise Vote Sets Stage for Cloakroom Battles," *State Newspaper* (December 25): 4.

Lind, Amy. 2013. "Heteronormativity and Sexuality." In *The Oxford Handbook of Gender and Politics*. Georgina Waylen, Karen Celis, Johanna Kantola, and S. Laurel Weldon, eds., 189–213. New York: Oxford University Press.

Lipton, Eric, Brooke Williams, and Nicholas Confessore. 2014. "Foreign Powers Buy Influence at Think Tanks," *New York Times* (September 7): 1.

Lizza, Ryan. 2012. "Fussbudget: How Paul Ryan Captured the G.O.P." *New Yorker* (August 6): 24–32.

Loeb, Paul Rogat. 1999. *Soul of a Citizen: Living with Conviction in a Cynical Time.* New York: St. Martin's Griffin.

Lorber, Judith. 2012. *Gender Inequality: Feminist Theories and Politics*, 5th ed. New York: Oxford University Press.

Lorde, Audre. 1984. *Sister Outsider.* Freedom, CA: Crossing Press.

Lore, Diane. 1994. "Hysterectomies Often Unneeded, Insurer Reports," *State News- paper* (February 8): 1D.

Loven, Jennifer. 2010. "Obama Signs It, Must Sell It," *State Newspaper* (March 24): 1, 4.

Lundberg, George D. 2001. "The Best Health Care Goes Only So Far," *Newsweek* (August 27): 15.

Lush, Tamara. 2009. "'You Fight for What You Need to Do': Miami Doctor Treats Uninsured with Dignity," *State Newspaper* (October 13): 4.

Lynch, Frederick R. 2011. *One Nation under AARP: The Fight over Medicare, Social Security, and America's Future.* Berkeley: University of California Press.

MacFarquhar, Larissa. 2016. "What Money Can Buy: The Ford Foundation's Quest to Fix the World," *New Yorker* (January 4): 38–51.

MacGillis, Alec. 2009. "Abortion a Key Fault Line in Health Fight," *Washington Post* (November 9).

MacKinnon, Catharine A. 1993. *Only Words.* Cambridge, MA: Harvard University Press.

MacManus, Doyle. 2011. "Touching the 'Third Rail.'" *State Newspaper* (September 16).

MacManus, Susan. 2010. "Voter Participation and Turnout Female Star Power At- tracts Women Voters." In *Gender and Elections: Shaping the Future of American Politics*, Susan J. Carroll and Richard L. Fox, eds., 78–116. New York: Cambridge University Press.

MacManus, Susan A. 2006. "Targeting [Specific Slices of] Female Voters: A Key Strat- egy of Democrats and Republicans Alike in 2004 . . . and Most Assuredly So in 2008," *Politics and Gender*, Vol. 2, No. 3: 374–387.

Madden, Ed. 2013. *My Father's House: Poems.* Lewisburg, PA: Seven Kitchens Press.

———. 2010. *Nest.* Lewisburg, PA: Seven Kitchens Press.

Madrick, Jeff. 2014. *Seven Bad Ideas: How Mainstream Economists Have Damaged America and the World.* New York: Vintage Books.

Maloney, Carolyn B. 2016. "Falling into Poverty: The Gender Pay Gap Is Perilous for Women in Their 'Golden Years,'" *Ms.* (Summer): 47.

———, [Representative]. 2008. *Rumors of Our Progress Have Been Greatly Exaggerated: Why Women's Lives Aren't Getting Any Easier and How We Can Make Real Progress for Ourselves and Our Daughters.* New York: Modern Times.

———, [Representative]. 2003. "Press Release: Ending Tax Deductions for Discrimi- nation" (June 11). In author files.

"Mammograms for Women in Their 40s Contested," 1995 *State Newspaper* (January 11): 7.

Mann, Judy. 2000. "Bush Proposal Would Hurt Women Worst," *Washington Post* (August 11).

"Many Factors Make Retirement Tough for Women." 2002. *Seattle Post-Intelligencer* (July 5).

Marcus, Ruth. 2009. "Abortion's New Battleground: Will Pro-Choice Democrats Kill Health-Care Reform? Probably Not—And That's a Good Thing," *Newsweek* (De- cember 7): 48–50.

Marilley, Suzanne M. 1996. *Woman Suffrage and the Origins of Liberal Feminism in the United States, 1820–1920.* Cambridge, MA: Harvard University Press.

Martin, Robert W. T. 2013. *Government by Dissent: Protest, Resistance, and Radical Democratic Thought in the Early American Republic.* New York: New York Univer- sity Press.

Matsuda, Mari. 2013. "Beside My Sister, Facing the Enemy: Legal Theory Out of Co-alition." In *Feminist Theory Reader: Local and Global Perspectives*, 3rd ed., Carole R. McCann and Seung-Kyung Kim, eds., 332–340. New York: Routledge (originally published in 1993).

Matsui, Robert T. 2002. "Introductory Statement by Robert T. Matsui on H.R. 4671 'The Social Security Widow's Benefit Guarantee Act of 2002'" (May 7). In author files.

Matthews, Nancy. 1995. "Feminist Clashes with the State: Tactical Choices by State-Funded Rape Crisis Centers." In *Feminist Organizations: Harvest of the New Women's Movement*, Myra Marx Ferree and Patricia Yancey Martin, eds., 291–305. Philadelphia: Temple University Press.

Matthews-Gardner, A. Lanathea. 2005. "The Political Development of Female Civic Engagement in Postwar America," *Politics and Gender*, Vol. 1, No. 4: 547–575.

May, Vivian M. 2015. *Pursuing Intersectionality, Unsettling Dominant Imaginaries*. New York: Routledge.

Mayer, Frederick W. 2014. *Narrative Politics: Stories and Collective Action*. New York: Oxford University Press.

Mayer, Jane. 2017. "Trump's Money Man: How Robert Mercer, a Reclusive Hedge-fund Tycoon, Exploited America's Populist Insurgency," *New Yorker* (March 27): 34–45.

McAdam, Doug. 1982. *Political Process and the Development of Black Insurgency, 1930–1970*. Chicago: University of Chicago Press.

McBride, Dorothy E., and Amy G. Mazur. 2008a. "Women's Movements, Feminism, and Feminist Movements." In *Politics, Gender, and Concepts: Theory and Methodology*, Goertz, Gary and Amy G. Mazur, eds., 219–243. New York: Cambridge University Press.

———. 2008b. "State Feminism." In *Politics, Gender, and Concepts: Theory and Methodology*, Goertz, Gary and Amy G. Mazur, eds., 244–269. Cambridge: Cambridge University Press.

McCann, Carole R., and Seung-Kyung Kim, eds. 2010. *Feminist Theory Reader: Local and Global Perspectives*. New York: Routledge.

McCleery, Peter. 2003. "Viewers' Guide: CBS Will Show the Tournament but What about the Protesters?" *Golf Digest* (April): 138–139.

McDonagh, Eileen. 2009. *The Motherless State: Women's Political Leadership and American Democracy*. Chicago: University of Chicago Press.

McFarland, Andrew S. 2011. *Boycotts and Dixie Chicks: Creative Political Participation at Home and Abroad*. Boulder, CO: Paradigm Publishers.

Mendelberg, Tali, Christopher F. Karpowitz, and J. Baxter Oliphant. 2014. "Gender Inequality in Deliberation: Unpacking the Black Box of Interaction," *Perspectives on Politics*, Vol. 12, No. 1 (March): 18–44.

"A Message from Heidi for Steering Committee." 2004. Xerox from NCWO archives (October 6). In author files.

Mettler, Suzanne. 2005. *Soldiers to Citizens: The G. I. Bill and the Making of the Greatest Generation*. New York: Oxford University Press.

———. 1998. *Dividing Citizens: Gender and Federalism in New Deal Public Policy*. Ithaca, NY: Cornell University Press.

Michelman, Kate, and Frances Kissling. 2009. "Trading Women's Rights for Political Power," *New York Times* (November 12): 31.

Milbank, Dana. 2011. "Republicans Color Abortion Debate," *State Newspaper* (December 8): 11.

Miller, Arthur. 1949. *Death of a Salesman*. New York: Viking Press.

Miller, Lisa. 2010. "When Bishops Play Politics: A New Generation Gets Righteous," *Newsweek* (March 15): 22.

Monroe, Linda Roach. 1992. "Women's Health Research Tries to Remedy Years of Neglect," *State Newspaper* (May 11): 1, 8.

Montoya, Celeste, and Lise Rolandsen Agustin. 2013. "The Othering of Domestic Violence: The EU and Cultural Framings of Violence against Women," *Social Politics: International Studies in Gender, State and Society*, Vol. 20, No. 4 (Winter): 534–557.

Morgan, Olivia, and Karen Skelton, eds. 2014. *The Shriver Report: A Woman's Nation Pushes Back from the Brink; A Study by Maria Shriver and the Center for American Progress*. New York: Palgrave MacMillan.

Morgen, Sandra. 2002. *Into Our Own Hands: The Women's Health Movement in the U.S., 1969–1990*. New Brunswick, NJ: Rutgers University Press.

———. 1995. "'It Was the Best of Times, It Was the Worst of Times': Emotional Discourse in the Work Cultures of Feminist Health Clinics." In *Feminist Organizations: Harvest of the New Women's Movement*, Myra Marx Ferree and Patricia Yancey Martin, eds., 234–247. Philadelphia: Temple University Press.

Morgenthau, Tom, and Mary Hager. 1993. "The Clinton Cure," *Newsweek* (October 4): 37–43.

Mosle, Sara. 1996. "Letter from Las Vegas: How the Maids Fought Back," *New Yorker* (February 26 and March 4 double issue): 148–156.

"Motorola Said the Internal Revenue Service." 2004. *Washington Post* (August 12). From NCWO archives.

Moyers, Bill. 2003. "This Is Your Story—The Progressive Story of America, Pass It On," Common Dreams News Center (June 16).

Moyo, Dambisa, and Niall Ferguson. 2009. *Dead Aid: Why Aid Is Not Working and How There Is a Better Way for Africa*. New York: Farrar, Straus, and Giroux.

Mueller, Carol. 1995. "The Organizational Basis of Conflict in Contemporary Feminism." In *Feminist Organizations: Harvest of the New Women's Movement*, Myra Marx Ferree and Patricia Yancey Martin, eds., 263–275. Philadelphia: Temple University Press.

Mulhauser, Karen, and Rene Redwood. 2008a. "Memo to Interested Leaders: re: Peace Impact 2008: Narrative Summary." In author files.

———. 2008b. "Peace Impact: Engaging an Under-Utilized Infrastructure for Electoral Impact; A Report for 2008." In author files.

Muncy, Robyn. 1991. *Creating a Female Dominion in American Reform, 1890–1935*. New York: Oxford University Press.

Murray, Pauli. 1987. *Pauli Murray: The Autobiography of a Black Activist, Feminist, Lawyer, Priest, and Poet*. Knoxville: University of Tennessee Press.

Murray, Rainbow. 2014. "Quotas for Men: Reframing Gender Quotas as a Means of Improving Representation for All," *American Political Science Review*, Vol. 108, No. 3 (August): 520–532.

Nainar, Vahida, and Pam Spees. 2000. *The International Criminal Court: The Beijing Platform in Action*. New York: Women's Caucus for Gender Justice.

Naples, Nancy A. 2005. "Confronting the Future, Learning from the Past: Feminist Praxis in the Twenty-First Century." In *Different Wavelengths: Studies of the Contemporary Women's Movement*, Jo Reger, ed., 215–235. New York: Routledge.

National Abortion Rights Action League (NARAL). n.d. "Title X: The Nation's Cornerstone Federal Family Planning Program." Washington, DC.

National Coalition against Domestic Violence. 1999. "The Hate Crimes Prevention Act: Strikes the Right Balance between Federal and State Interests" (March).

National Committee on Pay Equity. 1999. Wage Gap Briefing Materials, for National Council of Women's Organizations Women's Equality Summit (March 15).

National Committee to Preserve Social Security and Medicare. n.d. [probably 2001]. "5 Ways to Win the Privatization Debate." Fourfold pamphlet. In author files.

NCWO. 2011. "NCWO Older Women's Economic Security Task Force: Statement on Safeguarding Social Security" (January 24). In author files.

———. 2009. Staff. "NWLC Health Care Conference Call—Thurs, August 6" (August 4). Copy of email in author files.

———. 2009. Staff. "Senators Opening Statements on Privacy Choice Roe" (July 17). Copy of email in author files.

———. 2009. Staff. "Shireen Mitchell, NCWO Vice-Chair Featured in Washington Post" (July 30). Copy of email in author files.

———. 2009. Staff. "Urgent! Health Care Reform Sign-On" (August 30). Copy of email in author files.

———. 2006–2007. *Handbook of Women's Organizations and National Leaders*. Washington, DC: CWA.

———. 2006. "The 2006 ABC's of Women's Issues," pamphlet. Washington, DC: Pure CWA.

———. 2005a. "AFL-CIO, NCPSSM Polling on Social Security Notes: Confidential—Not for Wide Distribution" (January 18). From NCWO archives. In author files.

———. 2005b. *50 Ways to Improve Women's Lives: The Essential Women's Guide to Achieving Equality, Health, and Success*. Maui, HI: Inner Ocean.

———. 2005c. "Statement of the NCWO Task Force on Women and Social Security on 'Gender Adjustments'" (January 26). In author files.

———. 2004a. "A Safer, Better World Begins with Women: Your Guide to Global Issues," memo to Open Society Institute (May 28). In author files.

———. 2004b. "A Message from Heidi for Steering Committee" (October 6). Email. From NCWO archives. In author files.

———. 2004c. Steering Committee. "RE: National Council of Research on Women" (March 29). Email exchanges. From NCWO archives.

———. 2003. "Special Alert: National Council of Women's Organizations Statement on War with Iraq," *Ms.* (Spring): 64–65.

———. 2001a. "NCWO Statement on Domestic Priorities." Attachment to NCWO meeting minutes (November 13, 2001). In author files.

———. 2001b. Child Care Taskforce. "Working Families Need Access to Affordable, Quality Child Care Right Now!"

———. 2000a. Women and Social Security Project. "Media Advisory for Thursday, March 30, 2000: Joint Advisory with the Institute for Women's Policy Research: Opponents of Social Security Privatization Hold Press Conference to Offer Options to Address Solvency and Strengthen Benefits for Women" (March 30). In author files. Underline in original.

———. 2000b. "Dr. Martha Burk Elected New Chair of the National Council of Women's Organizations" (April 19). In author files.

————. 2000c. National Women's Equality Act for the 21st Century.

————. 2000d. "Statement to the Democratic Party Platform Committee." NCWO Archives. Copy in author files.

————. 2000e. "Statement to the Republican Party Platform Committee." NCWO Archives. Copy in author files.

————. 2000f. Task Force on Women and Social Security. "Congressional Staff Briefing and Q&A on: 'Strengthening Social Security for Women.'" Announcement and agenda (May 23). In author files.

————. 2000g. Testimony of the National Council of Women's Organizations to the Democratic Platform Committee (July 21).

————. 2000h. Testimony of the National Council of Women's Organizations to the Republican Platform Committee (July 21).

————. 1999–2009. "Minutes of Meetings."

————. 1999a. Social Security and Women Project: Keeping the Heart in Social Security. "Task Force on Women and Social Security's Policy Initiatives: Presented to the NCWO on September 21, 1999" [Confidential Draft—For Discussion Only]. In author files.

————. 1999b. Social Security and Women Project: Keeping the Heart in Social Security. "Women and Social Security Project Update" (September). In author files.

————. 1999c. "Steering Committee" (September). In author files.

————. 1999d. Task Force on Women and Social Security. "Working Conference on Women and Social Security: Draft Report" (November 16). In author files.

————. 1999e. *Women's Leadership Handbook.*

————. 1998. "Keep the HEART in Social Security." Press conference announcement, agenda, speaker introductions, talking points (December 2). In author files.

————. n.d. Organizational Document: (by-laws). In author files.

————. n.d. Organizational Description. In author files.

———— [and Fifty-One Separate Group Signatories]. 2006. NCWO Archives [regarding U.S. Department of Labor changes to Women's Bureau data gathering] (August 3). Xerox in author files.

————. n.d. [probably 2000]. Women and Social Security Project. "If You Don't Vote to Make Sure Social Security Is There for You in Your Retirement, It May Not Be." Pamphlet. In author files.

————. n.d. Women and Social Security Project. "Women's Checklist to Strengthening Social Security." In author files.

NCWO Task Force on Women and Social Security. 2000. "Congressional Staff Briefing and Q&A on: 'Strengthening Social Security for Women.'" Announcement and agenda (May 23). In author files.

————. 1999. "Working Conference on Women and Social Security: Draft Report" (November 16). In author files.

"National Council of Women's Organizations: Policy Agenda." Adopted November 1998. Xerox in author files.

National Family Planning and Reproductive Health Association. 1998. "Facts about the National Family Planning Program: Title X (ten) of the Public Health Service Act" (December).

National Partnership for Women and Girls. 2005. With 26 additional women groups signatories. "Letter to: United States House of Representatives; Re: The Small Business Health Fairness Act of 2005 (H.R. 525)" (July 25). In author files.

National Partnership for Women and Families. n.d. [maybe 2005]. "Reasons Social Security Privatization *Particularly* Harms Women." In author files. Italics in original.

National Women's Health Resource Center, Inc. 1999. "National Women's Health Report," Vol. 21, No. 1 (February).

National Women's Law Center (NWLC). 2011. *Poverty among Women and Families, 2000–2010: Extreme Poverty Reaches Record Levels as Congress Faces Critical Choices.* (September 15). Available at www.nwlc.org/povertydata.

National Women's Law Center. 2005. "Why Social Security Is a Better Deal Than Privatization for Women and Their Families." In author files.

Neergaard, Lauran. 2011. "U.S. Restricts Morning-After Pill Sales," *State Newspaper* (December 8): 4.

Ness, Debra, National Partnership Women and Girls. 2009. "Outrageous" (December 20). Copy of email in author files.

Neumann, Caryn E. 2008. "Enabled by the Holy Spirit: Church Women United and the Development of Ecumenical Christian Feminism." In *Feminist Coalitions: Historical Perspectives on Second-Wave Feminism in the United States*, Stephanie Gilmore, ed., 113–134. Urbana: University of Illinois Press.

Neuwirth, Jessica. 2015. *Equal Means Equal: Why the Time for an Equal Rights Amendment Is Now.* New York: New Press.

Newton, David. 2003. "Unexpected Exposure: Martha Burk Didn't Expect Her Letter to Augusta National President Hootie Johnson Asking the All-Male Club to Admit a Woman Would Ignite the Fight That Would Put Her in the National Spotlight," *State Newspaper* (March 30): 1, 3C.

"Nobody Asked Us but . . ." 2003. *Golf Magazine* (July): 38.

Norrander, Barbara, and Clyde Wilcox. 2008. "The Gender Gap in Ideology," *Political Behavior*, Vol. 30 (December): 503–523.

Norris, Pippa. 2003. "The Gender Gap: Old Challenges, New Approaches." In *Women and American Politics: New Questions, New Directions*, Susan J. Carroll, ed. New York: Oxford University Press.

NOW. 2005. "Facts: Social Security Is Vital to Women" (March 3). In author files.

———. 2005. "Women's Organizations Condemn Privatizers' Attacks on Stay-at-Home Moms, Cite Gross Hypocrisy of Party Claiming Mantle of Family Values" (March 30). In author files.

———. 2002. "Executive Summary of NOW's Comments on Notice of Proposed Rulemaking Regarding Single-Sex Classes and Schools" (July). In author files.

———. 2000. "News Release: Privatization = Poverty: Statement of NOW President Patricia Ireland on Social Security" (February 25). In author files.

NOW Legal Defense and Education Fund. 2000. "VAWA [Violence against Women Act] Reauthorization and Action Packet" (July).

———. 1998. "Child Care: Talking Points for Welfare Reform" (December).

NOW National Action Center. 2009a. "Reproductive Health Care in Reform Bills Threatened" (July 23): Copy of email in author files.

———. 2009b. "Oppose Stealth Stupack Provision in Senate Bill" (December 19). Copy of email in author files.

Nussbaum, Martha C. 1997. *Cultivating Humanity: A Classical Defense of Reform in Liberal Education.* Cambridge, MA: Harvard University Press.

"Obama Says Senate Close to Passing Health Care Plan," 2009. *State Newspaper* (December 16): 1, 6.

Obley, Patrick. 2003. "About 50 Attend Peaceful Burk Protest: Presentation Features Marionette Show, One Hour of Speeches," *State Newspaper* (April 13): 1, 10C.

———. 2003. "Latest Protest Supports Augusta: Movement Doesn't Appreciate Burk Speaking on Behalf of All Women," *State Newspaper* (April 7): 8C.

———. 2003. "Protesters to Square Off during Masters," *State Newspaper* (April 12): 1, 13A.

———. 2003. "Protester Says Burk Misrepresenting Women: Todd Manzi Has Problem with Power Being Accrued by NCWO Head," *State Newspaper* (April 11): 1, 10C.

O'Connell, Roselyn [president, National Women's Political Caucus] and Martha Burk [chair, National Council of Women's Organizations]. 2000. "Call for Women Candidates for Presidential Appointments" (November 27).

Office of House Democratic Leader Nancy Pelosi. 2004. "In Their Own Words: The Experts on the Republican Proposal to Privatize Social Security" (January 24). In author files.

Older Women's League (OWL). 2000. *Women, Work and Pensions: 2000* (June).

———. n.d. [probably 2005]. "Social Security Matters." In author files.

———. n.d. [probably 2000]. "Just the Facts: The Truth about Women and Social Security." Pamphlet.

O'Neill, Brenda, and Elizabeth Gidengill, eds. 2006. *Gender and Social Capital.* Oxford: Routledge.

O'Neill, Terry. 2014. "Am I Not Also My Sister's Keeper?" Blog posted on Huffington Post, July 24, 2014.

———. 2009. "Greetings from Terry O'Neill, Your New NOW President" (July 21). Copy of email in author files.

O'Neill, Terry, and Heidi Hartmann, cochairs. 2011. "Statement of Terry O'Neill and Heidi Hartmann, Co-Chairs on the President's Plan to Reduce the Deficit," Older Women's Economic Security Task Force, NCWO (April 14): In author files.

O'Neill, Terry, and Shireen Mitchell. 2014. "Letter to the Editor: Young Women of Color Need Support Too," *Washington Post* (July 30).

Outtz, Janice Hamilton. 1998. "Women Work, Poverty Still Persists: An Update on the Status of Displaced Homemakers and Single Mothers in the United States," *Women Work!* The National Network for Women's Employment (Fall). Washington, DC.

Paglia, Camille. 2003. "A Rock Meets a Hard Place," *Golf Digest* (April): 187–188.

Patterson, Martha Priddy. 1996. "Women's Employment Patterns, Pension Coverage, and Retirement Planning." In *The American Woman 1996–97: Women and Work*, Cynthia Costello and Barbara Kivimae Krimgold, eds., 148–165. New York: W. W. Norton.

Payne, Charles M. 2007. *I've Got the Light of Freedom: The Organizing Tradition and the Mississippi Freedom Struggle.* Berkeley: University of California Press.

Payne, Charles M. 1990. "'Men Led, but Women Organized': Movement Participation of Women in the Mississippi Delta." In *Women and Social Protest*, Guida West and Rhoda Lois Blumberg, eds., 156–165. New York: Oxford University Press.

Payne, Ruby K. 2005. *A Framework for Understanding Poverty*, 4th rev. ed. Highlands, TX: aha!Press.

Pear, Robert. 2009. "Home Care Patients Worry over Possible Cuts," *New York Times* (December 4).

————. 2009. "Long-Term Care Stirs Health Care Debate," *New York Times* (December 13).

————. 2009. "Obama Seeks Revision of Plan's Abortion Limits," *New York Times* (November 9).

Pear, Robert, and David M. Herszenhorn. 2010. "House Democrats Claim Votes for Landmark Health Bill: Poised to Win Hard-Fought Battle," *New York Times* (March 22): 1, 16.

————. 2009. "Senators Pitch to Women and Elderly on Health Bill," *New York Times* (December 1).

Perez, Amara H. 2007. "Between Radical Theory and Community Praxis: Reflections on Organizing and the Non-Profit Industrial Complex." In *The Revolution Will Not Be Funded: Beyond the Non-Profit Industrial Complex*, Incite! Women of Color against Violence, eds., 91–99. Cambridge, MA: South End Press.

Perry, Lewis. 2013. *Civil Disobedience: An American Tradition*. New Haven, CT: Yale University Press.

Peter D. Hart Research Associates. 2002. Memo to: The AFL-CIO. Re: Focus Groups on Social Security Privatization (April 4). In author files.

Phelan, Shane. 1994. *Getting Specific: Postmodern Lesbian Politics*. Minneapolis: University of Minnesota Press.

————. 1989. *Identity Politics: Lesbian Feminism and the Limits of Community*. Philadelphia: Temple University Press.

Phinney, David. 1995. "Boxer Heads Off Senate Vote on Anti-Abortion Bill," *San Francisco Examiner* (November 9).

Pimlott, Jamie Pamelia. 2010. *Women and the Democratic Party: The Evolution of Emily's List*. Amherst, NY: Cambria Press.

Piven, Frances Fox, and Richard A. Cloward. 1977. *Poor People's Movements*. New York: Pantheon.

Planned Parenthood Federation of America. 1998a. "Confidentiality and Teen Access to Family Planning" (August).

————. 1998b. "Title X: America's Family Planning Program" (December).

Polletta, Francesca. 2006. *It Was Like a Fever: Storytelling in Protest and Politics*. Chicago: University of Chicago Press.

————. 2002. *Freedom Is an Endless Meeting: Democracy in American Social Movements*. Chicago: University of Chicago Press.

Pollitt, Katha. 2007. "With Facts on Our Side," *The Nation* (November 5): 10.

Polsby, Nelson W., and Aaron Wildavsky. 2004. *Presidential Elections: Strategies and Structures of American Politics*, 11th ed. Lanham, MD: Rowman and Littlefield.

Poppendieck, Janet. 1998. *Sweet Charity? Emergency Food and the End of Entitlement*. New York: Penguin Books.

Preston, Larry. 1995. "Theorizing Difference: Voices from the Margins," *American Political Science Review*, Vol. 89, No. 4 (December): 941–953.

"Proposal: 2004 NCWO Voter Guide to Women's Issues: Executive Summary," n.d. In author files.

Proskauer, Rose, S. Harshbarger, and A. Crafts. 2009. "An Independent Governance Assessment of ACORN: The Path to Meaningful Reform" (December 7). Available at http://www.proskauer.com/files/uploads/report2.pdf.

Pugh, Tony. 2015. "Health Care Tax Credits: High Court Ruling Could Hurt Women," *State Newspaper* (April 12).

———. 2001. "Social Security Worries Intensify," *State Newspaper* (October 19).

Quindlen, Anna. 2012. *Lots of Candles, Plenty of Cake*. New York: Random House.

———. 2002. "The Sand Trap of Inequality," *Newsweek* (December 2): 92.

Rai, Shirin M. 2013. "Gender and (International) Political Economy." In *The Oxford Handbook of Gender and Politics*, Georgina Waylen, Karen Celis, Johanna Kantola, and S. Laurel Weldon, eds., 263–288. New York: Oxford University Press.

Rankine, Claudia. 2014. *Citizen: An American Lyric*. Minneapolis, MN: Graywolf Press.

Ransby, Barbara. 2003. *Ella Baker and the Black Freedom Movement: A Radical Democratic Vision*. Chapel Hill: University of North Carolina Press.

Raymond, Janice, Co-Executive Director, Coalition against Trafficking in Women (CATW) and Malka Marcovich, Representative, French Coordination of the European Women's Lobby: For the International Human Rights Network. 2000.

Reed, T. V. 2005. "The Poetical Is the Political: Feminist Poetry and the Poetics of Women's Rights." In *Feminist Theory Reader: Local and Global Perspectives*, 3rd ed. Carole R. McCann and Seung-Kyung Kim, eds., 85–97. New York: Routledge.

Reger, Jo. 2012. *Everywhere and Nowhere: Contemporary Feminism in the United States*. New York: Oxford University Press.

———, ed. 2005. *Different Wavelengths: Studies of the Contemporary Women's Movement*. New York: Routledge.

Reger, Jo, and Lacey Story. 2005. "When Feminism Is Your Job: Age and Power in Women's Policy Organizations." In *Different Wavelengths: Studies of the Contemporary Women's Movement*. Jo Reger, ed., 117–136. New York: Routledge.

Reich, Robert. 2007. *Supercapitalism: The Transformation of Business, Democracy, and Everyday Life*. New York: Alfred A. Knopf.

Reid, Czerne M. 2007. "Drug Abuse during Pregnancy Still Prevalent," *State Newspaper* (August 9): 2D.

Reid, T. R. 2009. "No Country for Sick Men: To Judge the Content of a Nation's Character, Look No Further Than Its Health-Care System," *Newsweek* (September 21): 42–45.

Reilly, Katie. 2017. "Trump Inauguration: Barack Obama Gives Final Remarks." *Time*. Accessed October 29, 2017. Available at http://time.com/4641336/president-obama-transcript-post-inauguration/.

Reilly, Rick. 2003. "A Three-Ring Masters," *Sports Illustrated* (April 21): 90.

Reingold, Beth, ed. 2008. *Legislative Women: Getting Elected, Getting Ahead*. Boulder, CO: Lynne Rienner.

Remnick, David. 2016. "It Happened Here: A President Confronts an Election That Changes Everything—and Imperils His Legacy," *New Yorker* (November 28): 34–65.

Rhode, Deborah L. 2014. *What Women Want: An Agenda for the Women's Movement*. New York: Oxford University Press.

Riccardi, Nicholas (Associated Press). 2012. "Fight for Women's Vote Defines Presidential Race." *Masslive.com* (August 27). Accessed April 2, 2018. http://www.masslive.com/politics/index.ssf/2012/08/fight_for_womens_vote_defines.html.

Rich, Adrienne. 1979. *On Lies, Secrets, and Silence: Selected Prose 1966–1978*. New York: W. W. Norton.

R.M.K. Political Cartoon. 2002. Caption "Hey, Lady, Do You Think We Could Talk You into Boycotting the World Series and the Super Bowl, Too? . . ." reprinted in *Detroit News* (September 9).

Rochon, Thomas. 1998. *Culture Moves: Ideas, Activism and Changing Values*. Princeton, NJ: Princeton University Press.

Roithmayr, Daria. 2014. *Reproducing Racism: How Everyday Choices Lock in White Advantage*. New York: New York University Press.

Rojas, Paula X. 2007. "Are the Cops in Our Heads and Hearts?" In *The Revolution Will Not Be Funded: Beyond the Non-Profit Industrial Complex*, Incite! Women of Color against Violence, eds., 197–214. Cambridge, MA: South End Press.

Rosen, James. 2010. "13 State Prosecutors Challenge Health Plan," *State Newspaper* (March 24): 5.

Rosenberg, Debra. 2005. "Roe's Army Reloads," *Newsweek* (August 8): 25–29.

Ross, Loretta J. 1999. "Epilogue: African American Women's Activism in the Global Arena." In *Different Wavelengths: Studies of the Contemporary Women's Movement*. Jo Reger, ed., 325–339. New York: Routledge.

Rosser, Sue V. 1994. *Women's Health—Missing from U.S. Medicine*. Bloomington: Indiana University Press.

———. 1991. "Gender Bias in Health Research: The Difference It Makes," *State of Women's Studies at South Carolina* (Fall): 1, 4. Newsletter in author files.

Roth, Benita. 2004. *Separate Roads to Feminism: Black, Chicana, and White Feminist Movements in America's Second Wave*. New York: Cambridge University Press.

———. 1999. "The Making of the Vanguard Center: Black Feminist Emergence in the 1960s and 1970s." In *Still Lifting, Still Climbing: African American Women's Contemporary Activism*, Kimberly Springer, ed., 70–90. New York: New York University Press.

Roy, Arundhati. 2014. "Arundhati Roy: How Corporate Power Converted Wealth into Philanthropy for Social Control," Alternet (August 27). Available at http://www.alternet.org.

Rubin, James H. 1993. "Money for Health Research Might Bridge Gender Gap," *State Newspaper* (March 31): 1, 10.

Ruzek, Sheryl Burt, and Julie Becker. 1999. "The Women's Health Movement in the United States: From Grass-Roots Activism to Professional Agendas," *JAMWA*, Vol. 54, No. 1 (Winter): 4–9.

Ryan, Gery W., and H. Russell Bernard. 2003. "Techniques to Identify Themes," *Field Methods*, Vol. 15, No. 1 (February): 85–109.

Sack, Kevin. 2009. "'Opt Out' Proposal Would Put State Leaders to the Test," *New York Times* (November 11): 18.

Said, Edward W. 1978. *Orientalism*. New York: Vintage Books.

Samuelson, Robert J. 2009. "The Burden on the Young," *Washington Post* (November 25): 7.

———. 2009. "Get Real About Health Care Costs," *State Newspaper* (December 13).

———. 2009. "A Parody of Leadership," *State Newspaper* (December 23): 13.

———. 1993. "Health Care: How We Got into This Mess," *Newsweek* (October 4): 31–35.

Sanbonmatsu, Kira. 2010. "State Elections: Why Do Women Fare Differently Across States?" In *Gender and Elections: Shaping the Future of American Politics*, Susan J. Carroll and Richard L. Fox, eds., 117–143. New York: Cambridge University Press.

————. 2006. *Where Women Run: Gender and Party in the American States.* Ann Arbor: University of Michigan Press.

"Sanford Asks Clyburn for Medicaid Help." 2009. *State Newspaper* (December 25): 4.

Sanger, David E. 2010. "A Big Victory, At What Cost?" *New York Times* (March 22): 1, 16.

Sanger-Katz, Margot. 2015. "What's at Stake in Health Law Case," *New York Times* (February 3): 3.

Scanlan, Susan (chair, NCWO). 2009a. "Please Urge Your Organization to Sign On to the Women and Health Care Reform Letter" (August 11). Copy of email in author files.

————, (chair, NCWO). 2009b. "Sept 10—Lobby Day for the Employee Free Choice Act" (July 29). Copy of email in author files.

Scanlan, Susan (chair), and Terry O'Neill (executive director), NCWO. n.d. "Letter to Senator Arlen Specter, Chairman, Committee on the Judiciary. Re: nomination of Samuel Alito to the U. S. Supreme Court." From NCWO website.

"Schedule and Participants for White House Conference on Social Security." 1998. In author files.

Schlozman, Kay Lehman. 1990. "Representing Women in Washington: Sisterhood and Pressure Politics." In *Women Politics and Change.* Louise A. Tilly and Patricia Gurin, eds., 339–382. New York: Russell Sage Foundation.

Schlozman, Kay Lehman, Sidney Verba, and Henry E. Brady. 2012. *The Unheavenly Chorus: Unequal Political Voice and the Broken Promise of American Democracy.* Princeton, NJ: Princeton University Press.

Schmidt, Steve, and Carl Forti. 2002. NRCC: National Republican Campaign / OR Congressional Committee. Memo to GOP Incumbents and Candidates. "Re: Words Matter in the Social Security Debate" (August 26). In author files.

Schneider, Anne Larason, and Helen Ingram. 1997. *Policy Design for Democracy.* Lawrence: University Press of Kansas.

Schoen, Johanna. 2005. *Choice and Coercion: Birth Control, Sterilization, and Abortion in Public Health and Welfare.* Chapel Hill: University of North Carolina Press.

Schreiber, Ronnee. 2008. *Righting Feminism: Conservative Women and American Politics.* New York: Oxford University Press.

Schulz, Kathryn. 2017. "Saint Pauli: She Advanced Two Movements for Equality— and Was at Home in Neither," *New Yorker* (April 17): 67–73.

Schuyler, Lorraine Gates. 2006. *The Weight of Their Votes: Southern Women and Political Leverage in the 1920s.* Chapel Hill: University of North Carolina Press.

Schwarz, John E. 1988. *America's Hidden Success: A Reassessment of Public Policy from Kennedy to Reagan*, rev. ed. New York: W. W. Norton.

"Scorecard: Where the Boys Are." 2002. *Sports Illustrated* (September 9): 21.

Scott, Anne Firor. 1992. *Natural Allies: Women's Associations in American History.* Urbana: University of Illinois Press.

Sedensky, Matt. 2009. "What about Long-Term Care?" *State Newspaper* (October 9): 7A.

Seelye, Katharine Q. 2009. "A Message after the Vote," *New York Times* (November 11): 18.

————. 2009. "Showing Support for Overhaul," *New York Times* (August 26): A14.

Seifter, A. 2009. "Police Report Filed by ACORN Exposes False Claims by Individuals behind Videos" (September 17). Available at http://mediamatters.org/research/2009/09/17/police-report-filed-by-acorn-exposes-false-clai/154723.

"Senate Votes against Abortion Funding Restrictions." 2009. *State Newspaper* (December 9).

Sergent, Jennifer. 2002. "Ex-prof Lives on $989 a Month," *Seattle Post-Intelligencer* (July 5).

———. 2002. "40 Years as Waitress, Bartender Brings Retiree $794 a Month," *Seattle Post-Intelligencer* (July 5).

Sexton, Jared Yates. 2017. *The People Are Going to Rise Like the Waters upon Your Shore: A Story of American Rage*. Berkeley, CA: Counterpoint.

Shaiko, Ronald G. 1999. *Voices and Echoes for the Environment: Public Interest Representation in the 1990s and Beyond*. New York: Columbia University Press.

Shaw, Todd C. 2017. "No Longer a Republic? Building a Coalition against Trump's White Nationalist Anti-Democracy." *Left Side of the Margin*, July 1, 2017. Available at http://www.leftsideofthemargin.net/2017/07/no-longer-republic-building-coalition.html.

———. 2009. *Now Is the Time! Detroit Black Politics and Grassroots Activism*. Durham, NC: Duke University Press.

Sheinin, Aaron Gould. 2007. "S.C. House: View Fetal Image Prior to Abortion: Bill Clears Early Hurdle," *State Newspaper* (March 22): 1, 7.

Shipnuck, Alan. 2012. "Southern, Charming and Successful, Moore Will Fit in with Augusta Power Brokers" (August 20). Available at golf.com/tour-and-news/darla-moore-joins-augusta-national.com.

———. 2004. *The Battle for Augusta National: Hootie, Martha, and the Masters of the Universe*. New York: Simon and Schuster.

Sholar, Megan A. 2016. *Getting Paid While Taking Time: The Women's Movement and the Development of Paid Family Leave Policies in the United States*. Philadelphia: Temple University Press.

Sicherman, Barbara. 2010. *Well-Read Lives: How Books Inspired a Generation of American Women*. Chapel Hill: University of North Carolina Press.

Sierra, Christine Marie. 2010. "Latinas and Electoral Politics: Movin' on Up." In *Gender and Elections: Shaping the Future of American Politics*, 2nd ed., Susan J. Carroll and Richard L. Fox, eds., 144–164. New York: Cambridge University Press.

Silliman, Jael, Marlene Gerber Fried, Loretta Ross, and Elena R. Gutierrez. 2004. *Undivided Rights Women of Color Organize for Reproductive Justice*. Cambridge, MA: South End Press.

Simien, Evelyn M. 2006. *Black Feminist Voices in Politics*. Albany: SUNY Press.

———. 2004. "Black Feminist Theory: Charting a Course for Black Women's Studies in Political Science," *Journal of Women, Politics and Policy*, Vol. 26, No. 2 (January): 81–93.

Sinderbrand, Rebecca. 2005. "A Shameful Little Secret: North Carolina Confronts Its History of Forced Sterilization," *Newsweek* (March 28): 33.

Singletary, Michelle. 2011. "If Everything Is on the Table, How Will Some Women Afford to Eat?" *Washington Post* (July 14): A14.

Sirak, Ron. 2002. "Bunker, Old Boys' Flub: Augusta National GCs All-Male Practice Questioned," *Golf World* (July 19): 6–8.

Skocpol, Theda. 1997. *Boomerang: Health Care Reform and the Turn against Government*. New York: W. W. Norton.

Slevin, Peter. 2009. "Antiabortion Efforts Move to the State Level: Legislatures Often Mandate Restrictions," *Washington Post* (June 8).

Sloan, Allan. 2001. "Bush's Social Security Plan Would Reduce Benefits by 40%," *Washington Post* (June 26): 3.

Smeal, Eleanor (president, FMF). 2010. "A Title IX for Health Care," *Ms.* (Spring): 12–14.

———, (president, FMF). 2009. "Feminist Majority Foundation Defends Targeted Nebraska Abortion Provider" (August 28). Copy of email in author files.

———, (president, FMF). 2009. "Invest in the Future of Equality" (December 21). Copy of email in author files.

———, (president, FMF). 2000. "Fall 2000 Letter Regarding the Campaign to Stop Gender Apartheid in Afghanistan." Xerox in author files.

Smith, Andrea. 2007. "Introduction: The Revolution Will Not Be Funded." In *The Revolution Will Not Be Funded: Beyond the Non-Profit Industrial Complex*, Incite! Women of Color against Violence, eds., 1–18. Cambridge, MA: South End Press.

Smith, Dorothy E. 2007. "Institutional Ethnography: From a Sociology for Women to a Sociology for People." In *Handbook of Feminist Research: Theory and Practice*, Sharlene Nagy Hesse-Biber, ed., 409–411. Thousand Oaks, CA: Sage.

Smith, Jackie, and Hank Johnston, eds. 2002. *Globalization and Resistance: Transnational Dimensions of Social Movements.* Lanham, MA: Rowman and Littlefield.

Smith, Mark A. 2000. *American Business and Political Power: Public Opinion, Elections, and Democracy.* Chicago: University of Chicago Press.

Smith-Evans, Leticia, Janel George, Fatima Gooss Graves, Lara S. Kaufmann, and Lauren Frohlich. 2014. "Unlocking Opportunity for African American Girls: A Call to Action for Educational Equity," NAACP LDF and National Women's Law Center. Washington, DC.

Smooth, Wendy. 2011. "Standing for Women? Which Women? The Substantive Representation of Women's Interests and the Research Imperative of Intersectionality," *Politics and Gender*, Vol. 7, No. 3 (September): 436–441.

———. 2010. "African American Women and Electoral Politics: A Challenge to the Post-Race Rhetoric of the Obama Moment." In *Gender and Elections: Shaping the Future of American Politics*, 2nd ed., Susan J. Carroll and Richard L. Fox, eds., 165–186. New York: Cambridge University Press.

———. 2006. "Intersectionality in Electoral Politics: A Mess Worth Making," *Politics and Gender*, Vol. 2, No. 3 (September): 400–414.

Snyder, R. Claire. 2008. "What Is Third-Wave Feminism? A New Directions Essay," *Signs: Journal of Women in Culture and Society*, Vol. 34, No. 1 (Autumn): 175–196.

"Social Security Groups Supporting Privatization," n.d. [probably 2005]. Xerox from NCWO archives. In author files.

Southworth, Ann. 2008. *Lawyers of the Right: Professionalizing the Conservative Coalition.* Chicago: University of Chicago Press.

Spalter-Roth, Roberta, and Ronnee Schreiber. 1995. "Outsider Issues and Insider Tactics: Strategic Tensions in the Women's Policy Network during the 1980s." In *Feminist Organizations: Harvest of the New Women's Movement*, Myra Marx Ferree and Patricia Yancey Martin, eds., 105–127. Philadelphia: Temple University Press.

Spillar, Katherine. 2016. "Betting on the Gender Gap: The Women's Vote in the High-Stakes Elections of 2016," *Ms.* (Summer): 20–23.

Springer, Kimberly. 2005. *Living for the Revolution: Black Feminist Organizations, 1968–1980*. Durham, NC: Duke University Press.

———, ed. 1999. *Still Lifting, Still Climbing: African American Women's Contemporary Activism*. New York: New York University Press.

Spruill, Marjorie J. 2017. *Divided We Stand: The Battle over Women's Rights and Family Values That Polarized American Politics*. New York: Bloomsbury.

Squires, Judith. 2013. "Equality and Universalism." In *The Oxford Handbook of Gender and Politics*, Georgina Waylen, Karen Celis, Johanna Kantola, and S. Laurel Weldon, eds., 731–755. New York: Oxford University Press.

Staggenborg, Suzanne. 1995. "Can Feminist Organizations Be Effective?" In *Feminist Organizations: Harvest of the New Women's Movement*, Myra Marx Ferree and Patricia Yancey Martin, eds., 339–355. Philadelphia: Temple University Press.

———. 1991. *The Pro-Choice Movement: Organization and Activism in the Abortion Conflict*. New York: Oxford University Press.

———. 1988. "The Consequences of Professionalization and Formalization in the Pro-Choice Movement," *American Sociological Review*, Vol. 53 (August): 585–606.

———. 1986. "Coalition Work in the Pro-Choice Movement: Organizational and Environmental Opportunities and Obstacles," *Social Problems*, Vol. 33, No. 5 (June): 374–390.

Steelman, Joseph F., Laura R. Woliver, and Lala Carr Steelman. 2009. "Gender, Race and Social Class in North Carolina Populist Movement." Paper presented at the Southeastern Women's Studies Conference, April 2–4, Boone, North Carolina.

Steinbreder, John. 2002. "What Drives Augusta's Nemesis?" *Golf Week* (September 21): 10–13.

Steinem, Gloria. 2015. *My Life on the Road*. New York: Penguin/Random House.

———. 1992. *Revolution from Within: A Book of Self-Esteem*. Boston: Little, Brown.

Stillman, Sarah. 2014. "Get Out of Jail, Inc.: Does the Alternatives-to-Incarceration Industry Profit from Injustice?" *New Yorker* (June 23): 48–62.

Stolberg, Sheryl Gay. 2009. "Delicate Dance for 2 Lobbyists on Health Bill," *New York Times* (October 28): 1, 23.

———. 2009. "In Support of Abortion, It's Personal vs. Political," *New York Times* (November 28).

———. 2009. "Obama Presses Senate to Pass Its Health Bill," *New York Times* (November 9): 1, 15.

Stolberg, Sheryl Gay, and David M. Herszenhorn. 2009. "Obama Health Care Meeting Aims to Rally Senators," *New York Times* (December 15).

Stout, Jeffrey. 2010. *Blessed Are the Organized: Grassroots Democracy in America*. Princeton, NJ: Princeton University Press.

Strid, Sofia, Sylvia Walby, and Jo Armstrong. 2013. "Intersectionality and Social Inequalities: Visibility in British Policy on Violence against Women," *Social Politics: International Studies in Gender, State and Society*, Vol. 20, No. 4 (Winter): 558–581.

Strolovitch, Dara Z. 2007. *Affirmative Advocacy: Race, Class, and Gender in Interest Group Politics*. Chicago: University of Chicago Press.

Strope, Leigh. 2001. "Panel Predicts Social Security Crisis," *State Newspaper* (July 20): 16A.

"Study: Female Doctors More Likely to Give Pap Smears, Mammograms." 1993. *State Newspaper* (September 12): 3.

"Study: More Women Need Birth Control to Save Lives." 1993. *State Newspaper* (August 16): 3A.

Stupak, Bart. 2010. "Health Care Hell," *Newsweek* (May 17): 10.

"Suggested Slogans—Social Security." [Probably 2000–2001]. Xerox from NCWO Archives. In author files.

Sullivan, Patricia. 2009. *Lift Every Voice: The NAACP and the Making of the Civil Rights Movement*. New York: New Press.

Superville, Darlene. 2010. "Slight Hike Seen in Health Costs," *State Newspaper* (January 10): 5.

Surowiecki, James. 2012. "Corporate Welfare Queens," *New Yorker* (October 8): 42.

Swers, Michele L. 2013. *Women in the Club: Gender and Policy Making in the Senate*. Chicago: University of Chicago Press.

———. 2002. *The Difference Women Make: The Policy Impact of Women in Congress*. Chicago: University of Chicago Press.

Tanden, Neera. 2014. "Preface." In *The Shriver Report: A Woman's Nation Pushes Back from the Brink; A Study by Maria Shriver and the Center for American Progress*. Olivia Morgan and Karen Skelton, eds., iv–viii. New York: Palgrave MacMillan.

Target Smart Communications. 2006. "Engaging Women 2006: Summary of Impact on Elections," one-page report to National Council of Women's Organizations. In author files.

———. 2006. "Engaging Women: Concept Paper" (March 21). In author files.

———. 2006. "Engaging Women: Executive Summary." In author files.

Tarrow, Sidney. 2013. *The Language of Contention: Revolution in Words, 1688–2012*. New York: Cambridge University Press.

———. 1998. *Power in Movement: Social Movements and Contentious Politics*, 2nd ed. New York: Cambridge University Press.

"Taxes, Insurance, Fairness: Who Should Pay for What?" 2009. *State Newspaper* (November 24): 3.

Taylor, Ula Y. 2010. "Black Feminisms and Human Agency." In *No Permanent Waves: Recasting Histories of U.S. Feminism*, Nancy A. Hewitt, ed., 61–76. New Brunswick, NJ: Rutgers University Press.

Taylor, Verta. 1995. "Watching for Vibes: Bringing Emotions into the Study of Feminist Organizations." In *Feminist Organizations: Harvest of the New Women's Movement*, Myra Marx Ferree and Patricia Yancey Martin, eds., 223–233. Philadelphia: Temple University Press.

"Tea Partyers Say Health Vote Clarifies Autumn Battle Lines," 2010. *State Newspaper* (March 24): 5.

Templeton, Robin. 2004. "She Who Believes in Freedom: Young Women Defy the Prison Industrial Complex." In *The Fire This Time: Young Activists and the New Feminism*, Vivien Labaton and Dawn Lundy Martin, eds., 254–277. New York: Anchor Books.

Thaler, Richard H. 2015. *Misbehaving: The Making of Behavioral Economics*. New York: W. W. Norton.

"This Is for . . . Ted Kennedy." 2009. *State Newspaper* (December 25): 4.

Thomas, Evan. 2009. "The Case for Killing Granny: Rethinking End-of-Life Care," *Newsweek* (September 21): 34–40.

Thomas, Rich. 1993. "'A Walk in Space': The Health Plan Is a Brilliant Political Document, but Take Another Look at the Numbers," *Newsweek* (October 4): 46, 49.

Thomas, Sue. 1994. *How Women Legislate.* New York: Oxford University Press.

Thompson, Becky. 2010. "Multiracial Feminism: Recasting the Chronology of Second Wave Feminism." In *No Permanent Waves: Recasting Histories of U.S. Feminism,* Nancy A. Hewitt, ed., 39–60. New Brunswick, NJ: Rutgers University Press.

Thompson, Douglas. "An Ill Fitting Coat: Reforming U.S. Political Boundaries for a Metropolitan Age," *The Journal of Politics,* forthcoming.

Thorpe, Rebecca U. 2014. *The American Warfare State: The Domestic Politics of Military Spending.* Chicago: University of Chicago Press.

Thurman, Karen M. [and 39 additional Congressional Women signatories]. 1998. "Letter to Honorable Al Gore, Vice President" (June 24). In author files.

Tickner, J. Ann. 2014. *A Feminist Voyage through International Relations.* New York: Oxford University Press.

Tison, Jennifer. 2012. "Gender and Public Policy: Comparative Political Analysis." Ph.D. dissertation. Department of Political Science. Columbia: University of South Carolina.

Tomasky, Michael. 2009. "Who Are the Blue Dogs?" *New York Review of Books,* Vol. LVI, No. 19 (December 3): 10, 12.

Toobin, Jeffrey. 2017. "Full Court Press: The Impresario behind Neil Gorsuch's Confirmation," *New Yorker* (April 17): 24–28.

———. 2009. "Not Covered," *New Yorker* (November 23): 37–38.

———. 2005. "Still Standing: The Resilience of *Roe v. Wade,*" *New Yorker* (November 28): 70, 72, 76–78, 80–81.

Towey, Shawn, Stephanie Poggi, and Rachel Roth. 2005. *Abortion Funding: A Matter of Justice.* Amherst, MA: National Network of Abortion Funds.

Traister, Rebecca. 2015. "The Body Politic: The Big Secret of Abortion, Women Already Know How It Works," *New York* (August 10–23): 34–35.

———. 2010. *Big Girls Don't Cry: The Election That Changed Everything for American Women.* New York: Free Press.

Triece, Mary E. 2013. *Tell It Like It Is: Women in the National Welfare Rights Movement.* Columbia: University of South Carolina Press.

True, Jacqui. 2012. *The Political Economy of Violence against Women.* New York: Oxford University Press.

Turman, Christopher. 2002. "News Release: Women's Groups: Congress Must Reject Social Security Privatization." Women and Social Security Project of the National Council of Women's Organizations (April 8). Xerox from NCWO archives. In author files.

———. 2001. "News Release: Women's Groups Question Social Security Commission": Women and Social Security Project, NCWO (May 2).

———. 2000. "Project Highlights": Women and Social Security Project, National Council of Women's Organizations (November 28). In author files.

"TV Ads Will Return to Next Year's Masters." 2004. *USA Today* (August 30). From NCWO archives.

Uchitelle, Louis. 2001. "Women Forced to Delay Retirement," *New York Times* (June 26).

Ulrich, Laurel Thatcher. 2007. *Well-Behaved Women Seldom Make History.* New York: Vintage Books.

Ungar, R. 2013. "James O'Keefe Pays $100,000 to ACORN Employee He Smeared— Conservative Media Yawns" (March 8). Available at http://www.forbes.com/sites

/rickungar/2013/03/08/james-okeefe-pays-100000-to-acorn-employee-he-smeared
-conservative-media-yawns/.

United Nations General Session. Report on the Ninth Session—June 5–9, 2000—of
the Ad Hoc Committee on the Elaboration of a Convention against Transnational
Organized Crime: Protocol to Prevent, Suppress and Punish Trafficking in Persons, Especially Women and Children. New York.

Valelly, Richard M. 2004. *The Two Reconstructions: The Struggle for Black Enfranchisement*. Chicago: University of Chicago Press.

VandeHei, Jim, and Juliet Eilperin. 2002. "Bush's Plan for Social Security Loses Favor," *Washington Post* (August 13).

Verloo, Mieke, ed. 2007. *Multiple Meanings of Gender Equality: A Critical Frame Analysis of Gender Politics in Europe*. Budapest, Hungary: Central European University Press.

Vives, Olga (vice president—Action, NOW). 2003. "Letter to South Carolina NOW Member," re: Augusta rally (March). In author files.

Walby, Sylvia. 2015. *Crisis*. Cambridge, U.K.: Polity.

———. 2011. *The Future of Feminism*. Malden, MA: Polity Books.

———. 2009. *Globalization and Inequalities: Complexity and Contested Modernities*. Los Angeles: Sage.

Walsh, Deirdre. 2009. "Democrats Ready with Tempered Public Option, Aides Say," CNN Politics. Accessed October 28. Available at www.cnn.com/2009/politics/10/28/Health.care/index.html.

Wang, Amy B. 2017. "'Nevertheless, She Persisted' Becomes New Battle Cry after McConnell Silences Elizabeth Warren," *Washington Post* (February 8).

Warren, Elizabeth. 2014. *A Fighting Chance*. New York: Henry Holt.

Wattleton, Faye. 1996. *Life on the Line*. New York: Random House.

Waylen, Georgina, Karen Celis, Johanna Kantola, and S. Laurel Weldon, eds. 2013. *The Oxford Handbook of Gender and Politics*. New York: Oxford University Press.

Weber, Lynn. 2010. *Understanding Race, Class, Gender, and Sexuality*, 2nd ed. New York: Oxford University Press.

Weisberg, Jacob. 2009. "Death, Republican Style: It's the GOP That's Out to Get Granny," *Newsweek* (September 7): 16.

Weldon, S. Laurel. 2011. *When Protest Makes Policy: How Social Movements Represent Disadvantaged Groups*. Ann Arbor: University of Michigan Press.

———. 2002a. "Beyond Bodies: Institutional Sources of Representation for Women in Democratic Policymaking," *Journal of Politics*, Vol. 64, No. 4: 1153–1174.

———. 2002b. *Violence against Women: Protest, Policy, and the Problem of Women*. Pittsburgh: University of Pittsburgh Press.

Wenger, Yvonne. 2010. "McMaster Fights Medicaid Provision," *State Newspaper* (January 5): 3B.

West, Guida, and Lois Blumberg, eds. 1990. *Women and Social Protest*. New York: Oxford University Press.

"What's in It for Me? Scenarios for 5 Americans." 2009. *State Newspaper* (December 20): 15.

Wheeler, Marjorie Spruill, ed. 1995. *Votes for Women! The Woman Suffrage Movement in Tennessee, the South, and the Nation*. Knoxville: University of Tennessee Press.

Whelan, Sloane. 2009. "Abortion Shouldn't Imperil Health Care Reform," *State Newspaper* (November 29): 3D.

"Where the Boys Are." 2002. *Sports Illustrated* (September 9): 21.

Whitaker, Lois Duke, ed. 2008. *Voting the Gender Gap*. Urbana: University of Illinois Press.

Whitby, Kenny J. 2014. *Strategic Decision-Making in Presidential Nominations: When and Why Party Elites Decide to Support a Candidate*. New York: SUNY Press.

White, Deborah Gray. 1999. *Too Heavy a Load: Black Women in Defense of Themselves 1894–1994*. New York: W. W. Norton.

"The White House Conference on Social Security: List of Attendees." 1998. Xerox from NCWO Archives. In author files.

Whittier, Nancy. 1995. *Feminist Generations: The Persistence of the Radical Women's Movement*. Philadelphia: Temple University Press.

Wider Opportunities for Women (WOW). n.d. [probably 2006]. "Older Women and the Impact of Housing Status on Economic Security." Washington, DC. In author files.

Wie, Michelle. 2003. "On the Tee, Ladies First: 10 Reasons the LPGA Tour Is More Fun Than the PGA Tour," *Golf Magazine* (July): 28, 30.

Wiegman, Robyn, ed. 2002. *Women's Studies on Its Own: A Next Wave Reader in Institutional Change*. Durham, NC: Duke University Press.

Wiggins, Ernest L. 2002. "Outside Augusta, Looking In," *State Newspaper* (September 18): 15A.

Wiley, Ralph. 2003. "Zip USA, Augusta, Georgia, 30904, Playing the Fairway," *National Geographic* (April): 126–131.

Wilkinson, Jeff. 2011. "S.C. Jobless Rate Spikes to 11 Percent: This Is the Fourth Month the Rate Increased," *State Newspaper* (September 17): 1, 9A.

Williams, Claudia, and Barbara Gault. 2014. "Paid Sick Days Access in the United States: Differences by Race/Ethnicity, Occupation, Earnings, and Work Schedule." IWPR Fact Sheet (March). Washington, DC.

Williams, Tonya M. 2016. "Why Are You under the Skirts of Women? Race, Gender, and Abortion Policy in the Georgia State Legislature." In *Distinct Identities: Minority Women in U.S. Politics*. Nadia E. Brown and Sarah Allen Gershon, eds., 282–303. New York: Routledge.

Wilson, Duff. 2009. "Drug Makers Raise Prices in Face of Health Care Reform," *New York Times* (November 15): 1.

Wilson, Jan Doolittle. 2007. *The Women's Joint Congressional Committee and the Politics of Maternalism, 1920–30*. Urbana: University of Illinois Press.

Wilson, Joshua C. 2013. *The Street Politics of Abortion: Speech, Violence, and America's Culture Wars*. Palo Alto, CA: Stanford University Press.

Witt, Linda, Karen M. Paget, and Glenna Matthews. 1995. *Running as a Woman: Gender and Power in American Politics*. New York: Free Press.

Wolbrecht, Christina. 2000. *The Politics of Women's Rights*. Princeton, NJ: Princeton University Press.

Wolbrecht, Christina, and Michael T. Hartney. 2014. "'Ideas about Interests': Explaining the Changing Partisan Politics of Education," *Perspectives on Politics*, Vol. 12, No. 3 (September): 603–630.

Wolbrecht, Christina, Karen Beckwith, and Lisa Baldez. 2008. *Political Women and American Democracy*. New York: Cambridge University Press.

Woliver, Laura R. 2017. "Essential yet Unspectacular: Women's Groups Shoring-Up Foundational Policies." Paper presented at the 2017 American Political Science Convention, August 31–September 3, San Francisco, CA.

————. 2016. "Economic Security Issues in the American Women's Movement." Paper presented at the 2016 Southern Political Science Convention, January 7–10, San Juan, Puerto Rico.

————. 2015. "Dissent Is Patriotic: Disobedient Founders, Narratives, and Street Battles," *Tulsa Law Review*, Vol. 50, No. 2 (Winter): 381–395.

————. 2013. "Keeping the Faith during a Backlash: National Women's Rights Lobbying to Retain Progress on Women's Issues," Southeastern Women's Studies Convention, April 18–20, Greensboro, NC.

————. 2013. "Pushing Back Neoliberal Agendas via Women's Coalitional Lobbying," Southern Political Science Convention, January 3–5, Orlando, FL.

————. 2012. "Master Narratives While the Masters Golf." Paper presented at the Southern Political Science Convention, New Orleans, LA.

————. 2010. "Framing Reproductive Politics in American Health Care Reform," Southern Political Science Convention, January 7–9, Atlanta, GA.

————. 2009. "National Coalition Work in the American Women's Movement," American Political Science Convention, September 3–6, Toronto, Canada.

————. 2008. "Lobbying Nationally on Women's Issues," Southeastern Women's Studies Convention, April 3–5, Charlotte, NC.

————. 2002a. "Ethical Dilemmas in Elite Interviewing," *PS: Political Science and Politics*, Vol. 35, No. 4 (December): 677–678.

————. 2002b. *The Political Geographies of Pregnancy*. Urbana: University of Illinois Press.

————. 1998a. "Abortion Interests: From the Usual Suspects to Expanded Coalitions." In *Interest Group Politics*, Allan J. Cigler and Burdett A. Loomis, eds., 327–342. Washington, DC: Congressional Quarterly Press.

————. 1998b. "Social Movements and Abortion Law." In *Social Movements and American Political Institutions*, Anne N. Costain and Andrew S. McFarland, eds., 233–247. Lanham, MA: Rowman and Littlefield.

————. 1993. *From Outrage to Action: The Politics of Grass Roots Dissent*. Urbana: University of Illinois Press.

"Women Give Most Care to Dying, Study Finds." 1999. *State Newspaper* (September 23): 4.

"Women on Drug Charges Fill Jails." 1992. *The State Newspaper* (March 23): 3.

Women and Social Security Project of the National Coalition of Women's Organizations. n.d. [probably 2000]. "Women's Checklist to Strengthen Social Security." In author files.

Women's Committee of 100. 2000. *An Immodest Proposal: Rewarding Women's Work to End Poverty*. In author files.

————. n.d. "TANF Reform." In author files.

Women's E News. 2008. "The Memo: Special Report: Status of U.S. Women" (August): Democratic National Convention Edition. In author files.

Women's Equality Summit, Congressional Action Day [WESCAD]; NCWO. 2008. Conference Packet of Materials (March 10–11). In author files.

————. 2002. "Dear Representative," sample letter from participant to congressperson (April 9). In author files.

"Women's Groups Press National Agenda." 1987. COP News Release (January 16). In author files.

Women's Health Research Coalition. 2000. Letter to Senator Olympia Snowe (July 21). In author files.

Women's Network for Change. 2001. "Get the Facts: Privatizing Social Security Will Hurt Women" (May 10). In author files.

Womens Way USA. 1994. "Womens Way USA: Guiding Principles for Forming a Women's Federation," (March 3). NCWO Archives. Xerox in author files.

Woods, Harriet. 1994. "Letter to Jill Miller; Re: 1995 COP Pledge" (December 26). [National Women's Political Caucus]. In author files.

Working Group on the Women's Human Rights Treaty. 1999. "Convention on the Elimination of All Forms of Discrimination against Women."

www.womensclearinghouse.org email. 2017. "Subject: Invitation to Feminist Organizations to Send Representatives to Noon Tuesday June 27 CWI Meeting on Enhancing Collaboration Among DC area Feminist Organizations," sent June 22. Copy in author files.

Yard, Molly. 1982. "Memo to ERA Support Organizations" (September 15). Xerox in author files.

Yen, Hope. 2011. "Nearly 1 in 6 in U.S. Live in Poverty," *State Newspaper* (September 14): 1, 7.

Yen, Yi-Wyn. 2003. "The Battle of Augusta, Hootie v. Martha," *Sports Illustrated* (April 8).

Yi, Youngmin. 2013. "IWPR's Paid Leave Convening Sparks New Research Collaborations," *IWPR Quarterly Newsletter*, (Winter): 1, 3.

Young, Laurie (executive director), Older Women's League (OWL). 2004. "OWL Statement on the 2004 Annual Report of the Board of Trustees of Social Security and Medicare" (March 24). In author files.

Young, Louise M. 1989. *In the Public Interest: The League of Women Voters, 1920–1970.* New York: Greenwood Press.

Young, McGee. 2010. *Developing Interests: Organizational Change and the Politics of Advocacy.* Lawrence: University of Kansas Press.

Zajac, Andrew. 2009. "How Health Lobbyists Influenced Reform Bill," *Chicago Tribune* (December 20): 1.

Zeleny, Jeff, and Sheryl Gay Stolberg. 2010. "Legal and Political Fights Ahead for the Democrats," *New York Times* (March 22): 17.

Zerubavel, Eviatar. 2006. *The Elephant in the Room: Silence and Denial in Everyday Life.* New York: Oxford University Press.

Zlotnick, Frances. 2010. "Social and Economic Status of Latina Immigrants in Phoenix," IWPR Fact Sheet (May).

Index

Linked fate: activism, cultural, 48; activism, intersectional, 10, 16, 43–44, 55, 121; coalitions, 4, 5, 134, 139, 145; neoliberalism, critique of, 5, 23, 70, 77; social programs, 90, 112

Maatz, Lisa, 3, 4
Maloney, Carolyn, 71, 123
Maloney/Sherman Bill, 44
Managerial conservatism, 22–23
Marcus, Ruth, 103, 107–108
Marriage as social construction, 9
Master narrative, 45, 48, 69, 131
Masters Golf Tournament, 41–51
McConnell, Mitch, 4
McCrory, Pat, 49
Metanarratives, 10, 41, 44
Milkulski, Barbara, 104
Miller, Jill, 29
Miller, Joyce, 26–27, 29
Mitchell, Shireen, 138, 139, 144
Ms. Magazine, 58, 111, 127
Mulhauser, Karen, 56–59, 66–67
Muncy, Robyn, 16, 72
Murray, Pauli, 15, 50–51, 70
My Brother's Keeper Initiative, 139
My Vote 2012, 64–65

Nadel, Ruth, 8
Narrative masculinity, 74
National Association of Colored Women (NACW), 14, 18
National Commission on Fiscal Responsibility and Reform, 95
National Committee on Pay Equity (NCPE), 29
National Committee to Preserve Social Security, 87, 97
National Council of Women's Organizations (NCWO): 1999 Working Conference, 8; Afghanistan, women's rights, 115–116, 123–125; CEDAW, 126–128; coalition-building, 32–37, 50; corporate accountability, 41–50; Corporate Accountability Taskforce, 58, 67–68; Democratic Party, alignment, 33; funding issues, 37–38; globalization and women's rights, 119, 121–123; GOTV/GOHV efforts, 55–62, 67–72; healthcare reform activism, 102–103, 105, 107–108, 111, 114; intersectional efforts, 9, 12, 32; origins, Council of Presidents, 5, 12, 13, 19, 27–31, 39, 126, 138; Social Security reform activism, 71–72, 76–101
National Economic Council, 82

National Education Association (NEA), 59
National Organization of Women (NOW), 18; coalition work, 39, 58, 135; COP, formation of, 26, 27; healthcare reform, 103, 104, 107–110, 112; Legal Defense and Education Fund, 32; My Brother's Keeper, criticism of, 139; Social Security reform, 86, 80, 92, 95, 100. *See also*, Ireland, Patricia; O'Neill, Terry; Smeal, Eleanor; Yard, Molly
National Partnership for Women and Families, 92, 112
National Partnership for Women and Girls, 110
National Plan of Action for Women, 28
National security as domestic issue, 90
National Women's Agenda, 19, 27–28
National Women's Equality Act for the 21st Century, 30
National Women's Law Center, 32, 82, 87, 89, 92, 110, 112
National Council of Negro Women (NCNW), 16, 57
Natividad, Irene, 27
Nelson, Ben, 7, 11
Neoliberalism: critique of, 5, 39–40, 70, 77; feminist ideology, 23; globalism, 115; healthcare, 130, 133; NCWO response, 5, 12; New Deal, response to, 22; paternalism, relation to, 131; women, impact on, 70, 117–118; linked fate, relation to, 77; Social Security reform, 82, 92, 96, 97
New Deal, 22, 67, 72–74, 105
Non-Governmental Organizations (NGOs): Coalition of Presidents, relation to, 19, 24, 29; danger of state control, 23; funding ethics, 38; global role, 118–122, 125, 126; health care reform, 112, 118
North Carolina HB2 Protest, 48–49

Obama, Barack: 2016 election, 145; Affordable Care Act efforts, 6, 107, 109–112; Church Ladies Project, 63; deficient reduction, 95–96; early voting, 60, 67; gender gap, 54; My Brother's Keeper, 139; Social Security reform, 81, 101, 134
Objective knowledge, critique of, 62, 66
Office of Women's Health Research, 104
O'Keefe, James, 35
Older Women's League (OWL), 32, 88
O'Neill, Terry, 20, 95–97, 139
Open Society Institute, 127
Otis, Kim, 38, 98
Our Bodies, Ourselves, 104

Laura R. Woliver is Distinguished Professor Emerita of Political Science and Gender and Women's Studies at the University of South Carolina. She is the author of *From Outrage to Action: The Politics of Grass-Roots Dissent* and *The Political Geographies of Pregnancy.*

www.ingramcontent.com/pod-product-compliance
Lightning Source LLC
Chambersburg PA
CBHW050808270326
41926CB00026B/4635